Aspirations and Affluence

COMPARATIVE STUDIES IN THE UNITED STATES AND WESTERN EUROPE

George Katona

THE UNIVERSITY OF MICHIGAN

Burkhard Strumpel

THE UNIVERSITY OF MICHIGAN AND
UNIVERSITY OF COLOGNE, GERMANY

Ernest Zahn

UNIVERSITY OF AMSTERDAM, HOLLAND

McGraw-Hill Book Company

*New York   St. Louis   San Francisco   Düsseldorf   London
Mexico   Panama   Sydney   Toronto*

Sponsoring Editors   M. Joseph Dooher/Dale L. Dutton
Director of Production   Stephen J. Boldish
Designer   Naomi Auerbach
Editing Supervisors   Barbara Church/Carolyn Nagy
Editing and Production Staff   Gretlyn Blau,
   Teresa F. Leaden, George E. Oechsner

ASPIRATIONS AND AFFLUENCE

07-033366-1

1234567890 VBVB 75432

Acknowledgments

$THIS$ book grew out of studies conducted over several years. Following discussions with social scientists in several countries and the collection of available data on the economic behavior in private households, comparative population surveys were conducted in Great Britain, Germany, Holland, and the United States in 1968.

The project was financed by a grant from The Ford Foundation to the Survey Research Center of The University of Michigan. Without the grant and without the broad leeway offered by The Ford Foundation in the utilization of the funds, the studies could not have been carried out.

The organizations conducting the interviews were: In Britain, Research Services Ltd., London; in Germany, the DIVO-Institute, Frankfurt am Main; in Holland, NIPO, Amsterdam; and in the United States, the Survey Research Center of The University of Michigan. The authors greatly appreciate the help, suggestions, and information received from these organizations as well as from several individual scholars. Professors Paul Albou, Paris, and Paul Deneffe and G. Deblaere, Louvain, Belgium, contributed data on consumer behavior in their countries. Professor Elisabeth Noelle-Neumann, University of Mainz, Germany, provided valuable advice and gave the authors access to the archive of the Institut fuer Demoskopie, Allensbach am Bodensee. Thanks are due also to Professor Guenter Schmoelders, Cologne, for help and encouragement during the first stage of the project.

Among the collaborators on the project, Sylvia Kafka and M. Susan Schwartz deserve foremost mention. Mrs. Kafka skillfully edited the entire manuscript. Her suggestions induced the authors to rethink and rewrite many passages of the book. Mrs. Schwartz compiled tables and statistics with great skill. Further assistance was rendered by Jay Schmiedeskamp in Ann Arbor and Horst Ermer, Klaus Novy, and Ernst Schaeffer in Cologne. The authors are indebted to all of them, as well as to Nancy McAllister and Virginia Eaton for typing the final manuscript and its numerous earlier versions.

The book represents a cooperative effort of three persons with backgrounds in different disciplines and in different countries. George Katona, Professor of Economics and of Psychology as well as Director of the Economic Behavior Program of the Survey Research Center of The University of Michigan, left Europe for America in 1933 but has traveled extensively in Europe during the last few years. Burkhard Strumpel began his cooperation in the project as Privatdozent at the University of Cologne where he directed a research group in empirical economics. In 1968, he moved to the United States where he serves as Senior Study Director of the Survey Research Center and Associate Professor of Economics at The University of Michigan. Ernest Zahn, Professor of Economic Sociology at the University of Amsterdam, Holland, looks back on experience over many years in European multinational corporations.

Although all parts of the book represent the result of a common undertaking, certain sections may be singled out as the work largely of one author: George Katona was mainly responsible for Chapters 4, 5, 7, and 13; Burkhard Strumpel for Chapters 9, 10, 11, and 12, and Ernest Zahn for Chapter 3 and the section on Holland in Chapter 12.

Contents

Aspirations
and Affluence

PART 1

Assumptions and Background

CHAPTER 1

Man in the Postindustrial Society

*C*LOSE to two-thirds of the many Americans who have experienced improvement in their financial situation over the past few years expect it to continue in the future. Only one-third of the Germans, French, and Dutch think that their progress will continue, although they, too, have enjoyed substantial and steady improvement in the past.

About one-half of all Americans both approve of and use installment credit. At the other extreme, only one-fourth of the Germans approve of it, and only one out of ten actually has any installment debt.

About forty percent of American husbands think it is a good idea for wives with school-age children to go out to work. Only one out of ten German household heads approves of mothers working if any children live at home, even if the children themselves are already working. Every second American wife, and only every

3

third Western European wife, between the ages of forty and fifty has a job outside her home.

More than two-thirds of American fathers expect their boys to go to college. Only one-third of German fathers approve of boys staying in school beyond the age of eighteen. In fact, today almost every second American youngster, boy or girl, eighteen years of age is in college, while in Western Europe only every tenth youngster of that age goes to school full time.

These are some of the findings that emerged from the comparative studies presented in this book, which were centered on the economic behavior of the people in the United States and some affluent countries of Western Europe, and therefore on the human element in economic affairs. The economies of these countries have undergone substantial changes during the last few decades. Consumers come to exert a great influence on the rate of growth of the economy, and—crucially for our purposes—a large share of consumers' demand now stems from their desires rather than from their needs. For the first time in history masses of consumers wield great economic power, and many of them are free to wield it at their own discretion, in accordance with their wishes, attitudes, aspirations, expectations. Designations such as mass-consumption economy, knowledge-oriented economy and, in view of the lessened importance of production compared with the preceding 100 years, postindustrial economy express various further aspects of the new developments. In choosing their subject matter, the methods used, and the nature of the empirical evidence collected, the authors set three tasks for themselves:

1. To indicate the similarities as well as the differences in the economic behavior of American and Western European people and to contribute to an understanding of economic trends and prospects in these countries by means of behavioral analysis.

2. To indicate what "affluence" means and how the participation of private households has contributed to its development and growth. Different ways of adaptation to changing conditions may have altered both the use consumers make of their income and the ways in which they attempt to increase their earning power.

3. To develop and enrich the new discipline of behavioral or psychological economics. Behavioral economists believe that in order to understand the functioning and the prospects of an economy, it is necessary to study people's behavior as influenced by psychological no less than by economic factors. It was thought, and our studies confirmed, that the influence of expectations and aspi-

rations on economic behavior would emerge more clearly in a comparative analysis of trends in different countries than in observations made in one country alone.

The three central aspects of our endeavor—the function of comparative studies, the relation of the affluent consumer to socioeconomic change, and the role of behavioral economics—will each be discussed in turn in the next sections of this chapter.

COMPARATIVE STUDIES IN THE UNITED STATES AND WESTERN EUROPE

The spread of affluence to a number of countries in the world opened up new vistas. It is not so long since the United States was the only highly developed country in which broad masses of people could engage in discretionary forms of consumer behavior. In recent years consumers in Canada, Australia, to some extent Japan, and, above all, several countries in Western Europe have acquired similar economic freedom.

It is sometimes said that America leads the way, so that what prevails there today will prevail in other affluent countries tomorrow. American tourists lament that Europe is getting to be just another United States when they find the picturesque old villages and towns surrounded by ever-spreading suburbs, modern housing developments, and industries. Superhighways, traffic jams and parking problems, skyscrapers and supermarkets, as well as air and water pollution, are clearly visible to everyone, as are modern heating and plumbing facilities, TV sets, washers and dryers to those who enter Western European homes. Progress in modern technology is international, and some differences in the availability of natural resources would hardly present an obstacle to similar developments on the two sides of the Atlantic. Will, then, the Old World, or at least an important part of it, soon resemble the New World? Is it just a matter of time until the economies of Western Europe and the United States will run parallel?

No doubt, with respect to the improvement of the common man's standard of living, America points the way. There are other areas, however, in which America has only recently begun to catch up with Europe as, for instance, social security and medical care, full employment, and the absence of substantial fluctuations in the business cycle, as well as the spread of paid vacations.

Whether future developments will run parallel on the two sides of the Atlantic depends above all on the people themselves. People change less rapidly than technology. The spread of automobiles and supermarkets, the introduction of computers, and the emergence of giant corporations producing ever-increasing quantities of goods do not suddenly efface traditions or old stereotypes and motivations. These traditions and motivations play a large role in economic developments and may be responsible for differences in the trends in different countries.

The development of the American consumer might have been influenced by the tradition of the frontier, which made self-reliance necessary, as well as by the experience of immigration, only one or two generations remote for many people. The European consumer, on the other hand, might have been fashioned by the not-yet-forgotten experience of distinct classes and class rigidity, as well as by the former absence of geographical and occupational mobility. It was such thinking that led the authors to launch studies in Western Europe comparable to those that had been going on in the United States. The question to be answered was whether differences in sociopsychological factors might be found that would result in differences in economic behavior and thus in economic developments.

Affluent societies other than the United States and Western Europe were not considered. Among the countries of Western Europe new data, comparable to those available in the United States, were collected in West Germany, Holland, and Great Britain and some also from France and Belgium.[1] Two smaller countries which probably have the highest standard of living in Europe, Sweden and Switzerland, were not included nor were other relatively affluent northern countries or Italy. It was thought to be sufficient to apply the new forms of research to a few crucial countries.

The countries chosen for study are the leaders not only in affluence but also in economic statistics. Many scholars have compiled a great variety of statistical indicators and compared the changes in them. This is particularly true in the realm of the business world—the capital expenditures and even the productivity of business firms—as well as of various aspects of economic policy.

---

[1] The term "Germany" as used throughout this book refers only to West Germany. The term "America" is also used throughout to refer only to the United States. The terms "Great Britain," "England," and "United Kingdom" are used interchangeably to refer to Great Britain.

What is missing in those studies is precisely what we placed at the center of ours—the sociopsychological factors influencing the economic behavior of private households. It is because of our concern with consumers that we found it necessary to conduct sample surveys on the reactions of masses of people to great changes in their economic lives.

SOCIOECONOMIC CHANGE AND THE AFFLUENT CONSUMER

Today's affluent societies are characterized by more for the many, rather than by much for the few. In rich societies over the past centuries, wealth and opportunities for advancement were restricted to a thin upper class. The living patterns of the nobility, of feudal landlords, of merchant princes, and of entrepreneurs differed greatly from those of the masses, and the actions of the masses exerted little influence on the course of the economy. During the hundred years prior to World War II, the living standard of the bourgeoisie improved greatly in industrial countries, but very broad groups of the population still remained at, or close to, the subsistence level. Today in the affluent societies the great majority of households have not only gone far beyond the level of mere subsistence but indeed acquire and constantly replace an extensive variety of consumer goods. Many goods and services formerly unknown or considered luxuries available to but a few now represent necessities of life for the masses.

During the last two decades in the affluent consumer economies compulsion arising from hunger or lack of shelter and clothing has given way to discretion about what to buy and when to buy it; a large proportion of consumers spend money not only on what they have to have but also on what they want to have. Affluent societies are characterized by a sharply increasing emancipation from material and external constraints and by growing freedom of choice about what to do with income received. Some latitude of action was always assumed to be available to the entrepreneur or business manager. Today, consumers are in the position of no longer being subjects who react to changes in their environment more or less automatically. Like businessmen, they are now actors who adapt their behavior to changes according to their past experiences, motives, and attitudes.

Wants and aspirations now influence the size, the composition, and the timing of much of consumer spending. The share consumers have been spending on optional purchases, especially on durable goods, housing, travel, and leisure-time pursuits, has been constantly increasing. They may choose to postpone purchases or to make them in advance, even in excess of immediate needs if they so desire. Their excess spending may involve curtailing the amounts they save, using previously accumulated savings, or resorting to borrowing.

Extensive empirical studies, initiated by the senior author of this book, have demonstrated that consumer attitudes and expectations have considerable influence on short-term changes in economic activities in the United States. The question to be raised in this book is whether psychological factors are equally powerful in shaping long-term trends. There was justification for believing that the extension of people's planning horizon and time perspective to fairly long future periods might exert a powerful influence on the growth rate of the economies. This was expected to be the case because people's horizons came to include such long-term goals as better housing, larger savings, and satisfactory conditions during retirement.

Freedom of action extends to the revenue as well as the expenditure side of consumers' budgets. For the great majority of those in the labor force full employment has become a reality, and the problem today is not so much how to get a job as how to get a better job. Income is therefore no longer determined solely by forces beyond the power of the individual. First, there is some latitude regarding how much to work—in terms of overtime, second jobs, timing of retirement. Secondly, there is great discretion on the part of married women as to whether or not to become part of the labor force. Finally, and most importantly, people make decisions concerning the acquisition of skills, additional education and training, striving toward a better position, and occupational mobility. All these choices influence economic growth even more than the choice between work and leisure. Extensive formal education as well as the acquisition of knowledge and skills during adult life have become the major avenues through which an increasing proportion of the population aspires to achieve better jobs and higher incomes.

Wealth no longer consists, as it formerly did, of productive facilities and financial assets alone. Today it is equally justified to consider the houses and durable goods individuals own as representing wealth or capital. When consumers spend money for items they do not immediately consume, their purchases, just as truly as the purchase of new machines by a manufacturer, constitute investment expenditures. More importantly still, national wealth is no longer restricted to fixed assets. Human capital—the sum total of the value of skills, and education and training, and the health of the people—has come to represent a most important productive asset. The "knowledge industry," concerned with the acquisition, transformation, and dissemination of knowledge, has indeed become the fastest-growing industry in societies with rapid technological as well as social changes.

BEHAVIORAL ECONOMICS

Traditionally, economics has been concerned with the analysis of the interrelationship among such financial variables as income, prices, interest rates, and expenditures. It was considered sufficient to establish cause and effect relations between changes in these variables and to assume that noneconomic or exogenous factors could be disregarded. The covering expression was "other things being equal." Thus most economists contented themselves with studying the results of economic behavior without concern for all the forces that might affect that behavior. Some of those forces, such as changes in taste and deviations from the postulated desire always to maximize one's profits or optimize one's situation, were often recognized but viewed as not falling within the realm of economics.

The new discipline of behavioral economics views economic behavior as a form of human behavior. Like all other behavioral sciences it applies the scientific method—observation, measurement, testing—to the actions of man himself. The area of study of prime interest is the process of decision making. Decisions on spending, saving, investing, and borrowing are studied, as well as decisions to work or to retire early, or women's decisions to enter the labor force, to mention some of the relevant examples. Behavioral economists believe that an analysis of the reasons—both economic and sociopsychological—for such decisions has much to contribute to an understanding of market processes and that only by combining this analysis with the traditional study of financial variables can one arrive at a complete picture of any economy where consumers have freedom of economic choice.

The importance of behavioral economics varies, of course, in direct proportion to the affluence of the economy, that is, to the degree of discretion the consumers have in their economic behavior. Then, too, its importance is heightened in times of rapid economic and social change. In such periods habitual behavior— doing what one has always done under similar circumstances—may be inappropriate, and people may have to adapt their behavior to changed circumstances. Changes in the environment represent stimuli to which consumers as well as businessmen and economic policy makers respond. However, human response does not depend on stimuli alone. It is a function both of the environment and of the person involved. Stimuli elicit responses according to the psychological predispositions of the responding individual. Motives, attitudes, expectations, and aspirations are intervening variables that mediate between stimuli and responses. They influence both the perception of changes in the environment and the response to them. They are relevant for the understanding of economic processes when they are general and do not cancel out, that is, when similar intervening variables arise among a large number of people at the same time and thus result in similar responses. The similarity of the response of very broad groups of people is enhanced by the mass media, which spread similar political and economic news from all over the world to people in all walks of life.

No consumer response can be predicted solely on the basis of the stimulus, be it a change in income, a change in prices, or any other economic factor. Discretionary expenditures depend both on ability to buy and on willingness to buy. How much money is available—from income and also from assets or credit—is very important but does not suffice to explain changes in discretionary expenditures. Changes in motives, attitudes, and expectations play a role by altering people's willingness to buy. When their time perspective extends beyond immediate requirements and when planning ahead is possible and common—as is especially true of relatively affluent people—expectations have a particularly great influence on spending and saving decisions.

Among the psychological factors considered in our studies, the presence or absence of felt progress and aspirations toward further progress were found to be of particular importance. Desires are not static and levels of aspiration are not given once for all time; they may be raised by success or lowered by failure. The subjective feeling of having made progress or of being disappointed or even frustrated depends on what has happened not only to the individual but also to his "group." Perceptions about developments in the fate of other people with whom a person identifies himself or is associated, and also of reference groups with whom he compares himself, influence the individual's attitudes. Thus notions about financial progress are at least partly dependent on one's perception of general economic trends.

The function of behavioral economics extends beyond studying people in their role as consumers. In our own studies we have considered the influence of psychological factors not only on the allocation but also on the acquisition of income. We have, however, excluded from our studies several other important areas of economic behavior even though they are susceptible to research by methods similar to those used in the field of consumer behavior. They include business and entrepreneurial behavior, government policy decisions, changes in management practices, and behavior on the job. It is increasingly recognized, for example, that progress by business firms depends to an ever-greater extent on management practices, on marketing, and on research and development, all of which are contingent on the human factor. Some headway has recently been made in psychological studies in these areas that fall outside the scope of the present work.

Behavioral economics is a young discipline, which has, however, made substantial progress in its brief history. Many of its propositions have been tested, especially in the United States and more recently also in Germany and several other countries, and have been found to contribute to the understanding and even the prediction of economic processes.[2]

ADAPTATION TO CHANGE

It is axiomatic to say that different people respond to changing conditions in different ways. Some may fail to perceive even substantial changes in their environment, in which case habitual patterns of behavior may persist, reinforced by inertia. To others, however, changes may be welcomed and may be reacted to by new forms of adaptation, which, in turn, may bring forth further changes. The latter may be designated as modern, progressive, or

[2] Regarding the principles of behavioral economics, see Katona,[32] [38] and regarding findings of behavioral economics, Katona,[34] [35] as well as Schmoelders.[68] [69] Exact references to these publications as well as to others cited in the text are cited in the Bibliography by number.

dynamic forms of the adaptive response; the former as traditional, habitual, or old-fashioned behavior.

It is not assumed that the two forms of behavior arise because of the existence of two different personality types. The behavior of any one individual is probably modern at certain times and traditional at others. The question is whether one or the other type of response is prevalent to a greater or lesser degree in the United States or in Western Europe.

The major features of the modern form of adaptation may be summarized as follows:

1. Progress or success makes for rising levels of aspiration. Getting what one wants results in stepping up one's sights rather than in being satisfied and desiring nothing more than to keep and maintain what one already has. The achievement of a higher income and an improved standard of living results not in saturation but in new wants.

2. Rising income, especially if the income increase is larger than that of colleagues, friends, and "everybody else," is seen as a personal accomplishment over which one has some control, or as progress in one's career, that will and must continue. Past changes are then projected into the future.

3. Social learning, consisting of the acquisition of new attitudes and behavior, comes easy. Innovation in the form of taking up new activities or accepting new products is common. New styles of living are readily adopted.

4. Actions oriented toward the future are undertaken even to the extent of foregoing immediate satisfaction. The dynamic person tends to extend his planning horizon. During the time devoted to education and training, or during a period of readjustment and starting new activities, he may be satisfied with a lower income for the sake of advancing more rapidly later. The dynamic consumer does not live from day to day. He purchases goods that will serve him in the future. He borrows to acquire housing and durable goods suitable to the status he expects to have and geared to his expected income. By thus committing future income in advance, his needs and wants exert great pressure toward obtaining a higher income.

5. Productive effort is stepped up to meet rising levels of aspiration. The effort can take two forms. The less dynamic pattern is characterized by providing more of the same kind of labor supply, that is, by adjusting upward the time devoted to gainful employ-

ment. The more dynamic form of adjustment consists of changing the quality of the labor supply, that is, of striving toward advancement by the acquisition of improved skills or education; or it may involve occupational and geographic mobility.

As the last point suggests, there are different degrees of positive reaction to change. The more limited response may be called participation and the more intensive, adaptation. A high and rising degree of participation in the economic process is a prerequisite for a growing consumer economy. The participative individual offers much to the economy, mainly in the form of labor, and demands much from it in goods, services, and security. Yet high levels of participation do not suffice to meet the challenge of progress. The purely participative individual, although tending to work harder or longer to raise his level of living, hesitates to take up new behavior patterns or to strive for more education or change in his status. Rapid socioeconomic change in industrial economies requires not just more of the same labor, goods, and services, but different inputs and outputs. The modern adaptive consumer not only participates intensely in market processes but also changes his behavior according to the requirements of the situation, and thus facilitates and even anticipates new technologies and styles of life.

Needless to say, extensive participation and modern forms of adaptation existed in earlier times as well as now, just as traditional and habitual forms of behavior also exist today. What is assumed here is that modern forms of adaptation have become more widespread in the last twenty-five years and that the extent to which they prevail differs in different countries. The assumptions presented about the behavior of the modern man served as guidelines for our comparative studies.

MALAISE OF AFFLUENCE

The dynamic modern man adapts himself to socioeconomic change and at the same time brings forth further change. Is this change beneficial? Does it represent progress? It is not enough to describe what has happened; questions about values must also be raised.

The beneficial nature of recent changes in the way most people earn their living is unequivocal. Arduous, tiring, and unpleasant jobs have been replaced, and will be increasingly replaced in the future, by physically easier and fairly interesting work carried out in pleasant surroundings. Work is no longer a way of life that occupies most waking hours. It not only provides the means for leisure and fun but is more often than ever self-fulfilling and should become increasingly so in the future. It enables more and more people to find satisfaction and enjoyment while "making money."

Arguments affirming the beneficial nature of consumer affluence are also readily marshaled. It is surely to the good when the necessities of life can be taken for granted and the standard of living of millions of people rises. But does the acquisition of more and more consumer goods represent progress? Our society has been criticized, no doubt with some justification, as being thing-minded and gadget-minded. Many young men and women have recently said "no" to the consumer society. Nonetheless, from the point of view of the individual, the acquisition of more and more consumer goods must be viewed as beneficial. It does not necessarily impede progress toward nonmaterial values, because the affluent consumer is free to extend his wants and aspirations from comfort and fun to cultural, artistic, and spiritual pursuits and indeed has more time and opportunity to do so than ever before.

It would be remiss, however, not to take note of some major problems that do arise in times of, and sometimes as the direct result of, affluence. First, rapidly growing expectations easily lead to disappointment—the greater the aspirations, the greater the danger of frustration. The more we feel we must have, the smaller the chance of gratifying all our wants and the greater the possibility of great expectations making for stress, tension, and anxiety.

Second, the extent to which different population groups participate in the generally improved standard of living is far from equal. Poverty, though it has been reduced, has not been eliminated. The awareness of rapid economic progress increases the dissatisfaction of those who do not participate in it. The poor feel discriminated against and alienated; rather than patiently waiting for gradual improvement, they demand and press for immediate change in their situation.

Third, on a different level, rising consumer demand may lead to difficulties by causing overheating of the economy, inflation, and balance of payments problems. While insufficient demand was the major calamity of the thirties, today it is the rapidly growing demand that threatens the economy. In England, in order to safeguard the national currency, it was found necessary in 1967–1969 to clamp down on consumer demand by introducing a pay freeze and making the acquisition of foreign as well as domestic durable consumer goods more difficult and more expensive. In France, likewise, the outflow of gold had to be counteracted in 1968–1969 by measures that have made it more difficult for the consumer to satisfy his wants. The increased rate of inflation that occurred in the United States in 1968–1969, although it had many causes, among which war expenditures were paramount, stemmed partially also from the attitudes and behavior of consumers. They demanded and obtained substantial pay increases in order to satisfy their ever-growing wants for goods and services and were opposed to paying higher taxes. Inflation has curtailed the beneficial effect of higher wages and salaries and greatly hurt those population groups whose income did not increase.

Clearly, consumer dynamism has its darker as well as its brighter aspects. In analyzing what has happened to the consumer and how he himself has contributed to what has happened, there are powerful reasons for not writing a story of unqualified success. Yet the greater the problems as well as the beneficial effects that result from consumer dynamism, the more reason there is to analyze and attempt to understand it.

2

The Economic Environment of the Western Consumer

BEFORE proceeding to the studies of psychological factors relevant for the economic behavior in different countries, it behooves us to review briefly the major economic changes of recent years. Each item listed in the "scenario" presented on the next page is familiar, and each occurred to a large extent in every one of the countries in which affluence had developed.

The average growth rate of the Gross National Product, although not identical or uniform, was unprecedentedly high after World War II in all the countries studied. There was no drop in real per capita GNP in any of the Western countries in any two consecutive years in the last two decades. In such instances when a drop did occur in a single year—more frequent in the United States than in Western Europe—it was rather small.

Between 1950 and 1967 the average yearly growth rates of real per capita GNP varied between the low of less than 2 percent in

MAJOR RECENT CHANGES IN THE ECONOMIC SITUATION

1. A high rate of economic growth: An annual rate of increase in GNP after World War II exceeding the rate of increase between the two world wars, and indeed during the first forty-five years of the century. No depressions and, in some countries, not even substantial recessions since 1945.

2. Considerable improvement in the standard of living: Improvement among practically all population groups with poverty persisting in certain sectors (the undereducated, the old, single women with children, and, in the United States, blacks).

3. Practically full employment: Continuous and substantial increases in the labor force. Shorter hours and fewer years spent working and greater security provided.

4. A decline in the proportion of farmers and blue-collar workers, and an increase in the proportion of white-collar, government, and professional workers. Occupational shifts and higher educational levels result in maximum incomes being earned at an ever-older age.

5. Increase in the net worth of broad population groups: Increase in home ownership, ownership of cars and household appliances, and also in financial assets.

6. Creeping inflation: Prices have increased continuously, albeit at a slow and gradual rate.

the United States and the high of more than 5 percent in Germany (see Table 2-1). The height of the latter was due in part to the low level at which the German economy started after the devastation of World War II, while the former was low largely because of the slow growth in the 1950s, when the United States alone experienced recessions. Growth rates were much more similar in all six countries in the early sixties than in the fifties. Even after two decades of substantial growth, the GNP in none of the West European countries has begun to approach that of the United States. In the late 1960s real per capita GNP was still much higher in the United States than in any other country.

In the postwar period the growth rate of wages and salaries per employee exceeded the GNP growth rate in all European countries and in the United States. In the thirteen years from 1947 to 1960 the real income of the average employee both in Europe and the United States rose by about as much as it had in the entire time from 1900 to 1947.

In considering the growth of per capita GNP as shown in Table 2-1, it is relevant to remember that the population increased sub-

TABLE 2-1   *Growth of Gross National Product in Affluent Countries*

Country	1950 Per capita GNP* dollars	Average annual percentage growth of real per capita GNP				1967 Per capita GNP† dollars
		1950–1955	1955–1960	1960–1967	1950–1967	
Belgium	816	2.88	1.90	3.67	2.92	2,036
France	655	3.14	3.72	3.90	3.62	1,940
Germany	486	7.81	6.45	2.79	5.34	2,211
Netherlands	504	3.47	2.76	3.20	3.15	1,803
United Kingdom .	731	2.85	2.16	2.18	2.37	1,722
United States	1,889	2.23	0.48	2.51	1.83	4,040

*Conversion in dollars on the basis of 1950 exchange rates.
†Conversion in dollars on the basis of January, 1970, exchange rates (chosen to reflect devaluations and revaluations in the late 1960s).

stantially in all the countries. Without adjustment for population growth, the changes in GNP would have been much greater. In the years 1950–1967, the population increase was the greatest in the United States. It was fairly small in the United Kingdom and Belgium (Table 2-2).

The increases in GNP have been presented in constant prices, thus eliminating price increases from the comparisons. Increases in the cost of living were similar and relatively moderate in the 1950s and 1960s in the United States, West Germany, and Belgium, somewhat larger in Holland and in the United Kingdom, and, for the entire period, much larger in France. From 1950 to 1967 cost of living indexes show an increase of 38 percent in the United States, 44 percent in Germany, 90 percent in Great Britain, and 123 percent in France.

During much of the first half of this century, the masses in all countries were hard hit by economic depressions. Unemployment, or at the very least the threat of it, was an experience common to a large part of the labor force. By contrast, in 1964 in the United States, three out of four members of the labor force said that they had never been unemployed. In Western Europe, where unemployment in the last twenty years has never presented a real threat and labor shortages made the importation of workers from the south necessary, that proportion must have been higher still.

In the highly developed Western European countries full employment was attained earlier than in the United States (Table 2-3). In the late 1960s, however, the United States unemployment rate dropped to about 3 percent for whites—and still lower for married whites—that is, to the level of France (where there was some increase in the late 1960s) and Great Britain. Black unemployment presents a special problem in the United States.

Depression as it was once known has disappeared from the Western economic scene. Economic fluctuations that still occur have less impact on the income of the masses than on business profits and government receipts. Important institutional changes usually referred to as automatic stabilizers allow the government to absorb much of the shock. Substantial social security and welfare payments to unemployed persons contribute to stabilizing incomes, regardless of short-term variations in business activity. Moreover, most people are protected by social security payments which provide for a minimum standard of living after retirement and in Europe also by health insurance. Practically the entire labor force is entitled to public old-age pensions in Germany, the United Kingdom, and the United States. The proportion of GNP devoted to social security expenditures is much higher in the large Western European countries than in the United States.

In all affluent countries the length of the working life of individuals has been reduced. In the United States the reduction in the number of hours worked per week was quite small in the 1950s and 1960s after having been substantial in the previous decades. The five-day workweek had become general by the end of World War II. Paid vacations, however, were extended only during the last two decades, when they were offered to many more people than before. The age at which retirement is compulsory was also lowered in that same period, and, to an increasing extent, members of the labor force now tend to retire even before reaching normal retirement age. Both trends were stimulated by old-age insurance pro-

TABLE 2-2 *Population and Its Growth*

Country	Percentage increase*		1967 (in millions)
	1950–1960	1960–1967	
Belgium	5.9	5.4	10
France	8.9	9.1	50
Germany	16.6	7.5	60
Netherlands	12.6	10.5	13
United Kingdom	3.8	5.5	55
United States	19.1	9.9	199

*The data include immigration and especially the influx of refugees into several European countries and therefore exceed the natural population growth.

TABLE 2-3   *Unemployment Rates**
(In percent of the labor
force)

Country	1959	1963	1967
United States:	5.5	5.7	3.8
White ....,....	4.8	5.0	3.4
Nonwhite	10.7	10.8	7.4
France	2.8	2.4	3.3
Germany	1.6	0.4	0.9
Netherlands	1.6	0.8	1.9
United Kingdom .	3.1	3.4	3.1

*Estimated proportions of unemployed,
adjusted to American concepts, Chandler,[10] p. 60.

vided by the government's social security system as well as by private pension plans set up by employers. Moreover, extended periods of formal education keep a large number of people from the
labor market until they are in their late teens or twenties.

Similar trends were observed in Western Europe, where the reduction in the workweek has been fairly extensive in the last two
decades. Legislation obligating employers to grant paid vacations
has been rather general, and particularly extensive in France
and Germany.

The major occupational shifts are universal. The first of the
large-scale movements from farms to the cities has long been
known. The second more recent one has been from blue-collar to
white-collar jobs. In the United States and Britain farm employment was already low in 1950, when it represented 12 and 5 percent
of total employment, respectively. In the late 1960s it dropped
even further to 7 and 4 percent. In 1950 farm employment constituted 25 percent of employment in Germany and 29 percent in
France. By the middle of the 1960s these proportions had decreased
to 11 and 18 percent, respectively. The emigration from farming
has made the affluent societies urban societies.

Farmers and blue-collar workers receive their peak lifetime
income early in life and may suffer income losses as early as in their
forties or fifties. White-collar workers and especially professional
workers and managers normally begin their working life at relatively low salaries and reach their peak income only late in life,
often just before retirement.

TABLE 2-4   *Percentage of Nonfarm Households Living in Their Own Homes, 1964*

United States	65
Belgium	51
Germany	32
France	19
Holland	18

Note: The proportion of home owners was 50
percent in 1946 in the United States. In Germany
the proportion rose from 26 percent in 1948 to 36
percent in 1967.

estate values, the wealth of home owners is growing fairly rapidly.

Ownership of automobiles has increased very substantially in
Western Europe yet still remains far below American rates (Table
2-5). Both automobiles and household appliances—refrigerators,
washing machines, and especially television sets—have caught the
fancy of the masses in Europe, so that further rapid increases in
ownership rates are inevitable.[3]

Expenditures on durables provide some leeway in balancing
household budgets in case of a temporary decline in income or an
increase in expenditures on necessities. Spending on consumer
durables is for the most part discretionary, postponable, and
prompted not so much by technical obsolescence as by the desire
to possess something better or more modern. Therefore these
expenditures can be waived temporarily without impairing the
general level of living.

The third important source of asset formation undergoing rapid
changes is liquid assets held in various forms of savings accounts
or in securities, which formerly were considered a privilege of a
very small group of "capitalists." The consumer savings revolution

[3] The recent increase in the percentage of German families owning durable goods
may be illustrated by the following data:

Ownership of	1962	1969
Passenger car	27	45
TV set	34	74
Refrigerator	52	85
Washing machine .	34	61
Telephone	14	32

TABLE 2-5   *Ownership of Passenger Cars per 1,000 Inhabitants*

Country	1958	1968
Germany	47	189
France	78	210
Italy	24	137
Netherlands	38	157
Sweden	114	252
United Kingdom	84	194
United States	321	410

SOURCE: Bundesministerium fuer Wirtschaft, *Leistung in Zahlen,* 1968, p. 32.

going on in most countries of the Western world has only been sketchily documented; its force, however, is undisputed.

For the first time in the history of the industrial societies, the majority of the population contributes significantly to capital formation, even beyond home ownership and household goods. Whereas the German national product doubled between 1958 and 1967 (in current prices), saving deposits in banks and building associations almost quadrupled. Saving deposits, the typical saving outlet for small and middle-income investors, constituted more than half of net financial savings during the sixties. In Europe, a large part of the smaller savings accounts is intended for purposes of consumption. They are a kind of down payment for consumer goods to be acquired later, particularly in countries where consumer credit is not easily accessible or is frowned upon.

In the United States, 60 percent of new cars, and a somewhat smaller but still sizable proportion of used cars and appliances, are purchased on the installment plan. The continuously growing and substantial volume of borrowing by American consumers depresses the overall rate of personal saving, which is therefore lower than in Europe. Yet Americans also engage in financial saving to a much larger extent than at earlier times. Today the common man both in America and in Western Europe has a financial stake in the economy. Furthermore, he is in a position to supplement his budget by drawing on his assets, and he is greatly interested in adding to his savings and reserve funds.[4]

[4] For detailed statistical or descriptive analyses of economic trends in postwar Europe see Denison;[14] Kindleberger;[41] Maddison;[49] Postan;[64] Dewhurst, Coppock, Yates and Associates,[16] as well as numerous publications by the OECD and the UN Statistical Office.

CHAPTER *3*

The Sociocultural Environment

*T*HE economic environment of the Western consumer, as described in the last chapter, is fairly similar in all highly developed countries. To be sure, there are differences in the economic position of the different countries as well as in their rate of progress. Yet they all participate in the trend toward improved well-being and increased opportunities for educational and occupational advancement.

Nevertheless, studies to be reported in this book revealed substantial differences in the economic behavior of the people in different nations and found those differences to be related to differences in their attitudes and expectations. These attitudes and expectations, in turn, may be traced to differences in the cultural and social structure of the different countries.

27

Whether or not individuals tend to take advantage of economic opportunities and participate in the modern affluent society may depend to a large extent on the traditions and behavioral patterns of the groups to which they belong. This chapter reviews some of the cross-national differences in social behavior the origin of which may be found in historical experiences and traditions and, most of all, in different roles imposed by society on the individual. The attempt to explain differences in people's responses to economic and social opportunities in various countries also requires an analysis of social stratification. Modern societies used to be divided into various classes based upon such considerations as wealth or income, education, religion, and occupation, particularly with regard to whether one's occupation involved manual or nonmanual work. Recent observers of the social scene have noted a tendency away from the conventional stratification into upper and lower classes and toward a more uniform society characterized by such middle-class values as making provisions and plans for the future, achievement in one's occupation and advancement in one's career, and education for one's children. Without attempting to deny that there is a certain degree—in the United States even a great degree —of this process of the "embourgeoisement" of manual workers taking place in all affluent countries, it should be pointed out that it is far from universal. Indeed the data presented in this chapter offer striking evidence of a rather surprising degree of rigidity among certain groups in certain countries in remaining within the life styles of their parents.

Nevertheless, modern society is no longer a class society with fixed categories of a social hierarchy. There is considerable social mobility. In feudal or early industrial societies, tradition-oriented patterns of behavior were transmitted from the older to the younger generation, and upward mobility was restricted to a small number of people. Today standards of behavior are often challenged by the young, and the authority of tradition is increasingly being replaced by the influence of the mass media and of reference groups—peer groups or groups to which an individual wants to belong. The latter are coming to function as initiators and transmitters of new ways of behavior in the complicated processes of social interaction. The extent to which traditions are transmitted from one generation to the next varies from country to country, as do degrees of class consciousness with its concomitant attitudes and expectations.

In 1950 the number of blue-collar workers in the United States was slightly higher than the number of white-collar workers. In 1965, however, the latter outnumbered the former by 20 percent. In Germany in 1950 there were 25 percent more blue-collar workers than white-collar workers; in 1961 the difference was only 11 percent. These changes resulted not only from increased automation but also from the decline of some industries and the growth of others. The stagnating industries—for instance, mining, railroads, textiles, personal service—have traditionally used blue-collar workers to a much greater extent than the growth industries, which include the "knowledge industries," trade, government, research.

Much has been written of the trend away from production and toward an increased role of services, to which Colin Clark called attention more than a quarter of a century ago. In the United States several service activities, defined broadly to include trade, utilities, and government, employed 43 million people in 1967, that is, the majority of the labor force, as against 26 1/2 million in 1947. But not fewer than 13 million of the 43 million were employed by the government, and much of the growth in the twenty-year period was due to increased government employment. By far the largest group of government employees are teachers. They perform a service rather than produce goods but are better classified as members of knowledge industries than of service industries. Although the number of people occupied by service activities increased greatly, their share in total consumer expenditures did not increase proportionately. When government is excluded from services and the relatively rapid price increases for services are neglected, in the United States consumer demand for services did not go up more than expenditures on goods during the last twenty years.

The number of people in the service sector of the economy is growing rapidly in Europe as well. The proportion of the labor force engaged in service trades, such as financial institutions, real estate, banks, and insurance, increased in Germany by one-seventh between 1960 and 1967. The number of government employees increased even more. The proportion of persons employed in manufacturing has remained essentially constant since 1956. Additions to services and to other growth industries stemmed primarily from the shrinking agricultural sector.

Intersectoral shifts of labor do not necessarily reflect broken or interrupted careers or even a change in jobs. In agriculture as in stagnating industries, retiring workers are often simply not replaced. Such shifts may nevertheless affect workers in several ways. Shrinking industries may not offer as much in fringe benefits and chances for advancement as expanding industries since they can afford and may even desire to lose employees. Furthermore, changes in the structure of industry may impair work routines, satisfaction, and the usefulness of the workers' education, training, or skill. Finally, there is, for some people, the danger of becoming useless, of being temporarily or permanently laid off as the result of changes in the technology or in the profitability of certain firms or industries.

Occupational shifts have been facilitated by changes in educational levels and in turn brought about further changes. In the United States, the average span of formal education of males in the labor force increased from 9.7 years in 1950 to over 11 years in 1968. At that time, approximately 40 percent of young people of college age participated in higher education. In both respects Western Europe lags far behind the United States, and much will be said later about this difference. It suffices to mention here that in 1950 in Germany and in France the mean years of formal education for males in the labor force were only 8 years; by 1962 this had increased but little, to 8.6 years in France and 8.2 in Germany.

Poverty has not been eliminated. But poverty can no longer be considered as stemming primarily from lack of employment opportunities. Not being qualified for available jobs because of lack of formal education and occupational training characterizes many of the poor. In the United States discriminatory practices and insufficiency of the welfare system are also responsible for poverty. Those who suffer from health handicaps or discrimination because of race, age, or sex constitute a high proportion of the poor—not only blacks but also older people and families without a male earner. Yet in the 1960s the number of the poor in the United States has greatly diminished, and their proportion has been somewhat reduced to, depending on the definition, 12 to 16 percent of the population.

In Europe poverty persists among the minorities of disadvantaged or handicapped people and those not adjusted to technological changes. The secular rise of incomes affects only the revenue side of the household budget. Yet the adequacy of a household's income is determined not only by the amount of money it receives but also by its needs as determined by family size and age of its members, and even by the commonly accepted standards of living. The welfare of the groups disadvantaged because of unusually large needs—mainly large families—thus may suffer from the relative affluence of the social environment that shapes their standards.

In Germany in 1962, 32 percent of four-person families and 26 percent of families with five or more persons had net incomes at the poverty level of less than $1,800.[1] In France, there is a generous government program of family allowances. It has been calculated that the German standard of living of a household with two adults and three children was at that time 35 percent lower than that of a childless family; the corresponding figure for France was only 9 percent. A French agricultural worker with four children may receive a higher income from family allowances than from wages.

In the United States, there had been some progress toward greater equality in income distribution between 1929 and 1949, as indicated by a declining share of the top income groups in total personal income. In the 1950s and 1960s, there was hardly any change in the extent of income inequality as measured by the share of top income receivers. Yet there was a sizable increase in the proportion of families in comfortable circumstances who partake in mass consumption and have an income at their disposal which is not required for necessities and permits them to undertake discretionary expenditures. American families may be divided into four groups according to income.[2] First, the poor, defined for the sake of convenience as families of any size with an income before taxes of less than $3,000, who composed somewhat less than 20 percent of all family units in 1968. Second, families with $3,000 to $6,000 income, many of which are young and have not yet reached their full earning capacity, constituting approximately another 20 percent of all families. Third, the mainstay of the mass consumption society: Families with an income between $6,000 and $20,000 represented in 1968 fifty-six percent of all households and received two-thirds of total personal income. The proportion of the first two groups has been decreasing, while the third has been growing. Finally, the "rich": In 1968 close to 5 percent of all families received over $20,000 income but had a share of almost 20 percent of total income.

For Germany, there is evidence that some striking inequities of

[1] Sozialenquete-Kommission,[73] p. 47.
[2] Survey Research Center,[37] 1969.

the reconstruction period were somewhat tempered in the second decade after the war. For several years after 1948, German unions showed great restraint in wage demands. Then capital formation was foremost on the agenda of economic policy. In the absence of a functioning capital market, business investment through retained earnings was heavily subsidized by tax privileges, resulting in a concentration of newly created income and wealth in the hands of entrepreneurs and large stockholders. After 1957, wages and salaries increased substantially, and the inequality in income distribution was somewhat reduced. A reform of the social security system drastically increased the relation of retirement income to working income so that the former now amounts to as much as 50 to 70 percent of the last earned cash income in most cases. Old-age pensions paid by social security were geared to the increase in wages and salaries and rose by 6 percent per year. While on the average in the years between 1950 and 1959 households accounted for only about 40 percent of newly-formed personal assets, this proportion was estimated at 52 percent for the last year of the period (1959).

A truly new characteristic of the present-day form of affluence is that masses of consumers have acquired sizable assets. A major factor in the increase in household wealth has been the spread of home ownership, which has resulted in part from the ever-growing tendency to move from city apartments to suburban houses. Wealth has also been accumulated in the form of automobiles, other durable goods, and liquid financial assets as well.

In the United States two-thirds of all families live in one-family houses they own. Rather than paying rent, they make regular payments on their mortgage. A large share of the mortgage payments represents repayment of debt, so that the net asset position of home owners improves continuously. Home ownership rates increased in Western Europe as well, but the proportion of families living in owner-occupied houses is very much smaller in Europe than in the United States. The proportion is particularly small in France and Holland (Table 2-4).

On the whole, home ownership does not immediately affect the family budget because its cost, including not only debt payments and taxes but also expenditures for upkeep and repairs, is usually as high as the regular expenditures of the renter. But home ownership adds greatly to a feeling of security. Furthermore, in view of the continuously declining mortgage debt and the rising real

TABLE 2-4　*Percentage of Nonfarm House-holds Living in Their Own Homes, 1964*

United States	65
Belgium	51
Germany	32
France	19
Holland	18

Note: The proportion of home owners was 50 percent in 1946 in the United States. In Germany the proportion rose from 26 percent in 1948 to 36 percent in 1967.

estate values, the wealth of home owners is growing fairly rapidly.

Ownership of automobiles has increased very substantially in Western Europe yet still remains far below American rates (Table 2-5). Both automobiles and household appliances—refrigerators, washing machines, and especially television sets—have caught the fancy of the masses in Europe, so that further rapid increases in ownership rates are inevitable.[3]

Expenditures on durables provide some leeway in balancing household budgets in case of a temporary decline in income or an increase in expenditures on necessities. Spending on consumer durables is for the most part discretionary, postponable, and prompted not so much by technical obsolescence as by the desire to possess something better or more modern. Therefore these expenditures can be waived temporarily without impairing the general level of living.

The third important source of asset formation undergoing rapid changes is liquid assets held in various forms of savings accounts or in securities, which formerly were considered a privilege of a very small group of "capitalists." The consumer savings revolution

[3] The recent increase in the percentage of German families owning durable goods may be illustrated by the following data:

Ownership of	1962	1969
Passenger car	27	45
TV set	34	74
Refrigerator	52	85
Washing machine .	34	61
Telephone	14	32

TABLE 2-5   *Ownership of Passenger Cars per 1,000 Inhabitants*

Country	1958	1968
Germany	47	189
France	78	210
Italy	24	137
Netherlands	38	157
Sweden	114	252
United Kingdom	84	194
United States	321	410

SOURCE: Bundesministerium   fuer   Wirtschaft, *Leistung in Zahlen,* 1968, p. 32.

going on in most countries of the Western world has only been sketchily documented; its force, however, is undisputed.

For the first time in the history of the industrial societies, the majority of the population contributes significantly to capital formation, even beyond home ownership and household goods. Whereas the German national product doubled between 1958 and 1967 (in current prices), saving deposits in banks and building associations almost quadrupled. Saving deposits, the typical saving outlet for small and middle-income investors, constituted more than half of net financial savings during the sixties. In Europe, a large part of the smaller savings accounts is intended for purposes of consumption. They are a kind of down payment for consumer goods to be acquired later, particularly in countries where consumer credit is not easily accessible or is frowned upon.

In the United States, 60 percent of new cars, and a somewhat smaller but still sizable proportion of used cars and appliances, are purchased on the installment plan. The continuously growing and substantial volume of borrowing by American consumers depresses the overall rate of personal saving, which is therefore lower than in Europe. Yet Americans also engage in financial saving to a much larger extent than at earlier times. Today the common man both in America and in Western Europe has a financial stake in the economy. Furthermore, he is in a position to supplement his budget by drawing on his assets, and he is greatly interested in adding to his savings and reserve funds.[4]

[4] For detailed statistical or descriptive analyses of economic trends in postwar Europe see Denison;[14] Kindleberger;[41] Maddison;[49] Postan;[64] Dewhurst, Coppock, Yates and Associates,[16] as well as numerous publications by the OECD and the UN Statistical Office.

CHAPTER *3*

The Sociocultural Environment

*T*HE economic environment of the Western consumer, as described in the last chapter, is fairly similar in all highly developed countries. To be sure, there are differences in the economic position of the different countries as well as in their rate of progress. Yet they all participate in the trend toward improved well-being and increased opportunities for educational and occupational advancement.

Nevertheless, studies to be reported in this book revealed substantial differences in the economic behavior of the people in different nations and found those differences to be related to differences in their attitudes and expectations. These attitudes and expectations, in turn, may be traced to differences in the cultural and social structure of the different countries.

27

Whether or not individuals tend to take advantage of economic opportunities and participate in the modern affluent society may depend to a large extent on the traditions and behavioral patterns of the groups to which they belong. This chapter reviews some of the cross-national differences in social behavior the origin of which may be found in historical experiences and traditions and, most of all, in different roles imposed by society on the individual. The attempt to explain differences in people's responses to economic and social opportunities in various countries also requires an analysis of social stratification. Modern societies used to be divided into various classes based upon such considerations as wealth or income, education, religion, and occupation, particularly with regard to whether one's occupation involved manual or nonmanual work. Recent observers of the social scene have noted a tendency away from the conventional stratification into upper and lower classes and toward a more uniform society characterized by such middle-class values as making provisions and plans for the future, achievement in one's occupation and advancement in one's career, and education for one's children. Without attempting to deny that there is a certain degree—in the United States even a great degree —of this process of the "embourgeoisement" of manual workers taking place in all affluent countries, it should be pointed out that it is far from universal. Indeed the data presented in this chapter offer striking evidence of a rather surprising degree of rigidity among certain groups in certain countries in remaining within the life styles of their parents.

Nevertheless, modern society is no longer a class society with fixed categories of a social hierarchy. There is considerable social mobility. In feudal or early industrial societies, tradition-oriented patterns of behavior were transmitted from the older to the younger generation, and upward mobility was restricted to a small number of people. Today standards of behavior are often challenged by the young, and the authority of tradition is increasingly being replaced by the influence of the mass media and of reference groups—peer groups or groups to which an individual wants to belong. The latter are coming to function as initiators and transmitters of new ways of behavior in the complicated processes of social interaction. The extent to which traditions are transmitted from one generation to the next varies from country to country, as do degrees of class consciousness with its concomitant attitudes and expectations.

TRUST IN PEOPLE AND
SELF-RELIANCE

Participative behavior and adaptation to change are facilitated if
the social environment is perceived as friendly and if there is trust
in people and confidence in the institutions. Adaptive behavior in
modern society means investing time, money, and energy in human
interaction. Experience in human interaction therefore is becoming
increasingly important. Success depends on the approval of other
people. Those who endeavor to succeed in a large organization,
who build up a business, or who run for public office can prevail
only if they can get along with people and if people respond
favorably to them. The ability and willingness of people to establish rapport with others, often with remote and anonymous others,
is a prerequisite in the network of social roles in modern society.
This is in contrast to traditional societies where interaction among
people has been more limited to enduring and intimate personal
relationships.

Belief in a benign human environment appears to be more widespread in the United States than in Germany or Italy. Civic com-
petence and pride in the political system characterize the political
culture of the United States. In contrast, a lack of general attachment to the political system and an orientation as a subject rather
than a participant are common in Germany.

Evidence for these statements has been provided by a cross-
cultural study of political attitudes conducted by Almond and
Verba.[1] The authors used questions developed by Morris Rosenberg to measure "faith in people."[2] The American and British
respondents are at the low end of the continuum on measures of
social distrust and at the high end on the measures of trust (Table
3-1). In all four countries confidence in the human environment
tends to increase among the better educated and the economically
more privileged sectors of the population.

A variety of additional findings by Almond and Verba is relevant in our context. In the Anglo-Saxon countries, young people
more frequently behave as members of a cooperative unit than in
Germany and Italy. The proportion of respondents who recall
having influenced family decisions when they were about sixteen

[1] Almond and Verba.[1]
[2] Rosenberg,[66] pp. 690 ff.

TABLE 3-1   *Social Trust and Distrust*

(Percent of respondents who expressed agreement with five statements in four countries)

Statements	United States	United Kingdom	Germany	Italy
Statements of distrust:				
"No one is going to care much what happens to you, when you get right down to it" ..	38	45	72	61
"If you don't watch yourself, people will take advantage of you"	68	75	81	73
Statements of trust:				
"Most people can be trusted"	55	49	19	7
"Most people are more inclined to help others than to think of themselves first"	31	28	15	5
"Human nature is fundamentally cooperative"	80	84	58	55
Number of respondents	970	963	955	995

SOURCE: Almond and Verba,[1] p. 213.

years old differs: 73 percent of Americans, 69 percent of British, 54 percent of Germans, and only 48 percent of Italians remember having had some influence. When asked whether they had felt free to complain of unfair treatment in school, or whether they had ever actually complained, American respondents answered in the affirmative far more often than any other nationality.

In the United States and Britain, the more cooperative attitudes of small groups and the prevailing belief that people are generally cooperative, trustworthy, and helpful have consequences for political behavior. Respondents who trust others are more wont to believe in their ability to do something about unjust local or even national regulations and feel inclined to form groups with others to join in political activity. "General social trust is translated into politically relevant trust," conclude Almond and Verba. Thus the proportion of people who feel they have some say is considerably higher in the Anglo-Saxon than in other countries. Only 28 percent of all Italians and 38 percent of Germans, but 62 percent of the British and 75 percent of Americans feel they personally can do something about national politics. About 13 percent of Italians, 22 percent of Germans, 43 percent of the British, but 74 percent of Americans say they would enlist the aid of an informal group to influence an unjust local regulation.

A greater sense of participation and involvement, of responsibility and self-reliance manifests itself also in people's behavior in their work. Thus attitudes of British as compared to American and Canadian workers have often been criticized. When workers finish a job in Great Britain, "they wait for the foreman to tell them what to do next. It is his responsibility; they do not worry about output at all. They work the slow steady gait they have been taught to maintain by their unions and fellow workers. In the United States and Canada they would not wait until they ran out of work to ask the foreman what to do next."[3]

Related evidence has been produced by an investigation carried out by Britain's Imperial Chemical Industries Ltd., the purpose of which was to discover why productivity was so much higher in the United States than in Britain. It is not because Americans work harder, the study concluded. It is because American hourly workers desire and expect to be personally responsible for much of their work. There are fewer managers and supervisors. A sense of involvement with the fortunes and prospects of the company and the units where they work is reflected in the workers' awareness of the need for efficiency and profitability. Flexibility in the allocation of work results in more interesting jobs. "American individual employees are self-reliant. They are frequently motivated by a desire for self-improvement, to seek training and education which increase their skill and knowledge, and the chances of advancement to better jobs."[4]

Lack of self-confidence and of aspirations, it should be noted, is found not only among blue-collar workers but also among certain groups of white-collar employees in Europe, as demonstrated by a survey of Dutch administrative employees carried out by J. Berting in nine big companies in Amsterdam.[5] Many feel locked in the organization, and there is little attachment to the job. By and large

---

[3] Ord,[59] p. 54.

[4] What ICI Discovered About Productivity, *The Financial Times*, November 18, 1966.

[5] Berting.[5]

they rate the opportunities for occupational advancement high, agreeing that "hardworking people with ability can get ahead." Despite this overall opinion they perceive a definite barrier separating them from the upper-middle class of department heads and managers and view their own specific chances for advancement as confined to the level of their present administrative duties.

Two other extensive studies on the attitudes and behavior of Dutch blue-collar workers and white-collar employees, respectively, carried out recently by P. J. A. Ter Hoeven and J. H. Buiter have supplied further data on the lack of occupational and educational aspirations in Holland.[6] Ter Hoeven concludes that the Dutch workers have become affluent consumers but that the higher level of consumption has hardly changed their mentality. Social subordination in the work organization continues to be prevalent. Both Ter Hoeven and Buiter found that people are by and large satisfied with their income and that they do not indulge in invidious comparisons with the income of other groups of people. Much of what has been called the managerial gap between the United States and Western Europe appears to consist not of a difference in know-how and organization but of a difference in occupational aspirations and in the employees' sense of self-reliance.

Interestingly enough, the persistence in Europe of traditional values of different social classes has not impeded occupational mobility. The process of industrialization, the movement from farms to cities, indeed the overall pattern of occupational mobility appear to be much the same in all industrial countries.[7] This is an important finding as it permits the conclusion that it is not impossible for traditional ways of behavior and patterns of authority to survive even in the midst of changes in the structure of the labor force. The move from manual to nonmanual jobs does not automatically result in the emergence of more dynamic forms of economic behavior.

Some indication of the extent to which patterns of obedience, self-confinement, and authority are being preserved in spite of economic progress and increasing social opportunities can be found in cross-national comparisons of educational standards and of patterns of childrearing. Recent studies, for instance, have shown that in many ways American children are treated differently from

[6] Ter Hoeven[82] and Buiter.[6]
[7] Lipset and Bendix.[46]

English children, just as middle-class children are treated differently from working-class children in both cultures. In the working classes, discipline tends to be inconsistent and sporadic, penalties and controls being imposed more for the convenience of the parents than for the welfare of the child. The American family is more egalitarian than the English family. The difference in the strength of parental authority might be even greater if Americans were to be compared with German and Italian families.[8]

WORKING-CLASS PATTERNS AND MIDDLE-CLASS VALUES

International differences in cultural patterns are most pronounced among blue-collar workers. Among white-collar employees and especially among people in professional or managerial positions living in different countries, differences in attitudes and in behavior are much less noticeable. The higher the education the less likely it is that people will be affected by the particular history and culture of their country. As will be shown in Chapter 11, there are striking differences in the amount of higher education prevalent in different nations, and they in turn can be traced at least in part to the lag in the educational attainment and aspirations of the blue-collar segments of the population.

Differences in the economic behavior of blue-collar and white-collar workers in Europe are worth studying. Do lower-class patterns of living resist modernization to a greater extent in Europe than in the United States? Have prosperous manual workers in Europe—unlike their American counterparts—failed to acquire new social perspectives and modes of behavior which reflect middle-class rather than working-class values? There is no doubt that in terms of income the relative position of manual workers in all affluent countries has improved in the last few decades. Many blue-collar families have acquired incomes comparable to or even larger than those of many members of the lower white-collar middle class—the families of clerks, small shopkeepers, or teachers. There do, of course, exist differences in security and in income expectations. The white-collar worker is more likely to be promoted and less liable to be laid off in times of recession.

Several European studies have provided evidence for persistent

[8] Devereux, Bronfenbrenner, and Rodgers.[15]

differences in the patterns of living of manual and nonmanual workers even when their economic situation is rather similar. The British sociologists Goldthorpe and Lockwood speak of "a far-reaching adaptation of the old working class subculture to a considerably changed physical and social context, rather than of any significant move towards a middle class mode of existence."[9] These authors disagree with others who have somewhat hastily assumed that with the coming of the affluent society the working class is being outmoded, that is, that manual workers are becoming indistinguishable from other groups in society. Goldthorpe and Lockwood find that although, with higher incomes and less threat of being unemployed, the workers have become more acquisitive and more concerned with maximizing their income, they have nonetheless not adopted middle-class attitudes, values, and modes of behavior. In Britain even affluent blue-collar workers, living in new communities, seem to have become more concerned with the style of their domestic living and with status distinctions between "rough" and "respectable" families than in moving across class lines. Segregation from the middle class still persists in neighborhood relations and in leisure activities. At the end of the 1950s in Britain only the TV set was equally represented among working-class and middle-class families. The washing machine was owned by 40 percent of middle-class but only 24 percent of working-class families; the respective figures for cars were 45 to 15, and for refrigerators 28 to 6 percent.

Similar findings have been made in Germany.[10] The proportion of middle-class families who own four standard items of durables (automobiles, refrigerators, cameras, and telephones) increased by 20 percentage points from 1953 to 1958, whereas ownership of the same package among working-class families increased by only 7 points. In the highest income class within the manual group only 18 percent owned all four items, while the proportion was somewhat higher among white-collar families in the next lower income category. Where the middle class had an automobile, the working class tended to have a motorcycle, a motorbike, or a motorscooter. When blue-collar families did buy automobiles, they tended to buy less expensive ones. These differences persisted even when differences in income level were controlled in the statistical analysis.

Homes and home entertainment devices like television sets and

[9] Goldthorpe and Lockwood,[23] p. 18.
[10] Hamilton,[28] pp. 144ff.

electric record players, in Germany as in England, rank relatively high on the scale of lower-class values. Whereas entertainment of middle-class families more frequently takes place outside the home, the radius of social contacts of workers is more limited. German blue-collar workers even after achieving a relatively high income level, spend less money on family outings, on cars, entertainment outside the home, and on vacations than do white-collar workers.[11] Television viewing all but monopolized the entertainment of the former. Food plays a very great role in working-class families, where common meals reflect family cohesion.[12]

According to data collected by the authors in 1968 there were hardly any differences in ownership rates of TV sets in England and Holland, either among income groups or among blue- and white-collar people. In Germany low-income blue-collar workers had an even higher ownership rate of TV sets than low-income white-collar workers. Car ownership rises greatly with income in all three countries both among blue- and white-collar families. Nevertheless, sizable class differences also prevail in the rate of car ownership in Germany and England (see Table 3-2).

The slow pace of higher income European manual workers in acquiring middle-class symbols of consumption suggests a lack of incentives to advance in status. It testifies to the persistence of a ceiling to their goals and horizons. As Popitz and his collaborators observed in an investigation of the workers in a German steel plant, they ignore changed reality and their opportunities in it. There is a peculiar mistrust of "those on the top," a feeling of being passive objects of decisions made in the upper-class power structure, and a retreat to the realm of leisure and television.[13]

In the United States less rigid class differences and the tradition of social mobility have joined forces with the rapid economic growth to make for faster adjustment and lesser survival of class or occupation-specific economic behavior. It should be said that the differences in this respect between America and Europe, though important, are differences in degree. In the first instance it must be acknowledged that in the United States too there prevails a fairly strong influence of the fathers' occupation and the fathers'

---

[11] In 1959, 43 percent of white-collar workers, but only 24 percent of blue-collar workers had made four or more vacation trips in the preceding five years. See: Forschungsstelle fuer empirische Sozialoekonomik.[18]

[12] Chombart de Lauwe.[11]

[13] Popitz et al.[63]

TABLE 3-2   *Relation of Occupation and Income to Ownership of Durables**

(Percentages of families)

Country and Occupation	Own a car		Own a TV set	
	Low income	High income	Low income	High income
Germany:				
Blue collar	27	45	82	84
White collar	33	56	65	85
All respondents .	25	50	77	84
England:				
Lower class	24	59	89	98
Middle class	44	71	95	96
All respondents .	34	73	92	95
Holland:				
Blue collar	31	51	87	86
White collar	31	59	87	85
All respondents .	26	56	84	85

*The income groups were selected according to the following annual disposable incomes:

Country	Low income	High income
Germany	7,200–9,599 DM	9,600–17,999 DM
England	Less than 1,200£	1,200–2,499 £
Holland	Less than 10,000 hfl.	10,000–21,000 hfl.

SOURCE: Surveys conducted by the authors in 1968. See Appendix A.

education on their children's education and on at least their first jobs as well. The American business elite is disproportionately derived from Protestant, Anglo-Saxon, native-born, well-to-do families although an increasing, if continuously small, proportion of business leaders do come from families other than this privileged group. Furthermore, according to studies by Richard F. Hamilton, many American skilled workers are opposed to social mobility.[14] Hamilton speaks of a "stable working class commitment" among workers and of values partly independent of the dominant values of the larger society.

All this is not to deny that there is a trend in blue-collar modes of living toward middle-class patterns in all industrial societies. The spread of the automobile among manual workers during the 1960s is eloquent warning against a wholesale rejection of the

[14] Hamilton,[27] pp. 42ff.

convergence hypothesis. Yet middle-class living patterns spread slowly, and their diffusion appears to be much slower in some countries than in others.

Contributing to a change in orientation away from the confined standards and values of blue-collar living are increased leisure time and the movement of many workers to new housing developments remote from the old working-class districts. In new communities, working-class life is no longer characterized by intimacy and gregariousness. The home in which one was once allowed a limited amount of rest and recreation in reward for working hard has increasingly often become the focus of life. The job and the degree of involvement it requires is valued to the extent that it contributes to satisfying the desired goals, including consumption and leisure.

The increasing home commitment of the worker, the changing orientation from the sociability of the pub, club, backyard, and corner shop toward his home and family life is, as we have seen, closely connected with a strong concern with home comfort and entertainment, in particular to massive exposure to nonlocal, non-class-bound mass media. TV, radio, and stereo set provide nonparochial, national, or regional information and entertainment contributing to quite a radical change in sources of influence, communication, and frames of reference.

It would be wrong to attribute the apparent lower level of aspirations in Europe exclusively to conservatism inherent in the traditional pattern of lower-class culture. It is necessary to consider as well the expectations with which Europeans are confronted today. Members of lower-income groups and of occupational groups with lower status are still expected by many people to behave in a manner appropriate to what was thought to be "their place" in society.

Later in this book we shall have ample opportunity to discuss a variety of European behavior patterns in which differences among occupational groups are conspicuous. Important examples are habits of saving, especially in financial institutions, credit buying, and leisure-time pursuits on the one hand, and educational attainment and educational aspirations on the other hand. It may suffice here to call attention to some manifestations of role expectations in Europe, which sometimes conflict with the values and goals of individuals.

A survey conducted in Holland found many married women with attitudes favorable to taking a job outside the home. However, they refrained from doing so because of their belief that their husbands would be opposed. They also knew that holding an outside job was not in harmony with the traditional role of a married woman in the middle classes. Female employment is not valued as a positive achievement but is seen as a deviation from the common pattern; moreover, it is associated with a bad state of financial affairs at home. Although many women express dissatisfaction with these norms, only a few decide to ignore them. A similar role conflict has been observed in France by Chombart de Lauwe.[15] In Germany social values define the role of the wife as a perfect housekeeper whose services cannot and should not be replaced by commercial products or services.

A further example are cultural taboos against credit buying. In Germany and Holland credit buying is widely perceived as living beyond one's means. The largest Dutch mail order company specializing in sales on credit uses unmarked packaging and unidentifiable trucks to make its deliveries!

Needless to say, in all Western societies strongly motivated individuals do go beyond the confines of traditional roles and norms. Cultural norms and values cannot be ignored in seeking an explanation of behavior and of cross-societal differences, but of course do not tell the whole story. Part of the story was found to reside in the attitudes, expectations, and aspirations of some individuals which appeared crucial in impelling them to cross lines and take themselves outside the social and economic patterns into which they had been born.

---

[15] Chombart de Lauwe.[11]

PART 2

Consumer Behavior

CHAPTER 4

Improvement in Well-being and Optimistic Expectations

W_E turn to the presentation of findings obtained in studies conducted in the United States and in several European countries. These studies were suggested by assumptions set forth in the first chapter on different possible forms of adaptation to changes in the environment and the impact of progress in personal financial conditions on consumer behavior. Only a few words are needed to recapitulate briefly and explain the rationale of the studies.

During the last twenty-odd years private households in affluent societies have experienced a substantial improvement in their standard of living. Since the end of World War II they have been, and are still today, in a position to make major choices about their spending, saving, and the allocation of their income. To an increasing extent people's perceptions of what has happened and their expectations about what will happen—rather than just their income—contribute to determining whether or not they engage in modern and forward-looking spending behavior. While the objective changes in the environment may have been fairly similar in several highly developed countries, people's perceptions of those changes as well as their attitudes and expectations may have differed greatly. How consumers in various countries viewed their past and expected personal financial situation and how they reacted to their own notions—these questions could be answered only by empirical studies. The studies were necessary in order to find out about (1) similarities and differences in consumer perceptions, expectations, and aspirations on the two sides of the Atlantic—this is the topic of this chapter—as well as (2) the relation of these psychological factors to expenditure patterns—the topic of the next chapter.

Because of the length and complexity of the argument and the data supporting it, the following summary of some major findings and conclusions of Chapters 4 and 5 may serve the purpose of orienting the reader.

▪ During the last decade a substantial proportion of Americans as well as West Europeans have perceived progress in their personal financial well-being; in this respect the differences are fairly small.

▪ Americans are more confident about further progress than West Europeans; the proportion of individuals who believe that they are making progress—not only that they are better off than a few years ago but that they will be still better off a few years hence —is much larger in the United States than in Germany, Holland, or England.

▪ Many more Americans than West Europeans attribute their progress to their own efforts rather than to any outside forces.

▪ On both sides of the Atlantic confidence in one's progress and optimism about the future stimulate discretionary consumer expenditures and make for high consumption aspirations.

SIMILARITIES AND DIFFERENCES
IN EUROPE AND AMERICA

Perceptions of personal financial advancement and expectations of further advancement were studied by asking the same set of fairly simple questions of representative samples in the United States, Germany, Holland, and England in the spring and summer of 1968.[1] We shall report first on the frequency of such statements as "We are financially better off than a year ago" or "four years ago"; second, on the frequency of such opinions as "We expect to be financially better off next year" or "four years from now." Third, we shall study the relation between the two kinds of attitudes.

People's perceptions and expectations reflect not only their actual situations but also their underlying attitudes. They reflect both the changes in the financial condition of the individual and his subjective notions about whether or not he has been making progress. Clearly, perceptions depend on experience. Yet even a substantial increase in income may be viewed as unsatisfactory and may not give rise to optimistic expectations. Whether or not an income increase is seen as satisfactory and as representing progress depends not only on its size and its relation to price increases, but also on the income increases of other people with whom an individual compares himself, on his previous expectations and aspirations, and even on the reasons for the increase as seen by him. Optimism or pessimism about future trends may be prompted not only by favorable or adverse circumstances but also by the presence or absence of confidence in one's abilities. Thus, information on objective changes alone does not suffice to predict any one individual's reactions to the changes. Correspondingly, information about the objective changes alone in the financial picture of all the people in any country cannot suffice to determine changes in either the quantity or the composition of aggregate consumer demand. Perceptions and expectations are usually similar among very many people at the same time and tend to reinforce one another rather than canceling out. What happens in the market for consumer goods—the macroeconomic consequences—can be understood only when information is available on the attitudes of the people concerned. In our studies the distribution of various attitudes of representative samples was determined in different countries and provided the key for an analysis of changes in the various consumer economies.

The survey question which asks for people's perception of changes in their personal situation has advantages beyond those just cited over a question about actual changes in income. Contrary to appearances, the latter question as well as the former calls

---

[1] The surveys conducted by or organized by the authors in these four countries are described in Appendix A. In addition, use was made of surveys conducted by others in the same as well as in some other European countries.

for subjective opinions. Memory is fallacious; detailed studies of answers to questions on income changes and a comparison of such answers with income data obtained from the same respondents interviewed over several years indicate that recollections are quite inaccurate. They do not always relate to all sources of income or to the earnings of all family members. Some people with relatively small income gains, and especially income gains that are smaller than price increases, say that their income was unchanged. Interviewing about satisfactions or dissatisfactions, as indicated by such answers as "We are better off" or "We are worse off," is much simpler and more welcome to respondents than questions that request factual information on income. Nevertheless, changes in money income are the most important consideration influencing the evaluation of changes in the financial situation. Changes in prices come next in importance. Thus to some extent the question "Are you better or worse off" represents a substitute for asking about changes in real income, which economic concept is not understood by many people and is not suitable for inclusion in a survey of the general population. In addition, some other considerations, such as changes in his assets and liabilities and even in general economic conditions, may also influence whether a person says he is better or worse off.

When survey respondents are asked for a comparison of changes over one year, specific recent developments influence the answers to a much greater extent than when the question calls for a comparison over several years. In the 1960s answers to the former question indicated greater fluctuations in the sense of well-being than did answers to the latter.

Information about people's feelings that they were better or worse off than "a year ago" has been collected in the United States for more than twenty years and in some European countries during the last ten years. Fewer data are available about their feelings covering a longer period of time. Some answers covering a period of four years, as obtained in surveys conducted in four countries in 1968, are presented in Figure 4-1.[2]

Both in the United States and in Western Europe a fairly substantial proportion of families felt better off than four years earlier, while a much smaller proportion felt worse off. The perception of improvement was much more frequent than the perception of ad-

[2] The detailed data on which Figure 4-1 is based are presented in Appendix A. The same is true for Figures 4-2 to 4-4.

Fig. 4-1 Evaluation of changes in the personal financial situation over four years, 1968

verse changes. The evaluation of changes was somewhat more favorable in the United States than in Germany and England in 1968, as it had been in earlier years as well. In 1968 in the United States 53 percent and in Germany 36 percent of heads of households said that they were better off than four years earlier.

Some related information is also available from Belgium and France. According to a survey conducted by the University of Leuven in 1966, 27 percent of Belgian families felt better off than a year earlier, while 21 percent felt worse off. In France in 1965, 35 percent of respondents of a survey conducted by INED said that their standards of living (*niveau de vie*) was better and 27 percent that it was worse than five years earlier.

Turning next to expectations as to their future personal financial situation, we find the differences between the United States on the one hand and Germany, Holland, and England on the other to be notably greater (Figure 4-2). Questions were again asked about whether respondents expected to be better or worse off in one as well as in four years. The frequency of "better off" answers was the highest in the United States. The index values (i.e., "better off" minus "worse off" responses) were lower and quite similar in the three European countries. The American index of 35 for four-year expectations compares with an average index of 10 for the three European countries, an excess of 25 percentage points. A similar calculation based on the data presented in Figure 4-1, referring to past rather than future progress, revealed an excess of the American over the European average index of only 13 percentage points (32 as against 19).

French and Belgian data are again quite similar to the other European data presented on Figure 4-2. For instance, five-year

Fig. 4-2   Expected changes in the personal financial situation during the next four years, 1968

expectations about the standard of living yielded an index of 11 in France as compared to 6, 8, and 17 in Germany, Holland, and England, respectively.

American studies revealed that people's expectations about their personal financial situation were not unrelated to their expectations about prospective business developments in the country. Thus, optimism was found to be more pronounced in the United States than in Europe regarding business expectations as well. In the same surveys from which the data presented in Figures 4-1 and 4-2 were taken, a question was also asked about expected business conditions during the next five years. The findings are presented in Figure 4-3.

Opinions about forthcoming business conditions are strongly influenced by recent past changes in those conditions. Therefore these notions vary over time to a greater extent than personal expectations. Business expectations were much less favorable in 1968 than a few years earlier. Nevertheless, it is worth noting that

Fig. 4-3   Opinions about the future course of business during the next five years, 1968

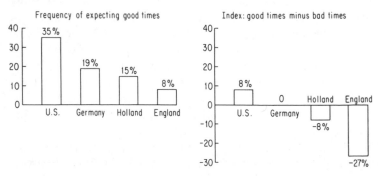

in 1968 only in America was a sizable proportion of families found to express optimism regarding the business outlook without any qualification. The ratio of optimistic to pessimistic answers was smaller in Germany and Holland, and much smaller in England, reflecting the depressed state of the British economy in 1968.

The data presented up to now may be viewed as an introduction to the most significant tabulation. People's time perspective extends both backward and forward. The separation of past trends from expected trends is somewhat artificial. Although there are always some people who expect progress even if there has been none in the past, and some who having experienced progress feel that they have reached their top, the crucial question concerns the prevalence of the notion of continuous advancement. Theoretical considerations suggest that people who have both experienced and expect to continue to experience progress will manifest dynamic behavior patterns to the greatest extent. The possibility of aspirations being raised as the result of accomplishment, in contrast to saturation following some advancement, may be studied by analyzing jointly the respondents' evaluations of past and expected changes.

Since three answers—"better," "same," or "worse"—were taken into account for both of the questions, "Are you better or worse off" and "Do you expect to be better or worse off," nine combinations of the answers were possible. These were condensed into six response patterns by disregarding differences in the time sequence, as follows: The first, which we shall call *Cumulative Gains,* represents the answer "better" to both questions. The term "cumulative" rather than, say, "continuous" was chosen for this pattern because, as will be shown later, there was found to be a causal link between past and expected progress. *Intermittent Gains* will be our term for combinations of "better" and "same" answers, and *Reversals* for combinations of "better" and "worse" answers without, as we said, considering the time sequence. Those who over fairly long periods neither experienced nor expected any change will be designated by the expression *Stagnation.* The fifth category, classified under the heading *Deterioration,* represents the combination of "same" and "worse" answers, again without regard to time. One final pattern, the answer "worse" to both questions, will be referred to as *Continuous Deterioration.*

It is apparent from Figure 4-4 that the attitude of Cumulative Gains is much more frequent in the United States than in Europe. There is little difference among the four countries in Inter-

Fig. 4-4 Past and expected changes in financial situation (during the past four years and during the next four years), 1968

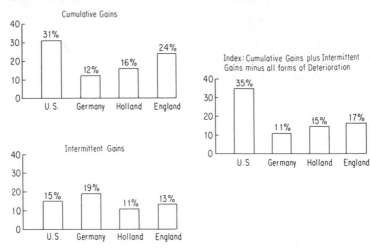

mittent Gains. Deterioration was reported most frequently in Germany and in England. Therefore even though Cumulative Gains are more frequent in England than in the other European countries, the index values are quite similar in all three countries studied in Europe and much lower than in the United States. The substantial differences on the two sides of the Atlantic, rather than variations in findings among European countries, represent the major topic of discussion in this chapter.

The proportion of people who expected future improvement among those who had experienced past improvement is of the greatest interest. This proportion was close to 60 percent in the United States in 1968. (In some other years it was as high as 66 percent.) In addition, some of those with past improvements said that they could not answer the question about their prospects. Thus less than one-fourth of American family heads with past progress expected that during the next four years they would not experience improvement in their financial situation.

The findings were quite different in Germany. In that country only one-third of those with improvement during the preceding four years expected further improvement, while one-half said that four years later they would be in the same situation as they then were. The data from Holland resemble those in Germany; in England, the proportion of those with past gains who expected further gains was somewhat higher.

These findings indicate that the association between past and expected trends is much stronger in the United States than in Europe. Yet even this pronounced association in the United States might not indicate that it was past progress in itself which influenced the expectation of further progress. It is possible that the feelings both of past and of expected progress are concentrated among certain population groups and that the association between the two attitudes is due exclusively to similarities among the people who experience them.

An initial perusal of our findings seems to support such an explanation. For example, many more families who share the characteristic of having a relatively high income report being better off and expecting to be better off than families with a relatively low income. This is as expected because the former must have experienced income increases much more frequently than the latter. Then again, the income of young people tends to increase more commonly than that of older people, and therefore the frequency of the answer "better" is inversely related to age. Both these relations were found to prevail in the United States as well as in all West European countries studied.[3]

It does not follow, of course, that the association between past and expected improvement is due entirely to the underlying factors of income and age. A multivariate analysis in which the influence of income and age were held constant was undertaken to shed further light on the relationship between past and expected trends. The results for the United States show that, indeed, income and age alone do not account for the association between being and expecting to be better off (Appendix Table A-6). After those two factors are partialed out, the association is less strong but still remains substantial. It seems evident that past experience does have an impact on expectations: the expectation of future progress is at least partly shaped by progress in the past. There is justification, therefore, for designating people who both had been and expected to be better off as people with "cumulative" gains. Their frequency was found to be much higher in the United States than in Western Europe.

[3] See the data in Appendix Table A-5, in which upper-income families as well as middle-aged families are singled out.

Far-reaching conclusions will be drawn from data on perceived and expected progress collected in the United States and Western Europe at one given time, in 1968. It must therefore be shown that the major results were similar in other recent years as well. Data on the two items referring to perceptions and expectations covering a one-year period in the past and one year in the future are available from the United States and from Germany for earlier years as well. In some thirty to forty surveys conducted between 1959 and 1968, the differences between the American and German data were found to be quite similar to those obtained in 1968. The differences between the two countries in answers to questions about past experiences were consistently much smaller than the differences in answers to questions about the expected situation, as shown in the following tabulation.

1959–1968	*"Better off" minus "worse off"** (plus 100)	
	Range	*Average*
United States	121–94	113
Germany	113–89	103
	"Will be better off"	
	*minus "will be worse off"** (plus 100)	
United States	145–114	122
Germany	110–88	103

*Compared with 12 months earlier or 12 months later.

In the United States, at most times and on the average, the index of optimistic expectations exceeded the index of past improvement. In Germany the two proportions were consistently similar.

There were some differences in the methods used in American and German surveys conducted prior to 1968, and the crucial questions were sometimes placed in different contexts. Therefore, we rely primarily on the 1968 surveys conducted under the same auspices with the same questionnaires (translated into different languages). Yet findings from earlier surveys justify our trust that the major finding of the 1968 surveys, namely, that there is some difference between the United States and Germany regarding the evaluation of past changes in personal financial situations and a much larger difference regarding the expectation of future changes, is not the result of special circumstances prevailing in 1968 alone. This conclusion is also true of the findings obtained regarding expected general business prospects; they have continuously been judged more favorably in the United States than in Germany.

Finally, some data collected in 1969 are also available. The frequency of "better" responses, referring both to the past and the future, increased from 1968 to 1969 both in the United States and in Germany. The extent of the gains was quite similar in both countries, so that the differences in expectations between the two countries prevailed in 1969 as well as in 1968.[4]

INFLATION AND WELL-BEING

A discussion of probable reasons for the differences in the frequency of optimistic expectations in America and Europe may best begin with a look at the relation of inflation and the rising cost of living to perceptions and expectations about changes in personal well-being. In all countries studied, people were aware of prices having risen during the preceding few years and expected them to go up further in the following few years. In 1968 the expected rate of inflation was least pronounced in Germany, somewhat larger and yet still moderate in the United States and Holland, and most pronounced in England. This is shown in Figure 4-5 on the basis of the same surveys in which the other data presented in this chapter were collected.

Extensive American surveys of the Survey Research Center over the past twenty years provide evidence that American consumers do not consider a rapid or runaway inflation probable or even possible. A slow and gradual advance in prices—i.e., creeping inflation—is, however, taken for granted with most people expecting prices in general to continue to rise by a few percentage points each year as they have in the past. Opinions about the reasons for the price increases varied greatly and, in most instances, were not held with great confidence. Inflation was considered a bad thing and was thoroughly disliked even by those people whose incomes had gone up more than prices. Price expectations and attitudes toward inflation had little influence on amounts saved or on the form of saving. Savings accounts, known not to be inflation-proof, remained the preferred form for the majority of savers. On the other hand, inflation did influence consumers' discretionary expenditures. In periods when inflation was perceived to be more ex-

---

[4] In the United States in June 1969, 57 percent of family heads in a representative sample said that they were better off than four years earlier (53 percent in 1968) and 50 percent that they expected to be better off four years later (43 percent in 1968). Cumulative Gains were reported by 37½ percent of all families (31 percent in 1968).

Fig. 4-5   Expected changes in prices during the next
year, 1968

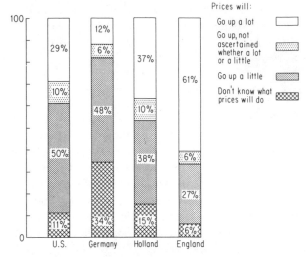

tensive and rapid, the ensuing dissatisfaction worsened sentiment
and induced some consumers to postpone some of their discretionary outlays, partly because of an expectation that a larger share
of income would be needed for necessary expenditures. This common reaction indicates that American consumers differentiate
sharply between creeping and runaway inflation. The latter would
have prompted purchases in excess of or in advance of immediate
needs. This, according to survey data, occurred rarely and only
with respect to a few specific consumer goods.

There is evidence that inflation detracts from satisfaction with
progress in one's personal situation and reduces the extent of optimism. In the United States, for instance, in 1968 sixty-two percent
of all family heads said that they were making more money than
four years earlier as against fifty-three percent who said that they
were better off. (The last figure is shown in Figure 4-1; the income
data were obtained in answer to the question, "Are you now making
more than four years ago" and should not be viewed as exact factual
findings.) At the same time 50 percent expected their income to be
higher four years later as against 43 percent who expected to be
better off. The relation between past and expected trends in income
closely resembles the relation between past and expected trends in
being better off. In both respects in 1968 in the United States

approximately 60 percent of those who perceived past improvements also expected future improvements.

Fragmentary data indicate that similar conclusions hold good for the European countries as well. To be sure, there is ample evidence that the German people are highly "inflation conscious," not having forgotten the ravages of the hyperinflations following both world wars, in which the national currency lost practically its entire value. While inflation is still greatly dreaded, the German people are aware of the fact that in the recent past prices have risen only slowly and gradually.[5] Their expectations of imminent price increases are moderate: Figure 4-5 shows that fewer Germans than Americans expect prices to go up "a lot." The proportion who reported income increases in the preceding four years in Germany hardly exceeded the proportion who felt they were better off. The Dutch data are rather similar to the American, while the English suggest somewhat more pronounced inflationary expectations. It appears, therefore, that the differences in optimistic expectations on the two sides of the Atlantic did not depend greatly on notions about inflation.

ON THE REASONS FOR OPTIMISM

Two considerations may help us to understand the differences in expectations of improvement in the various affluent countries. The first concerns the pattern of earnings over the life cycle and sheds light on the role played by age and education in determining the extent of income increases. The second concerns the relation of people's notions about *why* their income had increased and their financial situation had improved.

In the first instance, toward the beginning of this century, on both sides of the Atlantic, a substantial proportion of the labor force consisted of farmers and unskilled laborers. Today, however, white-collar employees in general and highly skilled or professional people in particular constitute a much larger proportion of the labor force. The former have always obtained, and still obtain, their peak lifetime income at a relatively early age. The latter pursue careers; after finishing their schooling, they start at what they rightfully consider low beginning salaries and receive, and expect

---

[5] More will be said of German people's attitudes toward inflation in Chapter 12.

to receive, raises over several decades. Many of them obtain their peak lifetime income only shortly before retirement. Acquisition of new skills and experience while gainfully employed is much more common and influences earning power to a much greater extent in the second than in the first group.

It follows that for a sizable and growing proportion of the population, income gains as well as expected income gains are associated with age. They are also associated with education; occupational careers are predominant among those with high school education and especially with college education. The transition from unskilled work to occupations requiring skill and experience could not have been very different on the two sides of the Atlantic. Yet higher education is much more common in the United States than in Western Europe—we shall discuss this point in some detail later—and this difference apparently contributes to the greater frequency of optimistic expectations in the United States. Survey findings indicate that Americans are well aware of the influence which not only age but also education exert on income trends.

As to the second consideration, our studies provided data on respondents' perceived reasons for their income increases. In the surveys conducted in Europe and in America in 1968, those who said in reply to a previous question that their income had advanced during the preceding four years were asked a question that sounded quite simple, namely, "What are the main reasons for your making more now than four years ago?" Many respondents found it difficult to answer this question and in spite of repeated queries gave no answer beyond saying that "I got a raise" or "My wages (salary) went up." But other respondents gave more information, the perusal of which proved revealing.

We shall describe first the findings obtained in the United States by interviewers of the Survey Research Center, who are trained and experienced in conducting conversational interviews, in probing in a nonsuggestive manner and in recording the answers received verbatim. Content analysis of those responses permitted their classification into relevant categories. The respondents who had had income increases in the preceding four years, and who were therefore asked the pertinent question, represented 63 percent of the total sample, 81 percent of those having more than $10,000 annual family income, 76 percent of those thirty-five to forty-four years of age, and 75 percent of those with a college education.

It is hardly necessary to say that the inquiry, the results of which are presented in Table 4-1, does not represent an analysis of the true causes of income gains. Answers to the single question cited above could but shed light on salient subjective notions. Yet these notions are particularly relevant for our purpose of exploring people's attitudes.

As shown in Table 4-1, 42 percent of all American respondents (46 percent of those with incomes over $10,000) made references to their own effort in explaining why they were making more than four years earlier. Such answers as "I did well" or "I worked hard" as well as references to advances in their careers were given primarily by upper-income and college-educated people. References to succeeding in getting better jobs were relatively frequent in other income and age groups as well and therefore in the entire sample. Some people, especially among those with incomes over $10,000, spoke of success in their own businesses. All those who gave answers in this first category indicated that, at least to some extent, they themselves were responsible for the improvement in their situation.

Not included in this category of "ego involvement" are those relatively few people who attributed their higher incomes to other family members who had started working, or those relatively many who said no more than that they had gotten a raise. Possibly some of the latter also belonged in the first but were included in this second category because they did not express themselves so as to be properly classified.

In the third category, consisting of 27 percent of all those with income increases, fall the respondents whose explanations indicated that they felt the income gains were due to something others had done or to something that had happened, rather than to their own efforts. We classified here those who explained income increases by price increases for which they were compensated, those who said that "everyone" got higher wages or salaries, those who referred to efforts by trade unions, as well as those who attributed their income gains to an improvement in business conditions.

Education was found to make a great difference in how Americans explained why their income had increased. Among the college-educated, 49 percent referred to their own efforts and only 16 percent to external causes, while among those with less than a twelfth-grade education the two proportions are 31 and 28 percent, respectively.

How do the American findings compare with the European in

TABLE 4-1   *Reasons Given for Making More Than Four Years Ago*

(Percentage distribution of *American* families with income increases, 1968)

Reasons	All families	Families With incomes over $10,000	Head's age 35 to 44	Head college educated
References to own efforts:				
Did good job, worked hard, deserved increase ..	6	9	8	6
Advanced in career, acquired more skill, experience ...	10	15	13	18
Changed job to a better one	18	10	16	15
Other reference to own effort*	8	12	8	10
Total	42	46	45	49
"Neutral" answers:				
Other family members started working	11	10	11	14
Received a raise	34	38	39	34
Total	45	48	50	48
References to "external" causes:				
Wages rose because of inflation	5	7	7	2
Everyone has higher incomes; union got us more	13	7	7	8
Business conditions better	9	10	7	6
Total	27	24	21	16
Not ascertained	2	1	1	2
Total	†	†	†	†
Proportion of those with income increases	63%	81%	76%	75%

*Related primarily to success in own business.
†Total exceeds 100 percent because some respondents gave two reasons.

this critical psychological respect? Unfortunately, it is not possible to give a numerical answer to this question. Although the same question was asked in the European surveys, it yielded answers much more often consisting of single words, ruling out such detailed tabulations as were possible for the United States. But some findings are clear: Explanations relating to actions by the government or by trade unions, as well as to the effects of inflation, and such statements as "Everyone is making more" were much more frequent in Europe than in the United States. The term "promotion" was often used by European respondents but without clear reference to their own efforts. On the other hand, references to their own efforts, or to the effects of additional training, were obtained from only 10 percent of the German respondents. Explanations in terms of changing jobs or of other family members working were likewise much less frequent in Germany than in America. No doubt, with detailed questioning more—perhaps even many more—Europeans might have given themselves the credit for the improvement in their situation. But the proportion could not conceivably have approached the 42 percent level that prevailed in the United States.

The differences between America and Europe in how people account for increases in their income are no doubt related to the prevailing large differences in the extent of higher education. As we noted above, in the United States references to personal efforts rose with level of education. Moreover, the frequency of perceived Cumulative Gains also increased with educational attainment on both sides of the Atlantic.

The finding that attribution of personal progress to one's own efforts is more common in the United States than in Western Europe is in accord with findings reported earlier in this chapter. In the United States a larger proportion than in Europe of those with past improvement expected further improvement. Cumulative Gains, the process of one gain leading to the expectation of further gains, must be a common occurrence when a person believes that he himself is responsible for his own progress. Those who have relied on themselves in the recent past may be expected to continue to do so in the future as well. On the other hand, favorable developments attributed to external influences or good breaks may not necessarily be expected to continue. Both the data on the contribution of personal efforts to past income gains and on notions about

Cumulative Gains indicate that more Americans than Europeans believe that they exert some control over their material well-being.

Findings obtained in some German and English surveys in which hypothetical questions were asked about income aspirations shed further light on the European situation. In England in 1966, in connection with a pay freeze imposed by the government, a representative sample was asked the following question: "If prices did not increase from now on, would you be satisfied if your household's income did not increase?"[6] The formulation of the question was far from perfect since assent to a question is easier than dissent and may occur without full awareness of the implications of the question. It is nonetheless worth reporting that at least 60 percent answered in the affirmative and only somewhat more than 30 percent in the negative. Thus the aspirations of the British for improvement in their financial situation appear to be severely restricted. In Germany in 1962 more than 60 percent of respondents said they would prefer unchanged wages and salaries, if prices were to remain stable, to rising prices and correspondingly rising wages and salaries.[7] The German findings do not exclude the possibility that the then prevailing situation, in which the increase in wages and salaries far exceeded the increase in prices, would have been preferred over stability of prices and incomes. Nevertheless, they too suggest that in the opinion of very many Germans a major function of income increases is simply to compensate for price increases. In 1965 two-thirds of German respondents said in reply to a survey question that they would be satisfied if during the succeeding five to ten years their economic situation were to remain as it was at that time.[8] The desire for continuous and substantial improvement in the standard of living, possible only through steady gains in real income, is apparently not very salient in Germany.

The notions of American families appear to be quite different. In the United States only a very small proportion of people see inflation as the cause for receiving higher wages and salaries. Price increases and income increases belong for most people in two

---

[6] Survey data published by Behrend et al.[4]

[7] See Noelle-Neumann.[58] Survey respondents were asked to choose between two alternatives: (1) stable prices with unchanged wages and salaries, and (2) rising prices compensated by wage and salary increases of the same size.

[8] Institut fuer Demoskopie, *Jahrbuch der Oeffentlichen Meinung 1965–1967*, 1967, p. 273.

different areas hardly connected with each other. Most people believe that their standard of living should steadily and continuously rise; inflation is viewed as bad because it detracts from the improvement they feel they should enjoy. If a question had been asked in America similar to that asked in England about income aspirations in case of stable prices, the great majority would have expressed the desire for rising income.[9] What was good yesterday is no longer satisfactory today—so most Americans think, and demand a higher and higher income.

Expectations are related to aspirations. People who confidently believe that their situation will improve are aware of concrete and attainable rewards that the future will bring. Awareness of such rewards represents a major motivating force which makes it worthwhile to strive for higher income and work hard to achieve it. At the same time, such awareness induces people to allocate part of their income to the purchase of goods that will be used over future years. The relation of optimism to changes in the allocation of income is the topic of the next chapter.

---

[9] In November, 1969, when inflation in the United States was fairly rapid, the Survey Research Center asked a series of questions on the damage caused by inflation and on attitudes toward anti-inflationary measures (see Chapter 13). Following these questions respondents were asked: "In order to slow down inflation, it has been suggested that increases in people's incomes should be limited to whatever amount the cost of living goes up; would you personally be willing to have a limit like this placed on the amount of your next year's income?" This question was asked only of respondents who expected their income to go up by 5 percent or more during the next year, since other respondents would probably not have been affected by the proposed limitation of incomes. Among the respondents asked, 24 percent answered in the affirmative and 67 percent in the negative (with 9 percent unable or unwilling to choose). Even though the wording of the question was somewhat suggestive—in effect asking the respondent to agree to making a sacrifice for a good cause without mentioning an alternative—the great majority of those who would have been hurt by the limitation of incomes refused to give up, even temporarily, their prospects for real income gains.

CHAPTER *5*

The Relation of Optimism to Consumption Patterns

INFORMATION on the relative frequency in different countries of optimistic expectations and cumulative financial gains is relevant if they play a significant role in influencing economic behavior. If such an influence exists, it should be most pronounced in the area of discretionary spending, especially for durable goods and fairly new products, rather than in expenditures on necessities, incidental goods or services, or contractual payments.

DISCRETIONARY TRANSACTIONS

Three considerations serve to explain the unique features of discretionary transactions and their relations to expectations.

1. Decision making by consumers is more careful and circumspect regarding some expenditures than regarding others. Delib-

eration and consideration of alternatives are fairly common, although far from universal, in connection with the purchase of goods such as durables which are bought infrequently, involve relatively large amounts of money, and are often planned in advance.[1] In contrast, smaller everyday expenditures, for instance on food, are often habitual and continue with little change over long periods of time. When a purchase is planned in advance and when it is decided upon on the basis of careful consideration, attitudes have the greatest chance to influence the purchase decision.

Advance planning and careful deliberation are not restricted to durables. Consumers also often make real decisions about whether or not to purchase products that are new—or at least new to them—and these may include a variety of fairly inexpensive nondurables. Such first-time discretionary purchases are obviously of lesser significance, however, either to the consumer or to the consumer goods market in general than the first-time purchase of major durables.

There are some major discretionary expenditures in the area of services as well, especially on travel and on major leisure-time pursuits. These expenditures are often connected with the purchase of durables. Many other service expenditures, on the other hand, become necessary as the result of external events (e.g., repairs) or are made routinely (e.g., payments for gas, electricity, laundry, etc.).

Finally, regarding savings, genuine decisions are also made as to the amounts of money to be saved. Some savings do accrue, however, simply because spending declines or income increases with no decision being made about spending the additional income. Then the result may be termed "residual savings." In addition, a substantial part of saving is contractual (e.g., mortgage payments) and is therefore not greatly influenced by changes in attitudes. The incurrence of debt—included as a negative item in the statistics on amounts saved—is a discretionary item which, however, is largely dependent on decisions to purchase houses, automobiles, appliances, and the like.

2. Durable goods are meant to be used over a period of years. Therefore they are related to people's planning horizon and may be more strongly influenced by expectations than expenditures on perishable goods or services intended for briefer use. When dur-

---

[1] This point will be taken up in greater detail in Chapter 8.

able goods are bought on the installment plan, the obligation to repay the debt in the future necessarily involves the financial expectations of the purchaser. Purchases of houses and durable goods represent investment expenditures, in many respects analogous to investments by business firms on plants and machinery. The latter also are often made on credit and prompted by expectations.

3. Consumers have great discretion regarding the timing of the purchase of durable goods. They may choose to buy cars, appliances, and furniture when their older possessions are still in excellent condition, or they may postpone for a considerable time replacing even older and less satisfactory products. In this respect again attitudes play a large role. Purchases are stimulated when buyers are inclined to be attracted to new products or new features of the products. Conversely, the absence of such purchases is related to a feeling of saturation. In prosperous years millions of consumers satisfy many of their needs and wants. If the gratification of needs and wants necessarily resulted in saturation, prosperity would become its own gravedigger; an upward trend would give way to stagnation if major expenditures were restricted to replacing goods that wore out or became unusable. Enduring improvement in the standard of living of consumers and in any total economy that depends largely on consumer purchases is possible only if satisfaction with progress stimulates the arousal of new wants. In the United States the highly valued goal of an improvement in the standard of living is identified by many people with better housing, the ownership of a larger number and better durables, as well as larger expenditures on leisure-time pursuits.

On the other hand, it must be pointed out that not all purchases of durable goods are discretionary. Some are made perforce as the result of such unexpected or unavoidable occurrences as breakdowns, accidents, and changes in residence necessitating expenditures for new cars, appliances, homes, etc. Available statistics make no distinction between truly discretionary purchases and those made with no advance planning or real choice. Thus in studying past purchases it is not possible to concentrate on the former. This can, however, be done by analyzing intentions to buy durables. When respondents are asked not what durables they have already purchased but what they intend or plan to purchase in the future, largely discretionary items are mentioned. The most pronounced correlation may be expected to be found between optimistic expectations and intentions to make major purchases which are not part of the "standard package" of consumption.[2]

SURVEY METHODS

Which purchases of and purchase plans for durables should be selected for the purpose of international comparisons? Clearly, a statistical analysis that relates to the same durables in all countries would have the advantage of comparability and simplicity. On the other hand, the spread of consumer durables and the modernization of living patterns began earlier in the United States than in Western Europe. In Europe the years following World War II saw not only the introduction of such newer products as television sets and automatic washing machines but also the diffusion of the automobile and even of modern plumbing and central heating. In these respects the transition from luxuries available to a few to felt necessities by the many occurred much earlier in America. For most Europeans in the 1950s the automobile represented a desire never before fulfilled, while at the same time the desires and wishes of Americans were already commonly directed toward owning a better car or two cars in the family. Even in the late 1960s, the great majority of European car owners remembered clearly the not-too-distant past when they had no car, while most American drivers were brought up with a car from early childhood on.

Theoretical considerations suggested that durable goods not yet accepted as standard items that everybody ought to have would be most suitable for our purposes. Accordingly, the relation of personal financial trends and attitudes to purchases and purchase plans was not studied for the same goods on the two sides of the Atlantic. In the United States only new cars and color TV sets, while in Western Europe all cars and black and white TV sets, were considered. In the American tabulations purchases of used cars were not included because in the United States they often involve relatively small amounts of money and do not represent major decisions; in Europe, color TV was excluded because it had

---

[2] The expressions discretionary "transactions" and discretionary forms of "behavior" will be used in this chapter even though data on intentions to buy and on unsatisfied wishes will also be considered which do not necessarily result in transactions.

only recently been introduced and had not yet attained any economic importance in 1968.

In addition, in the United States the studies extended to several forms of behavior not included in the European studies. Incurrence of installment debt, purchases of and purchase plans for two or more durable goods (rather than just one) within a year, and automobile turnover rates—the time period between the last purchase of a car and the expected next purchase—constitute such additional variables, which were expected to be sufficiently widespread to reveal the impact of personal financial trends only in America.

Buying automobiles and other durable goods on the installment plan represents an accepted and widely practiced form of behavior in the United States. Resorting to credit makes it possible to decide on purchases according to expected future income because it is from that income that the installments will be paid. In Europe, as will be shown in Chapter 7, installment buying does not represent a generally accepted form of behavior.

The length of the time span between car purchases by the same family is not only of great importance to the automobile industry but also provides a good indication of the buyer's urge toward upgrading his possessions. This is particularly true in America where the length of the time span between purchases is influenced not only by the desire to replace a car—often a fairly new one—by a newer or better car but also by the transition from a one-car family to a two-car family (or from a two to a three-car family).[3]

As a result of not having used the same questions for American and European respondents, the proportions of those who made or planned to make certain purchases are not comparable for the two groups. But the purpose of the studies was not to find out whether more or fewer families purchased or planned to purchase automobiles or other durables in America than in Europe. It was to compare the frequency of purchases and buying plans among people with different financial trends and expectations in the four countries. For that purpose the differences in questions or interviewing methods are hardly of any relevance.

---

[3] There were some additional differences between the surveys in the United States and in Western Europe concerning the time period for which past purchases and buying plans were studied. These differences, as well as differences in the wording of some questions, are discussed in Appendix B.

SURVEY FINDINGS IN FOUR COUNTRIES

The principal findings on the relation of discretionary forms of economic behavior to trends in attitudes are summarized in Table 5-1 for the United States and three European countries. The frequency of various forms of discretionary behavior in the trend group called Cumulative Gains in Chapter 4 is contrasted in the table with their frequency in all other trend groups. The purpose of the table is to illustrate the outstanding position of families who both are and expect to be better off. The major finding clearly shown in the table is that in all four countries the frequency of discretionary transactions is much larger among families who perceive Cumulative Gains than among families with other attitudes and expectations. Dynamic behavior was found not to be restricted to any one of the countries studied. Rising levels of aspiration and the absence of a feeling of saturation are concentrated among those who feel that they are advancing both in Europe and in America, although, as will be emphasized presently, they are not equally common on the two sides of the Atlantic.

The detailed data from which the summary presented in Table 5-1 was derived are shown in Appendix B. The Appendix also contains a report on an additional analysis which was made of both the American and the German data. It is conceivable that any relation found between felt progress and discretionary transactions could have been spurious in the sense that it was due to other factors. The higher the income and the younger the age, the more frequent are both felt progress and discretionary transactions. A multivariate analysis of the data indicates, however, that a significant relationship between progress and discretionary transactions prevails even when the considerable contribution of income and age is eliminated.

The following additional findings are apparent from the data collected:

1. In the United States the differences among the trend groups were small with respect to the proportion with different attitudes who had recently purchased a color TV set and who expressed unsatisfied desires. On the other hand, the predominant position of the Cumulative Gains group was notable with respect both to past purchases and intentions to purchase two or more appliances as well as intentions to purchase color TV sets. The same discrepancy

TABLE 5-1 *Discretionary Behavior Among Families with Cumulative Gains and Other Families*
(Proportion of families in each group in percent)

Behavior	United States		Germany		Holland		England	
	Cumulative Gains	All others	Cumulative Gains	All others	Cumulative Gains	All others	Cumulative Gains	All others
	Four years ago and four years hence							
Purchases:								
Car	21	14	16	8	23	15	35	17
TV set	11	10	14	12	15	14	n.a.	n.a.
Two or more appliances	16	10	n.a.*		n.a.		n.a.	
Intentions to buy:								
Car	13	10	20	12	32	16	32	14
TV set	13	6	12	9	9	7	14	6
Two or more appliances	13	6	n.a.		n.a.		n.a.	
Unsatisfied wishes	59	54	55	38	75	54	59	51
Wishes for better housing .	28	22	40	32	41	27	33	22
Proportion of sample in each group	31	69	12	88	16	84	24	76

	One year ago and one year hence							
Purchases:								
Car	22	15	22	8	20	16	39	18
TV set	13	10	16	12	17	14	n.a.	n.a.
Two or more appliances	19	10	n.a.	n.a.	n.a.	n.a.	n.a.	n.a.
Intentions to buy:								
Car	16	10	23	12	32	17	36	16
TV set	15	7	11	9	10	7	18	7
Two or more appliances	16	7	n.a.	n.a.	n.a.	n.a.	n.a.	n.a.
Unsatisfied wishes	65	53	58	39	75	56	64	51
Wishes for better housing	36	21	43	33	45	27	37	23
Proportion of sample in each group	20	80	4	96	10	90	13	87

*n.a. = not available.

Note: Only the relation of the percentages of families in the Cumulative Gains category to those of other families is comparable in the four countries. "Other families" include those with financial trends other than Cumulative Gains as well as not ascertained cases. For differences in absolute numbers, which are partly due to differences in definitions and questions, see text and Appendix B.

SOURCE: Surveys conducted by the authors in 1968.

was found with respect to automobile turnover rates and the recent incurrence of installment debt (see Appendix Table B-1). The relationship to felt progress is more common in purchases of durables made on credit than in cash purchases. The former may indicate a much greater involvement in the goal of improving the mode of living than the latter. It seems clear that the more discretionary a transaction is, and the more it relates to fairly new products or to the upgrading of one's possessions, the greater the influence of perceived progress.

2. In the three European countries the preponderance of discretionary transactions among respondents with Cumulative Gains appears to be as large as or even larger than in the United States. The large differences in the behavior of those with Cumulative Gains and those with other trends in Germany may be related to the fact that the former group is rather small in that country; in other words, the behavior of a relatively few select families is contrasted with the behavior of most people. In Europe, among those with Cumulative Gains, the relative frequency of purchases of and purchase plans for automobiles as well as of unsatisfied wishes is particularly pronounced. There was little difference among the trend groups in purchases or intentions to purchase a TV set, apparently indicating that in Europe in 1968 black and white sets were fairly standard rather than having the appeal of a new product.

3. The differences among the trend groups, especially in past and expected purchases of cars, were found to be substantially the same in Germany, England, and Holland.

4. Families classified under the headings Stagnation and Deterioration, particularly frequent in Germany, are conspicuous by a very low rate of participation in discretionary transactions (Appendix Table B-2). Those with Intermittent Gains — consisting overwhelmingly of people who after having experienced gains expected no further improvement — are in the middle and exhibit a much lower degree of participation in discretionary transactions than those with Cumulative Gains.

A major conclusion from the findings remains to be stated: It matters greatly to the economy what proportion of the population perceive Cumulative Gains. There are great differences in this regard in the four countries studied. This was shown in Chapter 4 and is illustrated again by the proportion of the population falling in that crucial trend group in Table 5-1. Dynamic forms of adaptation to changing conditions are by far the most frequent in the United States and the least frequent in Germany. Therefore the stimulating effect of perceived past progress coupled with expected progress on the economy must be greater in America than in Europe and, according to the findings in those countries, greater in England and Holland than in Germany.

The differences between Europe and America are not differences in the environment or in actual changes in income. Let us recall again that increases in real income during the past few years were at least as large, if not larger, and economic trends were at least as favorable in Germany as in the United States. It is the differences in the perception of and the expectation about personal financial progress which make for a greater frequency of purchases and plans to purchase new durable goods.

Dynamic forms of behavior appear to consist primarily of the acquisition of new or changed major products and the pace of upgrading family possessions. To illustrate this conclusion from further American findings: With respect to used cars the percentages of families who had made purchases and who planned to make purchases differed very little among the trend groups, whereas with respect to new cars they differed greatly. Again only in intentions to buy color TV sets, not black and white sets, is a preponderance of the Cumulative Gains group apparent; the same is true in the case of purchases of or purchase plans for two appliances rather than for just one. Finally, automobile turnover rates, indicating either a transition to multiple car ownership or an attraction to new or changed products, showed large differences among those with and without a perception of personal financial progress. It is the transition from satisfying needs to gratifying wants and aspirations which is related to the perception and expectation of progress.

There was a time when consumer goods were purchased by most people primarily for their utilitarian function. Today, with the great improvement in incomes and standards of living, satisfying the basic needs—for instance, the need for transportation in the case of an automobile—has become quite easy for masses of consumers. Their present wants and aspirations consist to an increasing extent of what were once considered luxuries or were unknown. It does not follow, however, that those who can afford to satisfy their wants all choose to buy and use the same kinds of goods. Much has been written of the uniformity of consumer goods in affluent countries; suburbia has been described as consisting of people owning the same kinds of houses, furnished by the same standard items, and satisfying the same needs and wants. Yet the dynamic consumer who perceives and expects progress is not inclined to buy what everybody else buys or even what he bought yesterday. He desires not only more and better products but wants also to express his individuality in the kinds of goods and services he uses. It is the producers and distributors who have catered to the consumer's desire to upgrade his possessions who have been most successful in the last two decades. They have understood the wishes of optimistic consumers for variety and betterment and have appealed to the incipient wants of the buyers by product differentiation. For instance, the American automobile industry became aware in the 1960s that consumers wanted a great assortment to choose from and were receptive to changes in cars—whether they consisted of automatic transmission, or air conditioning, or of such often criticized items as bucket seats, and sporty appearance. Information on the extent of dynamic forms of consumer behavior in a given country sheds light on the degree of receptivity that may be expected for product differentiation.

Today's well-to-do consumer, although he lives much better than he or his parents did ten or twenty years ago, still struggles to make ends meet. Interviews with many American families who have incomes of $15,000 or even $25,000 a year disclose that they find it difficult to fulfill the great variety of "obligations" they feel they have. Instead of considering themselves rich, they do not have enough to pay for what they think they must have. Clearly, the major reason for this situation is to be found in people's new needs and wants, unknown in the past, which arose after it became fairly easy to satisfy the traditional needs and wants.

THE GERMAN CONSUMER

West Germany, the country which rose to great prosperity in a period of two decades (a feat commonly referred to as "Wirtschaftswunder," or economic miracle), appears to be low in consumer aspirations and in dynamic consumer behavior. This finding is worthy of further study.

Data supplementing those presented above are available from surveys conducted over several years by a German market research organization in Nürnberg.[4] The questions asked in those surveys differed from those in the surveys directed by the authors of this book, but their import was similar. Most significantly, the Nürnberg surveys yielded data for earlier as well as more recent periods.

Early in 1967 the Nürnberg organization asked the following question: "In your household, are there any 'major outlays' contemplated for yourself, or other members of your family, or the household in general, for 1967?" The German expression, translated here as "major outlays," is *Anschaffungen*. It means infrequent and more or less enduring purchases that may fall in any of the following categories (on which specific questions were asked following the general question quoted above): automobiles, motorcycles and bicycles; household appliances; furniture, house furnishings and kitchenware; and clothing. Thus the term is broader than the concept of durable goods since it includes semidurables and clothing, but both the American and the German term exclude habitual or everyday expenditures. The proportion of families contemplating major expenditures declined continuously from 1956 to 1967:

Proportion of families with planned major outlays in percent

	1956	1959	1962	1967
All German households	84	80	69	54

Economic conditions were less prosperous in Germany in 1967–1968 than in the preceding years or in 1969. Nonetheless, the trend in the percentages over the eleven years leads to the conclusion that this was not the only cause of the decline in plans to make major purchases. An additional question asked in the 1967 survey yields the same conclusion. When respondents who had no plans to buy any large items—46 percent of all households—were asked why, more than half said that they "had everything," while fewer than one in five said that they "had no money." (A few others said that they were too old or that they had to save.)

Further relevant information may be cited from the Nürnberg

---

[4] The data in the next few paragraphs are taken from the studies of the Gesellschaft fuer Konsum-, Markt- und Absatzforschung in Nürnberg, Germany. They are reported in three volumes issued in June, 1967, under the title, "The Consumer, Motor or Brake of Economic Growth in 1967?"[22] The survey, conducted early in 1967, was based on a representative sample of 3,877 respondents; the earlier surveys had samples of over 4,000 respondents.

survey. Respondents were asked, "How do you feel about your standard of living?" and were given five possible answers from which they chose as follows:

I have acquired . . .	Frequency, Germany, 1967, percent	
	All families	Families with more than 15,000 DM income
Everything I wanted	14	21
Many of the things I wanted	30	40
Some of the things I wanted	38	31
Only a few of the things I wanted	14	6
Very few of the things I wanted . .	4	2
Total	100	100

The small proportion of families who indicated that they had many unsatisfied desires led the Nürnberg organization to conclude that in 1967 consumers would impede rather than stimulate the German economy. For our purposes attention must be called to the finding that the frequency of the first two answers—"I have acquired everything" or "I have acquired many things I wanted"—was not only much larger among older than among younger people, as was expected, but was also much larger among high-income than among middle- and low-income families. (An annual income of 15,000 DM represents a fairly high income in Germany, obtained by less than 30 percent of all families.) The higher their income, the more often did families say that they had what they wanted.

The German data collected by the authors in 1968 on unsatisfied wishes, which are not fully comparable with the Nürnberg data, also indicate that special wishes were expressed by fewer high-income than middle-income respondents. Such wishes were expressed least frequently by those with low incomes. The last finding coincided with those obtained in the United States and in other countries. It indicates that even wishes and desires are reality-bound; what one knows to be unobtainable is rarely mentioned when one is asked about unsatisfied wishes.

In the United States, in contrast to Germany, there was hardly any difference in the proportion of high-income and middle-income respondents expressing unsatisfied desires. Furthermore, the proportion of American families who, in answer to the question, mentioned things they would like to spend money on has changed very little over the last ten years. The composition of the desires mentioned did change, however. While shortly after World War II only a few basic products were mentioned by a substantial proportion of respondents—a house, a car, a refrigerator, etc.—in the 1960s sizable proportions were found to desire a greater variety of items, especially those connected with leisure-time pursuits. As a result, the average number of wishes expressed increased substantially in the 1950s and also in the 1960s. Thus, over twenty years, there has been no indication of any increased feeling of saturation on the part of the American people.

The low frequency of optimistic expectations must be viewed as the major reason for the apparently high degree of a feeling of saturation in Germany. In that country only 4 percent of all families fell in the Cumulative Gains group over one year and only 12 percent over four years. It was those families who expressed unsatisfied wishes with the greatest frequency and who both made and intended to make the most purchases of newer and better products. The number of such families who continuously upgrade their possessions is, of course, crucial to any consideration of the impact of consumers on economic trends. This may not have been true shortly after World War II when replacement needs were very common. In devastated Germany the period of replacement no doubt extended over many more years than in the United States. But at present, on both continents, there seems little doubt that consumers' feelings and expectations of progress in their financial situation constitute the very basis of dynamic consumer economies.

CHAPTER 6

Economic Fluctuations
and the Consumer

T *HUS* far we have found that Europeans, and particularly Germans, are less optimistic than Americans about their personal financial progress and, furthermore, that people who perceive continuous favorable income trends make the largest number of purchases of new durable goods. These findings, arrived at by comparing the behavior of people with different attitudes, left yet unanswered many other questions on the relation of attitudes to behavior. In the United States studies carried out over twenty years have indicated that data on changes in attitudes have a predictive value for subsequent short-run changes in aggregate spending behavior.[1] Whether the same was or was not true in other highly developed countries as well was not known prior to the investigations reported in this chapter.

[1] Katona,[34] and the annually published volumes, *Survey of Consumer Finances.*[37]

THE PREDICTIVE VALUE OF
ATTITUDES IN THE UNITED STATES

The theory behind the ongoing studies of the Survey Research Center of The University of Michigan, which are aimed at forecasting short-term changes in discretionary consumer demand, may be summarized briefly. Survey measures of attitudes indicate the general psychological frame of reference (willingness to buy) which determines whether a larger or smaller proportion of the disposable economic resources of the household (ability to buy) is to be used for major purchases which could be postponed. Short-term changes in consumer sentiment depend on information, not necessarily economic or financial, of which the consumers become aware. The timing of discretionary spending is subject to changes in sentiment, which usually occur earlier than changes in the level of business activity.

Consumers' discretionary expenditures are dependent on diverse attitudes. Attitudes toward one's personal financial situation provide important indications of willingness to buy but do not tell the whole story. It is relevant whether it is felt that income and the overall personal situation have improved and will improve further. But beyond that, people are members of groups; they feel that their well-being and progress are influenced by what happens to others with whom they are associated, as well as by what happens to their community and country. Even if they are not directly affected, they are made to feel uneasy by unfavorable developments in the broader systems to which they belong, just as they are stimulated by favorable developments. Therefore, what people believe has happened to the entire economy as well as their expectations as to what will happen are important components of consumer attitudes.

An Index of Consumer Sentiment was constructed in 1952 by the Survey Research Center to provide a summary measure of changes in attitudes and has been used since then in quarterly surveys with representative samples of respondents. The Index is based on answers to five questions, two about personal financial attitudes, two about attitudes toward business conditions, and one about attitudes toward market conditions. The answers are grouped in three categories: 1) up, better, or good, 2) same, no change, or uncertain, 3) down, worse, or bad. The Index reflects the changes in differences between the number of respondents in representative samples that fall in the first and the third category.

There is a lagged impact of attitudes on purchasing behavior; tomorrow's outlays are shaped by today's psychological disposition. The psychological frame of reference—barring a rare radical restructuring of consumer outlook by major events—changes only slowly. Thus, even in the face of changed environmental conditions, later consumer behavior is usually influenced by attitudes and expectations that prevailed several months earlier. The time lag in the impact of consumer sentiment is also due to the fact that large purchasing decisions, as a rule, are not made suddenly but require some advance planning. By contributing to the formation of decisions to be realized later, a psychological state, even after it has changed, may still influence outlays at a later period. This time lag is particularly useful to the forecaster because additudinal data are usually available well in advance of national account figures for the same period.

The impact of sentiment on purchases has been studied primarily with respect to automobiles and other consumer durable goods. As explained earlier, not all purchases of durables are discretionary, and discretionary spending is by no means confined to durables (it extends, for instance, to leisure-time expenses). Therefore it was not possible to test the theoretical propositions in their pure form. Nevertheless, a high degree of correspondence was found over many years between the Index of Consumer Sentiment, as measured several months in advance and adjusted for changes in income and in the population, and fluctuations in (1) expenditures on durables, (2) the number of new cars bought by consumers, and (3) installment debt incurred. Figure 6-1 reflects this correspondence with regard to the first of these. Actual expenditures on durables are compared in the chart with expenditures as estimated on the basis of an equation which makes use of two sets of data, namely income and the Index of Consumer Sentiment, both available at a time when expenditure data are not yet known. Income was considered as a measure of ability to buy and the Index as a measure of willingness to buy. Fluctuations in income—aside from a continuous upward income trend—were much less related to durable expenditures than those in consumer attitudes and expectations, so that a large share of the predictive power of the equation can be traced to movements in consumer sentiment.[2]

[2] The estimated expenditures are derived from a regression equation, calculated for the period 1953 to 1965 inclusive and published in Katona, *American Statistician*, 1967, p. 12, and *Katona et al.,*[37] 1967, p. 167. The continuation of the estimates for the eight quarters of 1966 and 1967 are true predictions from the equation fitted to

Fig. 6-1   Actual and estimated durable goods expenditures, 1953–1967 (annual rates adjusted for seasonal variations and for changes in prices and population)

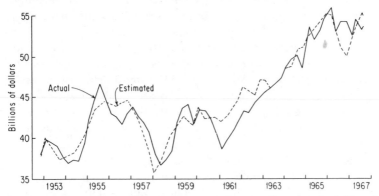

ACTUAL: Department of Commerce, quarterly expenditures at the indicated dates.

ESTIMATED: Projected expenditures, calculated on the basis of a regression equation in which the Survey Research Center's Index of Consumer Sentiment and previous period disposable income, available at the dates indicated, are the explanatory variables. The equation was fitted through the fourth quarter of 1965.

The chart indicates consistently correct estimates as concerns the *direction* of change, although the *magnitude* of change was sometimes over or underestimated. The most relevant test of the predictive value of the Index consists of an analysis of turning points in expenditures for consumer durables. Consumer sentiment improved sharply in 1954 prior to the great auto year of 1955; it declined significantly in 1957 prior to the recession of 1958; it began to decline as early as January, 1966, foreshadowing a short but steep slump in auto sales in the second half of 1966, and again moved upward in time to pick up the recovery of sales in 1967. Finally, and not shown in the chart, the Index of Consumer Sentiment dropped sharply and continuously in 1969, after having reached a high in February of that year, and thus served to predict the sharp reduction in car sales that began in the winter of 1969–1970.

The studies of the Survey Research Center extend also to an analysis of the reasons for changes in consumer sentiment. For

earlier data. The equation is as follows: $D_{+1} = 0.15Y_{-1} + 0.47A - 52$, with both terms being highly significant. D_{+1} stands for durable expenditures during six months after the survey; Y_{-1} for disposable personal income during six months prior to the survey; A for the Survey Research Center Index of Consumer Sentiment published at the dates indicated on the chart.

that purpose, many more questions are asked in its quarterly surveys than are included in the Index. Thus, to mention only a few previously published findings,[3] the deterioration of consumer sentiment in 1966 could be attributed to dissatisfaction with price increases, to a threat of tax increases, to rising interest rates as well as, to a large extent, uneasiness about the Vietnam war. Studies of changes in attitudes and of the reasons for them were found to contribute to "conditional forecasts" by providing indications of what would happen if inflation were to accelerate or slow down, or if the Vietnam war would end. The studies also served to assess fiscal and monetary policy by indicating how the expectation of changes in taxes and interest rates influenced consumer and business behavior. The Index itself has been incorporated in some major American econometric models which serve to predict future trends of GNP and its principal components, such as consumer durable expenditures.

The sharp slowdown of the American economy in early 1970 again demonstrated the role of the human element in economic affairs. At a time when their incomes and liquid assets continued to grow and their debt burden was far from heavy, consumers turned pessimistic because of an accelerated rate of price increases, rising interest rates, and because they saw no end to the war in Vietnam. Late in 1969 surveys revealed a great increase in consumer apprehension because recession and unemployment were feared as the price to be paid for slowing down inflation. Fluctuations in business conditions were thus precipitated, and predicted, by prior changes in consumer sentiment and in willingness to buy.

ATTITUDES AND AUTOMOBILE PURCHASES IN GERMANY

Clear indications of the predictive value of consumer attitudes have also been obtained in Canada.[4] However, until recently, the psychological approach to economic behavior had not been employed in a systematic, quantitative manner in Europe. It could be argued that changes in consumer sentiment would play a larger role in America than in Western Europe. The United States was the first consumption society; the standard of living of the masses is

[3] Cf. *Survey of Consumer Finances,* published annually by the Survey Research Center of the University of Michigan.

[4] Shapiro and Angevine.[72]

the highest as is the penetration of durable goods, particularly auto-mobiles. The proportion of disposable income spent on discretionary outlays is considerably larger in the United States than anywhere else. Americans may also have more reason than Europeans to watch the changing signals of the economy. Exposure to the hazards of changes in business conditions is more real in the United States than in most European countries, where unemployment has virtually become a thing of the past and job and old-age security are more effective. It was thus far from clear whether European consumers would react to new information about business conditions as promptly as do Americans. Even if they were to do so, an increase in pessimism might not result in lesser discretionary spending in Europe, as it does in America; Europeans, having undergone some catastrophic experiences in the not-too-distant past, might succumb to an "apocalyptic" attitude and speed up their purchases in the face of adverse news.

The German economy was selected as the test case. In Germany, consumer sentiment, as measured by the proportion of people expressing an optimistic or pessimistic evaluation of personal and general economic trends, exhibited significant short-term variations in spite of the continuous and, with one exception, recession-free upward trend in income and employment. Did these variations influence purchasing patterns?[5] The answer is an unqualified "yes" with respect to automobile purchases—the most important component of the demand for durables. In Figure 6-2, automobile expenditures, two attitude indexes[6] and income are plotted over time. The expenditure curve was transferred one-quarter to the left to indicate the anticipatory character of the attitude variable.

[5] The analysis that follows is based on a time series of survey results collected since 1958 by the DIVO-Institute, Frankfurt am Main. The Institute irregularly but frequently inserted three questions dealing with economic attitudes in its surveys of a cross section of the German population. These questions related to personal financial conditions compared to one year earlier, the expected personal situation one year later, and expected business conditions in the five years to come. The wording of the questions was similar to that in the United States. It should be noted that assessment of buying conditions and of the short-term business outlook—powerful explanatory variables in the United States and Canada—are not available in Germany. The discussion in the text is based on Strumpel, Novy, and Schwartz.[80]

[6] The attitude indexes were constructed from the differences between the number of optimistic and pessimistic answers to each question. The attitude questions were not adjusted for the growth of either income or population. Therefore they are compared with the deviations in automobile expenditures from the trend of these expenditures exhibited over the period 1959–1967.

Fig. 6-2   Germany—Attitudes and subsequent automobile expenditures.

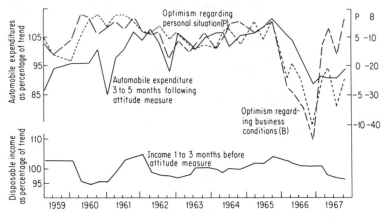

Note: Automobile expenditures have been plotted three to five months in advance.

The correspondence between expenditure changes and preceding changes in expectations for the economy as a whole and—to a somewhat lesser degree—in personal expectations is pronounced, as is the failure of income alone to reflect changes in the demand variable. Data on automobile sales, adjusted for the long-range trend and for seasonal variations, showed large slumps three times during the period considered: in spring 1961, in winter 1962–63, and during the year 1966. The strong advance indication by attitudes of a substantial decrease in sales at the beginning of 1966 is particularly noteworthy.

We conclude therefore that automobile purchases are no less influenced by earlier changes in sentiment in Germany than in the United States and Canada.[7] Although the level of discretionary expenditures is smaller, and the level of optimism is consistently lower in Germany than in the United States, short-run changes in demand appear to follow the same laws. There still remain, however, some interesting differences between the two countries in reactions to changes in attitudes. These differences emerge from data on the recession during the years 1966 and 1967.

---

[7] Analysis of British data by Gordon Heald likewise suggests a considerable and consistent lead of attitude changes over automobile expenditures between 1964 and 1969.

SPENDING AND SAVING IN
GERMANY IN 1966 AND 1967

In 1966, there was a deterioration in the attitudes of German consumers (Figure 6-2) which was out of proportion to the actual
impact of the recession. At the end of that year, the people expecting bad times to come for the economy exceeded the optimists
by 40 percentage points. Yet neither in 1966 nor in 1967 was there
a decline in people's incomes. Only the rate of increase in wages
and salaries, which amounted to 9 percent per employed person
(6.1 percent in real terms) in 1964 and 1965, dropped to 7.2 percent
in 1966 (3.7 percent in real terms) and to 3.3 percent in 1967 (1.9
percent in real terms). The overreaction in attitudes may be
explained in part by the fact that these changes followed what had
been a continuous upward movement of virtually all economic indicators over a period of more than 15 years.

The great sensitivity of German consumers became apparent as
early as January, 1966, when the attitudes as measured by the
DIVO-Institute declined drastically. Symptoms of political and
economic instability were seen by consumers in the success of the
rightist party at the polls, in the failure of the Erhard government
to balance the budget, and in a widely publicized though very small
decline in foreign currency reserves in 1965. These and similar
developments evidently made many people feel that they were in
a new and unfamiliar situation. In the middle of 1966, about six
months after the slump in attitudes, outlays for automobiles
dropped sharply. During the year from September, 1966, to
September, 1967, the value of retail sales of cars declined by 13
percent. Consumer durables was the only large expenditure category negatively affected by popular apprehension.

Although total savings remained fairly stable in 1966 and 1967,
data on monthly household budgets indicate that substantial
changes occurred not only in expenditures on durables but also
in amounts saved by wage and salary earners. Figures on household
budgets are compiled monthly by the German Central Statistical
Office for four-person households headed by employed workers
with modest incomes, as well as for four-person households of
managerial and supervisory personnel (including government
employees) with higher incomes. As Table 6-1 shows, the economic
behavior of lower- and higher-income families differed considerably. Even in the lower-income groups the proportion of income

used for the purchase of cars declined, and the proportion used for savings increased in 1966 and 1967. Yet, naturally, rearranging their budget is easier for higher-income families, and since the rates of saving and expenditures for durables of these households are considerably higher, their reactions are particularly significant for the consumer economy as a whole. This latter group stepped up their savings from 1965 to 1966 at a rate of more than 50 percent, from 6.5 percent to 10.3 percent of disposable income.

Americans, according to the available evidence, do not increase the amounts they save in times of recession. In the United States as in Germany, expenditures on durables vary cyclically, and less money is withdrawn from savings accounts to finance purchases in bad times than in good times. Furthermore, motivations to save may also be stronger when recessions threaten. But, as will be shown in the next chapter, in the United States, income increases, frequent in good times, stimulate additions to reserve funds. Thus, during an upswing there is more money both withdrawn from and added to savings with the result that there is little cyclical variation. The most volatile component in the American economy is the rate of debt incurred: buying on the installment plan is much less common in recessions than in periods of prosperity. A consumer relying on financing through credit will be primarily concerned with the relation of his future income to his obligations, while one who contemplates using part of his liquid savings for large purchases will be concerned primarily with the adequacy of his remaining

TABLE 6-1   *Allocation of Income by German Households to Durables and Savings, in percent*

Disposable income used for . . .	1965	1966	1967	1968
	Low-income families			
Durable purchases (including cars)	8.7	7.9	6.7	7.2
Car expenditures*	8.9	8.2	6.7	8.7
Additions to net savings	3.0	3.8	4.2	3.6
	High-income families			
Durable purchases (including cars)	11.1	9.6	9.6	9.1
Car expenditures*	13.6	11.7	12.4	11.9
Additions to net savings	6.5	10.3	7.2	8.7

*Purchases of *and* current expenditures for cars, motorcycles, bicycles.
SOURCE: Statistisches Bundesamt, Fachserie M, Reihe 13.

reserve funds for security. How people assess either their future income or their future needs for reserve funds depends greatly on their attitudes and expectations. Thus the potential for drastic shifts in expenditures for durables is equally great regardless of whether the purchases are financed out of savings or by borrowing.

Our findings suggest that the German consumer, who finances many of his major purchases out of savings, is tempted by a shift toward optimism to reallocate part of his accumulated reserves and make them available for the purchases of durables. Conversely, a shift toward pessimism leads him to regard his stock of savings as inadequate to meet anticipated future needs. Over the period from early 1961 to early 1964 the proportion of pessimistic expectations in Germany increased and savings grew greatly. In the years beginning in 1965, the correlation between pessimism and amounts saved was likewise pronounced, and in the first half of 1966 and in 1967 the increased flow of funds into savings accounts was again anticipated by a substantial increase in the proportion of consumers with pessimistic views about their personal economic future.[8]

AMERICAN VERSUS GERMAN
ATTITUDES AND REACTIONS

It appears that consumer attitudes and expectations influence automobile demand to a sizable extent in both the United States and Germany. This may seem surprising since we noted before that the more dynamic an economy the greater the role played by consumer attitudes, and Germans were found to be unquestionably less dynamic than Americans. The seeming contradiction is explained by the fact that attitudes affect discretionary much more than necessary expenditures and that a car is still considered to be a luxury by many German, and a necessity by most American, buyers.

A consideration of the influence of attitudes on the German

---

[8] The statistical relationship between changes in attitudes and subsequent changes in savings is demonstrated in the paper by Strumpel, Novy, and Schwartz.[30] Earlier changes in attitudes, considered together with changes in income and preceding automobile sales, were found to explain about 75 percent of the short-term variations in additions to savings accounts in Germany. In the United States, about 75 percent of the variance in the extension of installment debt for cars and other durables was found to be explained by attitudes, in conjunction with income.

people's saving practices in times of recessions, as outlined above, reinforces the picture of the Germans as notably less dynamic than the Americans. The common American way of reacting to improved expectations may be called expansive and the German pattern defensive. In times of rising optimism, the American consumer is willing to commit expected income to satisfying his consumption aspirations by buying on the installment plan; he thus increases the burden of fixed costs in future periods. By so doing, he takes a certain risk; if his expectations of income increases are not realized, he has to cut down on his consumption or fall back on his savings.

The German consumer behaves differently. He typically does not accept the risk of restricting his future budgets by commitments made in advance. We noted before that the proportion of optimists is consistently lower in Germany than in the United States. When there is a favorable shift in attitudes it consists in Germany, much more frequently than in the United States, of respondents' switching from the pessimistic ("will be worse") to the neutral ("will be the same") response. Thus an improvement in sentiment often means simply that consumers expect things not to get worse rather than that they expect them to get better. This in turn means that, although there is less felt need to add to savings for rainy days if one expects fewer such days, there is still little willingness to commit future income increases to purchases of durables. Conversely, in periods of unfavorable consumer sentiment, there is an unusually large number of people concerned with the danger of income losses rather than merely with stagnation, and savings are stepped up accordingly. Defense of the status quo is valued beyond rapid adjustment to long-term income gains.

In short, the average American consumer, convinced of a gradually rising income trend, tends to adjust his consumption levels in anticipation of the expected favorable developments. He tends to expect the present constantly improving economic situation to continue; it is the minimum which he takes for granted. In the United States optimism relates to improvement in the status quo, pessimism to its continuation. In contrast, German consumers hesitate to consider the extensive recent gains in prosperity as anything to be counted on for the future. Their confidence, when it prevails, is primarily oriented toward the continuation of the status quo; their pessimism reflects fear of the loss of some part of what they have achieved. While Americans contemplate how to spend tomorrow's higher income, Germans are more concerned with how to allocate yesterday's savings.

IS THE BUSINESS CYCLE OBSOLETE?

During the last ten years some experts have asserted that the business cycle is obsolete. The mere fact that this proposition has been seriously discussed points up the very great difference in the situation in highly developed countries in the 1950s and 1960s as compared to earlier times. The boom-bust cycle belongs to the past, and the recurrence of a severe depression in which unemployment affects as many as one-fifth or one-fourth of the labor force— as it did in the thirties—has become practically impossible. It seems unlikely, however, that we have arrived at an era in which we can count on continuing periods of steady growth or even uninterrupted economic stability. It appears probable that some economic fluctuations resulting in an alternation of periods of upswing and of probably shorter periods of stagnation or deterioration will continue to prevail in the future. This assumption is supported by the findings presented in this chapter indicating that the human factor exerts a significant influence on shaping economic trends. Attitudes and expectations fluctuate autonomously, that is, not necessarily in accordance with movements in income, and their improvement accelerates and their deterioration retards demand. This has been shown here only for the consumer sector, the influence of which on the total economy is growing, but is known to be true of business expectations and their influence on business investment as well.

One major factor reinforcing the opinion that economic cycles are obsolete consists of confidence in the power of new and sophisticated kinds of government policy which are thought to be capable of stabilizing the economy. A discussion of automatic stabilizers and of methods of countercyclical fiscal and monetary policy does not belong in this book. But it should be pointed out that people's attitudes toward government policy play a great role in determining its effectiveness. Whether or not a change in taxes or interest rates helps to curtail a boom or to overcome a threatening recession depends on people's reactions to the measures. These reactions are not automatic; a tax increase of X billion dollars does not necessarily reduce consumer demand by the same X billion dollars, or even a fixed proportion thereof.

Studies of consumer reactions to changes in income tax rates in the United States indicate that they vary greatly at different times and under different circumstances.[9] The large tax cut of 1964 had an impact on consumer behavior even before March of that year when withholdings from pay were actually reduced. Expenditures on durable goods and the incurrence of installment debt increased in the winter of 1963–1964 in anticipation of the tax cut, which was seen as ensuring an improvement in business conditions. On the other hand, during the first few months following the enactment of the cut, a sizable proportion of the gains in disposable income went into liquid assets rather than expenditures. Later in 1964 and in 1965, frequent and substantial increases in wages and salaries as well as the slowly accumulating gains from the tax cut again greatly stimulated consumer demand.

An aftermath of the satisfaction American taxpayers felt with the tax cut of 1964 was noticeable in 1966. Surveys conducted in that year disclosed that the majority of consumers had heard of the possibility of an increase in income tax rates and fully expected it to come about. Most informed people thought that a tax increase would depress economic activity, not simply because they did not cherish the prospect of paying higher taxes but also and primarily because they viewed the tax increase as the opposite of the tax cut of 1964, which they still remembered clearly as having been favorable to the economy.

Yet by the time the surtax became law in the summer of 1968, its psychological effect was very slight. People considered the impact of the surtax on their personal situation as temporary or, in a period of rapidly rising real wages, even nonexistent. In view of their optimistic attitudes, as determined by attitude surveys, people did not adjust their consumption downward and did not refrain from making planned expenditures. Naturally, a tax increase reduces the ability to buy, but changes in willingness to buy may counteract or even cancel out that factor, as they did in 1968. On the other hand, if a government manages to convince people of the serious and lasting impact of its restrictive measures, consumers may overreact by cutting down their discretionary expenditures in excess of the reduction in their income, as happened in Germany in 1966.

These experiences indicate that there are almost insurmount-

[9] Katona and Mueller.[39] See also Katona et al.[37] and Katona.[40]

able problems of timing which appear to preclude the management of consumer demand. Consumer reactions over the short term are far from being amenable to guidance. Although to some extent they can now be predicted from surveys of consumer attitudes, this information does not appear to suffice to enable the government to accomplish a "fine tuning" of its policy.

CHAPTER 7

Saving and Borrowing

BETWEEN the mid-fifties and the late sixties net
personal saving was relatively large in Germany and relatively
small in the United States; according to the conventional definition
of saving, the proportion of income saved by German households
substantially exceeded the proportion saved by American households. It will be shown in this chapter that financial practices in the
two countries, as determined by people's attitudes toward saving
and borrowing, serve to explain much of that difference. The German people save substantial amounts of money in various kinds
of savings institutions for the purpose of paying for future purchases, including dwellings and automobiles. Americans, on the
other hand, rather than saving in advance, borrow the money to
pay for a large share of their purchases of durables and repay their
debts out of income while using the goods. In the United States
consumer debt rose greatly both in the 1950s and the 1960s.

Hardly any financial statistics are more tenuous and questionable than those on amounts saved by individuals or households. Because of differences in definitions and in methods of measurement, the statement applies to international comparisons to a still greater extent than to data from each country.[1] In spite of the tenuous character of the measures used, data on the overall saving rates in the countries with which we are concerned are presented in Table 7-1.

We shall concentrate in this chapter on differences between the United States and Germany, the two countries for which the most

TABLE 7-1 *Aggregate   Personal Saving in Percent of Disposable Income*
(Approximate   averages for the period 1955 to 1965)

Germany	13 1/2
Holland	13 1/2
Belgium	10
France	7 1/2
United Kingdom	5 1/2
United States	6

Notes: In Germany the rate of saving was rather uniform, varying only from 12 to 14 1/2 percent during the ten-year period. In 1966 and 1967 it was on the low side, 12 1/2 and 12 percent, respectively.

In the United States the rate of saving rose to approximately 7 percent in 1966–1968.

SOURCE: Government statistics in each country compiled by the United Nations Statistical Office.

[1] Most commonly, amounts saved are determined as a "residual," representing the difference between disposable income and consumer expenditures. In the residuals, errors in measuring expenditures and income are confounded. In addition, the definitions used for savings and for "individuals" make for discrepancies in the estimates in different countries. Unincorporated business firms, welfare and pension funds, and the like, are often not distinguished from individuals. Many forms of household or personal saving represent residuals even in more recent and more sophisticated flow-of-funds accounts. Only statistics on net changes in deposits with financial institutions — as provided, for instance, in the United States by the Securities and Exchange Commission — make use of direct measurements of some amounts saved. Even in that case, the problem of distinguishing individuals from business firms and funds is not solved.

extensive information is available. The difference in the saving rate between these two countries is so large that lack of comparability in definitions or methods of compilation can hardly account for it. In many respects, German saving practices are typical for continental Western Europe.

In attempting to understand the difference in the saving rate between Germany and the United States we shall discuss separately two major elements that enter into personal savings: (1) financial saving, consisting of net additions to deposits in banks and other financial institutions and net purchases of stocks and bonds; (2) incurring and repaying debt, the former constituting negative and the latter positive saving.

THE EXTENT OF FINANCIAL SAVING

Financial saving by individuals in the form of putting money into banks and other savings institutions is reflected in the balance sheets of those institutions. These statistics indicate a high rate of growth in the last several years in Germany as well as in the United States. The growth of savings deposits has been spectacular in Germany, where they amounted to 2,500 DM per capita in 1968 against 1,450 DM in 1964 and 850 DM in 1960. Yet the total accumulated savings deposits, resulting from ten to fifteen years of high rates of saving, are far from impressive: Savings and time deposits per capita in the United States appear to be three to four times as large as in Germany, while disposable income per capita is only about twice as large. Furthermore, these calculations exclude securities, in which Americans have very much larger investments than Germans.

Turning from aggregate data to information on individuals, we likewise find indications of a high degree of financial saving in the 1960s in Germany. Recent surveys found the proportion of German families having savings accounts with banks, building associations, or the post office to be as high as 85 percent of all families. A survey conducted in 1959 estimated that proportion at only 53 percent. In that year only 34 percent of households had a savings book, while by 1965 that proportion had risen to 61 percent. In the United States a smaller proportion of the population has savings accounts than in Germany. The proportion of families with savings deposits or time deposits at commercial banks, savings banks, savings and loan institutions, or credit unions was estimated at less than two-thirds in the late sixties. This represented a substantial increase from the early fifties when the proportion was less than 50 percent.

The proportion of American savers appears to be smaller than the proportion of German savers. Among holders of savings accounts in the United States less than 40 percent in each of the last few years indicated in surveys that they had increased their deposits. (This proportion excludes small increments resulting primarily from the accrual of interest.) Every year close to one-fifth of all those with savings accounts were net dissavers, having reduced their deposits by larger amounts than they had added to them. Finally, each year a sizable proportion of all American families, and a very large proportion of low-income families, neither added to nor subtracted from their financial assets.

Checking accounts are much more common in the United States than in Germany, the proportion of families having such accounts being estimated at 70 percent and 30 percent, respectively. In 1959 in Germany only one in four survey respondents said that they had *ever* written a check.[2] This difference between the two countries, although interesting, is hardly relevant to an assessment of saving practices since few people use checking accounts for the purpose of saving.

Ownership of bonds is uncommon in both Germany and the United States, with the single exception of Government Savings Bonds in the United States. These discount bonds, popularized as War Bonds during World War II, are still held by close to one-fourth of all American families but no longer represent an important outlet for additional saving.

Differences do prevail between the two countries with respect to the ownership of common stock. In the United States the number of stockholders increased continuously and substantially during the 1950s and 1960s. According to Survey Research Center data, in 1969 approximately 25 percent of the 62 million American family units owned common stock (including shares of mutual funds).[3] Twenty years earlier the proportion had been as low as 6 to 8 percent of the then less than 50 million family units.

It should be noted, however, that most of the newer stockholders

[2] Instead of writing checks, Germans fairly commonly pay their bills by instructing their banks to transfer money from their account to the account of a business firm.

[3] These survey findings correspond fairly well with data compiled by the New York Stock Exchange on stock ownership by individuals (counting separately wives, etc.), which show that there were 26 million stock owners.

own fairly small amounts of stock. The fact that in the United States the value of individual holdings of stocks has increased substantially and now constitutes by far the largest proportion of individual savings is due primarily to the appreciation of stock values rather than to new money invested in stocks.[4]

In Germany the proportion of households owning stocks is very much smaller than in the United States. It was estimated at 5 percent in 1961 and at 8 to 9 percent in 1965.[5] The postwar increase in the number of stockholders resulted partly from the distribution of shares of publicly owned companies (e.g., Volkswagen) to private holders. In Germany as in the United States, stocks are held primarily by upper income people. In general German households have larger amounts of money in savings deposits than in securities, and stockholdings represent a much smaller share of the total of individually owned assets than in the United States.

In Western Europe as in America there is of course indirect as well as direct stock ownership by virtue of having savings in institutions, especially life insurance companies and pension funds, which in turn own large amounts of stock. Nevertheless, the data on the small amounts of direct stockholdings by German households make it understandable that for the past few years there have been frequent complaints about the insufficiency of risk capital available in that country.

Data on a few other forms of savings may be mentioned briefly, although they do little to change the total picture. Some part of payments of life insurance premiums represents savings; in the mid-sixties only somewhat more than one-half of all German families carried any life insurance as against close to three-fourths of American families. Saving through government insurance (social security) was once much more widespread in Germany than in the United States, where it has, however, greatly expanded in the last decades. A new development, the introduction of numerous private pension plans, has also substantially increased the American people's contribution to savings for retirement. Private pension plans also exist in Germany, but they are not as widespread as in the United States.

----

[4] Stockholdings are highly concentrated in the United States among the rich. An analysis of tax returns indicated that 1 percent of American families, those with the largest stockholdings, hold as much as 50 percent of the value of all individually owned stocks.

[5] The source of the 1961 data is Schmoelders.[69] The 1965 data are from a survey conducted by the DIVO organization.

To sum up, the available data do not warrant the conclusion that the great difference between Germany and the United States in overall saving rates is due to differences in the extent of financial saving in the two countries.[6] The explanation must lie elsewhere.

THE IMPACT OF BORROWING ON TOTAL SAVING

The most substantial differences in economic behavior between the United States and Western Europe were found to prevail in the use made of consumer credit. These differences greatly influence the total saving performance of people on both sides of the Atlantic.

There are, first, some differences with respect to the use made of mortgages in financing the purchase of homes. In Germany about 40 percent and in the United States about 67 percent of all families live in houses they own. Home ownership and mortgage debt have increased in the postwar years in both countries but much more in America than in Germany. In America homes are purchased typically with relatively small down payments, and about 40 percent of all families save every year by repaying some of their mortgage debt. In Germany much of the large-scale residential building is financed by individuals making deposits with building associations *(Bausparkassen)* over many years and obtaining from them some additional funds when the purchase is concluded. According to a German survey, in 1965 nineteen percent of all families had savings contracts with building associations. Yet about one-third of these people did not intend to build or purchase a new dwelling. They explained that saving contracts with building associations simply represented a very good way to save. Thus continuous and substantial accumulations of "deposits for building" often do not result in house purchases.

---

[6] The *Capital Markets Study* of the OECD[60] also concluded that in "the four western countries (United States, United Kingdom, Germany, and France) the rate of household financial savings out of income is quite close" (1967, p. 17). The American and German data may be supplemented by the information that in the early 1960s less than 30 percent of families in France and Holland had savings accounts. Much of the financial saving in France is in currency and demand deposits. In Britain the proportion with savings accounts is estimated at 60 percent, and holdings of bonds are also relatively common in that country. The proportion of families owning common stocks was estimated at 10 percent or somewhat lower in Britain and France as well as in Holland and Belgium. The rate of growth in stock ownership appears to be fairly small in all these countries. Life insurance is relatively common in Great Britain and uncommon in France.

There are radical differences between Germany and the United States with respect to consumer credit other than mortgages and especially in installment credit. In the United States in the late 1960s close to one-half of all families had some installment debt, and close to 40 percent of all families bought something on the installment plan each year in the 1960s. Every year more than 60 percent of all new cars and about one-half of all used cars and major appliances are bought on the installment plan. The best figure available for Germany is that in the late 1960s eleven percent of all families were making monthly installment payments. This proportion did not increase at all in the 1960s and, according to some surveys, may even have declined somewhat. Only 14 percent of German buyers of durable goods used credit as the primary method of financing their purchases in the late 1960s.

The average monthly payment on installment debt is likewise much higher in the United States than in Germany. In America by far the largest proportion of installment debt is owed for purchases of automobiles; in Germany, for purchases of household appliances, furniture, and semidurables. In the United States families in the middle and upper-middle income groups make the greatest use of installment credit; in Germany, low-income families. Total installment debt outstanding was slightly over $2 billion in Germany at the end of 1967, as against $80 billion in the United States (approximately $30 as against $400 per capita).

The difference between the two countries is much greater than could be explained by the fact that a larger proportion of families buy cars every year in America than in Germany. Established habits and attitudes constitute the primary explanation of the difference in the incidence of installment debt. In Germany the most usual form of purchasing durable goods is to save in advance of the purchase; in the United States it is to buy on the installment plan. Americans in general choose to use their cars and appliances while paying for them. By contrast, a very large proportion of the German people is absolutely opposed to debt. The accepted form of behavior in Germany is *Ansparen,* meaning saving in advance of purchases, rather than *Absparen,* denoting repayment of debt after the purchase has been made.

Before discussing the differences in German and American attitudes toward borrowing, the relevance of the different forms of behavior for total saving should be clarified. The difference between saving in advance of a purchase and saving afterwards through repaying debt does not necessarily result in a difference in overall saving rates. If in the United States incurrence of new installment debt were balanced every year by repayment of such debt, and if in Germany the amounts saved in advance were balanced by withdrawals from liquid funds to make cash purchases, the overall saving rates of the two countries would not be affected by the different practices. The fact is, however, that in the last ten years in Germany families have accumulated liquid funds beyond the amounts they have used while in the United States outstanding installment debt has risen year after year far beyond the amounts of repayments made.

The impact on aggregate saving of the American practice of borrowing to finance large expenditures can be illustrated from saving data compiled by the Securities and Exchange Commission. In Table 7-2 averages are presented for the years 1967 and 1968; the general picture was similar in earlier years as well.

The fact that in the United States in practically every one of the postwar years the amounts of consumer debt incurred greatly exceeded the amounts repaid substantially lowered the overall American saving rate. For instance, if there had not been an increase in consumer debt outstanding in 1967 or in 1968, $62 billion saved (see Table 7-2) would have represented close to 11 percent of disposable income; net savings, however, amounted to only $41 billion, or less than 7 percent of disposable income. We may safely conclude that a substantial part of the difference between the saving rates of American and German households has been due to the continuous increase in consumer debt in the United States.[7]

TABLE 7-2 *Personal Saving, United States*

	Approximate averages for 1967 and 1968
Net additions to liquid assets by individuals	$42 1/2 billion
Net saving through private pensions and insurance ...	14
Net saving through government insurance	5 1/2
Total	62
Deduct net dissaving due to increase in consumer debt	21
Total personal financial saving*	$41 billion

* A large net increase in mortgage debt is excluded, as is the increase in the value of owner-occupied houses, other real estate, as well as in the stock of consumer durables.

[7] Saving by business firms is excluded from discussion. The contribution by corporations to total saving is very large in both countries. In Germany ownership of businesses by individuals and partnerships is probably more common than in the

ATTITUDES TOWARD FINANCING CONSUMER INVESTMENT EXPENDITURES

For both the United States and Germany a variety of survey data are available on people's attitudes toward saving and borrowing, and they contribute to an understanding of the basic differences in the behavior of the peoples of the two countries. In the light of such data Guenter Schmoelders has for many years emphasized the importance for the German people of *Konsumsparen* (saving for consumption) and *Bausparen* (saving for housing).[8] When in surveys Germans were asked about the purposes of saving, they mentioned most frequently purchases they wanted to make in the near or even fairly distant future and for the sake of which they were putting money aside in savings institutions. As an example, the results of a 1967 survey are cited in Table 7-3.

TABLE 7-3 *Purposes of Saving in Germany in 1967, percent*

For emergencies, for the sake of security	44
For *Anschaffungen**	59
For vacation and travel	23
For education and training	7
Purpose uncertain, not ascertained	15
Do not save	12
Total	†

*This German term means large purchases which include not only automobiles and appliances, but also house furnishings and some clothing items.

†Greatly exceeds 100 percent because many respondents mentioned more than one purpose.
SOURCE: Gesellschaft fuer Konsum-, Markt- und Absatzforschung.[22]

Similar conclusions emerge from an earlier survey in which respondents were asked how they planned to use the various kinds of savings accounts they had. The answers most frequently given were grouped into three rather descriptive categories as explained in Table 7-4.

United States. Saving rates by self-employed people are relatively high in both countries. The inclusion of saving by the self-employed in the statistics on personal saving may explain some of the differences apparent in Table 7-1.

    [8] Schmoelders.[69]

TABLE 7-4 *Contemplated Use of Savings Accounts,*
Germany, 1959, by percent

Use of savings accounts	Accounts with		
	Savings banks	Commercial banks	Post office
*Konsumsparen**	45	41	65
Vorsorgesparen†	39	41	18
Vermoegensparen‡	37	33	16
For current expenditures	9	3	9
Total	¶	¶	¶

*Included here is the mention of specific consumer goods and of *Anschaffungen.*
†For medical expenses, needed repairs; also for security in general.
‡For the purchase of houses and securities, also for accumulation of funds in general.
¶Total exceeds 100 percent because some people mentioned more than one purpose.
SOURCE: Schmoelders, *Der Umgang.*[69]

The share of total savings represented by money saved for future purchases is very large in Germany. Amounts saved for consumption and building have been estimated at close to one-half of total savings.[9]

American answers to questions about the purposes of saving are quite different from the German answers. As can be seen in Table 7-5 the answers of most members of representative samples of Americans could be grouped into three categories—for a rainy day, for retirement and old age, and for the needs of children, primarily their education and other fairly long-range needs. Only a minority mentioned contemplated large purchases—especially a house and consumer durables—among their reasons for saving.

Data on the purposes of saving reflect differences in underlying attitudes even greater than the differences in actual practices. Actually, although relatively few Americans save for the specific purpose of buying a car or a household appliance at some later time, many do use savings for down payments or even to make the entire payment for such purchases (beyond the money received from trading in old goods). The total amounts withdrawn from savings accounts for such purposes are, however, usually small; and

[9] OECD,[60] vol. II, p. 160. This report also indicates that saving for the purpose of paying for consumer expenditures at a later time is widespread in France as well.

TABLE 7-5   *Purposes of Saving in the United States*
(Frequency, in percent, of purposes mentioned by
more than 3 percent of each group)

Purposes	All family units		Family units with incomes of $10,000 or more	
	1960	1966	1960	1966
Rainy days (emergencies, illness, unemployment) ..	46	45	45	39
Retirement, old age	27	31	39	46
Children's needs (primarily education)	25	22	33	32
Buying a house	8	8	6	6
Buying durable goods	6	7	4	7
Total	*	*	*	*

*Total adds to more than 100 percent because some respondents
mentioned more than one purpose.
The questions were: "Different people have different reasons for
saving. In your case, what are the purposes of saving? Anything else?"
SOURCE: Surveys of Consumer Finances, conducted by the Survey
Research Center of The University of Michigan.

the proportion of buyers who make such withdrawals is much
smaller in the United States than in Germany.[10]

Turning now to attitudes toward borrowing, we find widespread
acceptance of the use of consumer credit in the United States and
overwhelming disapproval in Germany. Let us look first at a few
of the relevant data collected in the United States.[11] In the 1960s
about one-half of all American family heads said without qualification that they approved of buying on the installment plan. When
attitudes toward purchasing specific goods on credit were queried,
about two-thirds thought that borrowing was appropriate to finance the purchase of a car, and more than half that it was appropriate to finance the purchase of furniture. The main argument
given in favor of installment buying was that it was the right thing
to pay for large purchases while using the goods. Buying on the installment plan meant paying for consumer goods out of income.
The reasons for putting money in savings accounts were considered
to be different, namely, to accumulate funds for long-term purposes.

Every year many Americans, about one-fourth of all borrowers,

[10] On the use of savings accounts for financing major transactions, see Mueller
and Lean.[56]
[11] They have been presented in Katona et al.,[37] 1967, Chap. 7.

buy their automobiles and large durables on credit even though they have enough money in savings accounts to pay cash for them. Surveys revealed that people who did so were usually aware of the great difference between borrowing costs and the interest earned on savings. They knowingly paid a price to make certain that their savings remained intact; buying on the installment plan made the repayment the first charge on income and thus compelled them to save, which they feared they would not do just to replenish savings accounts once they had been reduced.

The most frequent arguments against buying on credit in the United States are that it is expensive and that it offers too great a temptation to buy. Neither notion was held by more than one out of six people in the late 1960s. The proportion of those who are against borrowing in principle and who believe that debt is morally wrong is fairly small in the United States.

Surveys in Germany indicated approval of installment buying by only 20 to 30 percent of respondents. In replying to questions formulated in various ways, in the 1960s two-thirds or more of all German respondents indicated unqualified opposition to buying on credit. Such approval as existed tended to be found largely among the inhabitants of large cities and blue-collar workers. Guenter Schmoelders called attention to a peculiarity of the German language which may offer a clue to the origin of the opposition of so many Germans to borrowing. The German word for debt, *Schuld*, is the same as the word for guilt!

In the United States, unlike the European countries studied, the association of debt with distress and even with the necessity to resort to borrowing because of illness, unemployment, or other catastrophes has become very weak in the twentieth century. Indeed consumer credit is used in prosperous years more than in years of economic downturn or stagnation. Installment buying has become a symptom of as well as a contributor to good times. Furthermore, old people, poor people, and people with income declines use installment credit to the smallest extent. It is primarily young people with small children and families in the middle and upper-middle income groups ($6,000 to $15,000 income in 1968) who buy on the installment plan. Recent income gains as well as favorable income expectations stimulate installment buying. As discussed in Chapter 5, people with rising incomes set their sights high, are impatient to acquire needed goods, and so purchase them on credit. Credit is repaid from future income, which is expected to be higher than current income.

A few words may be added on credit buying in other European countries. Attitudes toward this practice appear to be somewhat more favorable in Holland than in Germany and much more favorable in the two European countries in which it is the most widespread—Sweden and England. Yet in England, and in 1968 also in France, installment buying has been severely restricted by government regulations. Late in 1968 English regulations required that 40 percent of the price of a car be paid in cash and that the debt be repaid within twenty-four months.

SAVINGS AND SECURITY

Further information on attitudes toward saving sheds light both on similarities and on differences between the United States and Germany. To most people in both countries the accumulation of reserve funds is a highly valued goal. Germans have always placed great emphasis on the virtue of thrift; following the depletion of savings during the great inflation after World War II the need for financial reserves was very strongly felt in that country. The desire for reserve funds was reflected in surveys in which a large proportion of the German population said "We are spending too much," or "We are living beyond our means," and deplored an alleged decline in the traditional value of thrift. The low frequency of optimistic expectations and the increase in amounts saved when business slowed down, shown in the previous chapters, likewise suggest the presence of a strong urge to save among very many Germans.

The American people, on the other hand, have been described by social critics as concerned solely with the acquisition of a great variety of consumer goods, including unnecessary but widely advertised gadgets, and willing to incur debt for the sake of purchases of little real value. As one popular American writer put it, "We buy goods we don't need with money we don't have." Even though the replacement of older by newer products may occasionally involve nothing more than changes in appearance, the views of some social critics that American economic behavior reflects an inordinate interest in gadgets and irresponsible or unnecessary borrowing are so greatly exaggerated that they must be branded as false in substance.[12]

[12] Katona.[35]

At this point we are concerned with just one of the implications of the argument: Does the American consumers' great desire to improve their standard of living impede their desire to save and thus curtail the amounts saved? No doubt, pressures to spend have reduced the amounts saved in the United States as elsewhere, but our studies yielded many indications that the American people are pursuing at the same time both the goal of improving their standard of living and the goal of acquiring financial reserves. Among numerous survey findings on widespread desires to save in the United States two may be mentioned:

1. In studies of transactions during the first few months following an increase in income, the income increments were found to have served to raise primarily two budget items: the purchase of durable goods and additions to financial reserves.[13]

2. In surveys made in both the 1950s and 1960s the majority of respondents were found to be dissatisfied with the amount of savings they had. They said that they would like to have larger savings even when those they already had were quite sizable. By contrast, the majority expressed satisfaction both with their income and with their standard of living.

Somewhat conflicting views are often held by the same people at the same time. Even people who are confident that their income will continually grow acknowledge that the future is uncertain. The higher the standard of living, the larger the financial reserves that are deemed to be necessary. Buying houses and other goods on credit means imposing financial obligations upon oneself. Then, since something untoward might happen, an absence or insufficiency of reserve funds makes for uneasiness or even anxiety. To be sure, the relative strength of motives to spend and to save differs in different age groups: for younger people the desire to improve their standard of living, and for older people the desire to acquire reserve funds, was found to be more powerful.

Saving for security or for "rainy days," for retirement or old age, and for the education of children have been described as the three most powerful saving motives of the American people. In all these respects Americans may have greater need to save than the Germans. To mention the third motive first, let it be said simply

---

[13] These findings were obtained from a panel study in which the same sample was interviewed at quarterly intervals in 1964–1965 and respondents with income increases during the preceding three or six months were singled out. See Katona and Mueller.[39]

that higher education is much more common in the United States and generally requires much greater financial contributions on the part of the students' parents. Provisions for retirement are made more completely by the government in Germany, and also in the other European countries, than in the United States. Finally, during the postwar period people in continental Europe have had much less experience with cyclical unemployment than the Americans.

Old-age pensions and health insurance were both introduced a very long time ago in Germany. Only a few of the relevant facts will be mentioned here. About nine out of every ten Germans in the labor force are entitled to old-age security, and old-age pensions by the government amount to 50 to 70 percent of income earned before retirement. Similarly, nine out of ten Germans have health insurance (mostly government insurance). This pays not only for hospitalization but for all medical care, including drugs, and also provides compensation for lost earnings for a limited time. Only in one respect may the German social security system be called incomplete, for instance, in comparison to France: It provides only a limited contribution to the additional needs of families with children.

In the United States, as is well known, public health insurance was unknown until recently and was then introduced only for people sixty-five years of age or over (Medicare). Private hospital insurance, which is widespread, is far from sufficient to cover the expenses of prolonged severe illness. Old-age security, as provided for by the government, was expanded after World War II, but the amount of public pensions remained woefully inadequate. Therefore during the last twenty years labor has placed great emphasis on the introduction of private pension plans, and trade unions have succeeded in inducing most large employers to institute such plans. Although they are not universal, often not very generous, and commonly not vested in the individual, they do represent some compulsory saving, usually by both the employer and the employee. The introduction of private pension plans therefore caused many experts to believe that individual saving would be reduced: why should people put as much money into banks and securities as before when the new pension plans would give them retirement income, and when they themselves and their employers would be saving through the contractual arrangements?

Recent studies of this problem shed further light on American attitudes toward saving: It was found that the rate of individual saving of people with private pension plans was larger than that of people without such plans, other things being held constant.[14] The prospect of receiving private pensions made many people feel that they were close enough to their goal of achieving a satisfactory income after retirement so that with some additional individual saving effort they would be able to reach that goal. On the other hand, people without private pension plans often felt that it was not possible to assure themselves a satisfactory standard of living during their old age; whatever they could save would not suffice, so that they were not greatly motivated to save. Aspirations appear to rise with accomplishment, and attainable rewards have a stimulating effect not only on spending but on saving as well because both are held to be of great value.

Because the reward of spending is more immediate than the reward of saving, many people tend to impose obligations on themselves to make sure that they will save. Contractual saving arrangements became popular in the United States in the form of payroll deductions for war bonds and later for government savings bonds. Buying on the installment plan likewise results in contractual saving. Savings contracts are widespread in Germany as well. In that country the government provides incentives in the form of tax advantages and bonuses for various forms of regular saving, including saving in building associations, provided they are not withdrawn for fairly long periods.

There are great differences in the extent to which different population groups engage in saving activities. In the United States savers are concentrated among upper-income groups and also among families the head of which is between thirty-five and fifty-five years of age. Among younger families with small children the common form of behavior is to acquire a one-family house, a car, and a variety of durable goods rather than deposits in banks or securities. Financial saving occurs primarily in the middle years of life when income is typically the highest and when concern with retirement has become salient.

Studies in Germany reveal that there age plays a relatively small role in differentiating between savers and nonsavers. Little difference was found in the proportion of younger people and middle-age people who were saving. This is understandable since saving in

14 Katona[36]; Cagan.[7]

that country is largely for consumption purposes, which is of course very important for younger married couples. The influence of occupation and social status on the saving performance of the German people is, however, considerable, probably exceeding even that of income. On the basis of a survey conducted in 1959 it was estimated that self-employed people saved 16 percent of disposable income, white-collar employees 11 percent, and blue-collar workers only 4½ percent. Net capital formation by the self-employed was estimated to amount to 50 percent of all capital formation in the 1950s although the self-employed represented only 17 percent of all households. The difference in saving rates between *Beamte* (officials) and salaried employees on the one hand and wage earners on the other hand was related by Schmoelders[15] to the degree of familiarity of the various social groups with financial institutions and forms of saving. Among blue-collar workers (whose numbers are declining) apparently not only securities but even banks represented unfamiliar and remote institutions. They were more concerned with immediate consumption than with making provisions for the future.

The discussion of factors promoting or impeding saving would be incomplete without considering the relation of saving to inflation. It appears that both in the United States and in Germany inflation has had little impact on amounts saved or even on the choice of the savings media. In both countries savings deposits remained the most popular form in which reserve funds were kept. Most savers do not view stocks or real estate as suitable alternatives to savings deposits because they are not considered as safe as money in the bank. Although desires for inflation-proof assets are noticeable in all countries, the large increase in the number of American stockholders cannot be attributed to attempts to safeguard against inflation. Data on the timing of stock purchases by individuals and inquiries about the reasons for stock purchases point to a different explanation. The typical American saver purchased stock when a bullish trend prevailed on the stock market, not when the cost of living rose or was expected to rise rapidly. The prospect of capital gains represents the prime attraction of the stock market; a saver is drawn to invest in stocks when he hears from friends and colleagues that they have made profits. The substantial appreciation of stock values in the 1960s induced a

---

[15] Schmoelders.[69]

growing proportion of American savers to speculate in stocks— most commonly with a relatively small proportion of their savings. In the late 1960s holders of large assets—a small minority of the savers responsible, however, for a very large share of total savings —were the only population group which invested more in stocks than in savings deposits.

To summarize: In the proportion of income put into financial savings there is no substantial difference between Germans and Americans. Yet in the United States a sizable number of people —not only those with low incomes but also young people in general —do not participate in the practice of accumulating financial reserves. In Germany putting part of one's income into various forms of savings institutions is more general, although it is least common among blue-collar workers. The most important difference between Americans and Europeans lies, however, not in saving practices but in the use made of consumer credit. Attitudes toward credit are primarily responsible for the fact that the rate of total saving, as conventionally defined, is larger in the affluent countries of the European continent than in the United States.

CHAPTER 8

Trends in Purchasing Behavior

THERE remain certain similarities and differences in the behavior of consumers in the highly developed countries with respect to a variety of goods and services that have not yet been discussed. People's behavior in making their purchases and doing their shopping needs to be reviewed because it, too, may exhibit more traditional features in certain countries and adapt itself more rapidly to changing conditions in other countries. Even with respect to the most important durable consumer product of our day, automobiles, little attention has been paid to the changing pattern of consumer attitudes and behavior. Let us look first therefore at some of the differences in the manner in which Americans and Europeans regard their cars.

ON THE ROLE OF THE
AUTOMOBILE

The American people's attitudes toward their automobiles have undergone some changes in the last two decades. Studies conducted by the Survey Research Center in the late 1960s indicate that the car has increasingly become a means for serving important ends, rather than the highly prized possession it once was in the United States and still is in much of Europe. According to answers to recent survey questions about the purposes of driving, very many Americans considered the car essential for a number of daily activities which required, in most cases, driving short distances: commuting to and from work, taking children to school, shopping, and visiting. In addition, the car had become a very important factor in the use of free time: Driving around in the evening and on weekends and also family travel by car during vacations constituted some of the leisure-time activities most frequently mentioned. Although the most favored or most desired way of spending free time was not in a car but in the country or in a second home—sometimes a cabin at a lake or in the mountains—or in motorboats or sailboats, a car was needed to reach them. A vacation spent at home was not considered a good vacation. The longer the vacation trip, in time and also in distance covered, the better. Family travel by car was not always seen as the best possible holiday—flying to distant places and renting a car there was preferred by some well-to-do people—but was undertaken in the majority of cases not only because of its lower cost but also because it provided mobility. A vacation consisting of going to one resort and spending several weeks there—formerly not uncommon in the United States and still common in Europe—was apparently either unheard of by modern Americans or not preferred by them. The present American custom of moving around during vacations, going to many places and seeing many things, clearly depends largely on travel by car.

Ownership of two or more cars spread from 10 percent of family units in 1955 to 26 percent in the late 1960s. At the same time, the proportion of one-car owners who expressed a desire to own two cars also increased. Absence or insufficiency of public transportation in most American towns and the growing proportion of the population living in often distant suburbs resulted in many respondents saying that it created a hardship if the husband used the one family car for commuting to work. The diversity of needs of various family members, notably teenage children, also increased aspirations to own at least two cars. Because of differences in the purposes for which the cars were to be used, frequently two different types of cars were wanted. Long-distance family travel—and probably also prestige, although this was rarely mentioned by survey respondents—called for the ownership of a large car. But even prestige obviously did not require that the second car be large. In the 1960s when American auto producers introduced many different kinds of cars—compacts, intermediates, station wagons, sport cars—they were responding to widely felt consumer desires.

Although in the late 1960s American auto companies produced a greater variety of cars than ever before, interviews revealed that the major problems confronting consumers no longer concerned the car purchase itself—the make, type, or price of the car bought. Their concerns had become centered around accessories and, more particularly, around problems that arise after the purchase. Because of the broad acceptance of such "extras" as automatic transmission, power steering, and even car air conditioning, it was quite common for the total price paid for a less expensive car to exceed the basic price of a more expensive car. Concern with the resale value also loomed large in the minds of respondents. Among the problems of automobile ownership parking, congestion, insurance, and repairs were most frequently mentioned. Concern with the quality of cars probably increased with the publicity given to the recall of faulty series of new cars and to safety features. Repairs had become a major problem not only because of their high cost and often inconvenient timing but also because of the difficulty in getting them done properly. Some respondents said that often it was better to trade in a fairly new car than to fix it even if it was only slightly damaged. Should the number of skilled mechanics decline further, as many expect, this statement may be rather generally true in a decade or two.

In Europe during the last two decades, there has been a great increase in car ownership. Great numbers of people have increased their mobility, and traffic congestion and parking problems have become as commonplace as in America. In cities where there are fewer and smaller cars, there are also narrower streets! Alongside these visible similarities, there exist very real differences in the attitudes of Europeans toward their cars and in their behavior as car buyers. The fact that most of them still recall the not-very-distant past when they did not own a car makes it a more valued possession, which is cleaned and polished regularly and carefully and expected to last. While in America cars are turned over fairly rapidly and purchases of used cars are more frequent than purchases of new cars, the typical European buys a new car and desires to keep it for a fairly long time. In Europe both cars and gasoline are heavily taxed, which partly explains the preponderance of small cars. In the United States some used cars are quite inexpensive, and the European type of small car is preferred by a small minority only. The proportion of two-car families among car owners is much larger in the United States than in Europe. Public transportation is better in most European cities than in America, and even well-to-do people use it and are accustomed to walking fairly long distances. The proportion of working wives is smaller in Europe than in the United States, and this also reduces the felt need for two cars. Finally, annual model changes are a standard feature of the American car market only. It has been charged, probably with some justification, that some parts of large annual expenditures on model changes in the United States are wasteful. Nevertheless, the changes do appear to stimulate demand for the new, the more modern, or the more fashionable and thereby result in a quicker turnover of cars. Changes in products tend to appeal to dynamic people. Whether or not Europeans will eventually duplicate the American pattern depends as much on whether or not traditional social and cultural attitudes will change as on a further growth of European prosperity.

LEISURE-TIME PURSUITS

With increased well-being has come a great increase in interest, in time, and in money devoted to leisure-time activities in all the affluent countries. What they do evenings, on weekends, and during their vacations has become a very important matter not only for most people but also for the national economies since many leisure-time pursuits are expensive involving money spent not only for services but also for the purchase of a great variety of products. The decisions as to how to spend that money vary greatly as reflections of different life styles in different countries.

A few words may first be said of the time available for leisure. At present the differences in working time, to be discussed in Chapter 9, are not large between the United States and Western Europe. But in the last two decades working time has been greatly reduced in Europe, while it has changed little in the United States. Vacation rights for workers were introduced earlier in Europe and are at present more extensive there than in America. For instance, German salaried as well as hourly employees now have on the average close to four weeks of paid vacation time. Many employees are also entitled to a vacation bonus in addition to their regular salaries. The number of paid holidays also appears to be larger in Europe than in America.

Vacation travel is somewhat more common in Europe than in the United States. According to a survey in 1965, 55 percent of German adults had made a vacation trip that year. It is well known that in the month of August there is an exodus from French and Dutch cities with a very substantial proportion of the people leaving their homes for a vacation trip. Winter vacations, and two vacations during the year, have become common in Western Europe. By contrast, according to surveys conducted in the early 1960s, only 45 percent of American families had taken a vacation trip during the year. This proportion is, however, growing, as are the vacation rights of the American labor force.

The fact that Americans spend a greater total amount of money on foreign travel than any other nationality is due solely to their number; the amount spent per capita is rather small. In Europe, with the relatively small size of the countries and the nearness of borders to most population centers, travel across national boundaries is very common. That inhabitants of a small country, such as Holland, commonly take their vacations in foreign countries is hardly surprising. Yet recent information according to which close to 50 percent of German vacations are taken in foreign countries may hardly be explained by the size of the country alone. Interest in spending time in a foreign environment and the desire to enjoy different and better climates appear to play a great role in determining vacation plans in Western Europe.[1]

Visiting relatives is frequently mentioned as the purpose of vacation trips in the United States, but not in Europe. This difference may be explained by the geographic mobility of Americans, who

[1] Abolition of extensive passport and customs controls have greatly contributed to foreign travel. The notion that travel in the countries belonging to the Common Market is no longer foreign travel may also have played a role, although it may be noted that the country which has grown most as a vacationland, Spain, is not in the Common Market.

frequently live in cities and states at some distance from their parents or close relatives.

In Europe there are many famous resorts and spas, each with a great number of hotels and boarding houses catering to vacationers. Yet the trend away from the traditional form of vacation—spending it entirely at one place—is clearly observable. Even though Europeans still use the railroad more frequently than the family car for vacation travel, there is a growing tendency to visit several places in the course of a vacation. Travel organized by travel agencies and all-inclusive tours are widely advertised and have become very popular in Europe during the last few years.

Survey questions about what the American people do and about what they like to do in their free time evenings and weekends have indicated the great popularity of outdoor recreation. When given a long list of activities, the largest number of respondents indicated that they had engaged in "automobile riding for sightseeing and recreation," as mentioned above. Picnicking, swimming, boating, hunting, and camping were also frequently cited by many as activities in which they had participated.[2] Since about two-thirds of Americans live in their own one-family houses, it was not surprising to find that much of their free time was spent in taking care of their houses and backyard. Among indoor activities, do-it-yourself hobbies are common, in addition to the ubiquitous viewing of television. Nevertheless, apparently the American people—primarily of course the younger people—tend to prefer to spend many of their evenings and weekends away from central cities and also away from the suburbs and small towns in which they live. Moving around and visiting outdoor places of recreation were often seen as the best use of free time.

Unlike Americans, most Europeans live in apartments, without the benefit of their own backyard or garden, and it might be expected that they, too, might seek to find their recreation outside the cities in which they live. The continental European, however, is traditionally city-oriented. True, the younger generations have always engaged in excursions and hiking. But neighborhood coffee houses and beer halls still form a major attraction for many Europeans in their free time; they meet other people there, read papers, and play cards, chess, or billiards. Recreation in the city

[2] Mueller and Gurin.[55]

and especially in one's own neighborhood appears to be more popular on the European continent than in the Anglo-Saxon countries.

Differences between members of the working class and the middle class in the use of their free time are still widely observed in Europe. Spending much time at home or in his own neighborhood is characteristic of the European manual worker and his family. The relatively low car ownership rates of this group referred to in Chapter 3 are related to leisure time spent at home. Both leisure activities and car ownership rates of the working class can be explained only in sociopsychological terms.

While leisure-time activities, especially in the United States, are often thought of as no more than fun or entertainment, they must also be viewed as important outlets of energy and expressions of values and goals. Since many jobs are not self-fulfilling or not even interesting, what people do in their free time plays a great role in their lives. Once it was said to be wrong to play so hard that it might affect one's work; now it is said to be wrong to work so hard that it might affect one's family life and leisure.[3] Leisure time is used not only for play but also for spiritual and cultural activities. Well-to-do people spend their free time to an increasing extent in reading, painting, and a variety of other artistic pursuits, and also in the acquisition of new skills and education. In these respects again, wants proliferate and new kinds of activities are taken up when work both inside and outside the home becomes less strenuous and less absorbing, and money is no longer scarce. As new values emerge among affluent people in all countries, they are inevitably reflected in leisure-time pursuits.

PURCHASING BEHAVIOR

Supermarkets and large suburban shopping centers spread first in the United States, and the decline of small stores, and of neighborhood stores in general, also started in America. But similar trends have developed in Western Europe as well. The threat of the demise of downtown or central city shopping areas has been extensively discussed on both sides of the Atlantic, as has the problem of the concentration of retail trade among a smaller number of sellers.

At the same time there appear some divergent trends which may reflect different habits and attitudes of people in Europe and Amer-

[3] *Mead,*[50] pp. 14–15.

ica. Many American shopping centers have been built in previously open areas that can be reached only by car and are thus accessible to shoppers who live fairly far away. The most conspicuous European trend has consisted of the establishment of shopping centers in the middle of residential suburbs, frequented by people who go there by public transportation or even on foot. Considerable effort and money has been spent in Europe not only on the renewal of central shopping districts but also on building large new shopping areas in the center of cities, as illustrated by the widely known developments in Rotterdam, Stockholm, and Duesseldorf.

The disappearance in the United States of the small shopkeeper, who was personally known to the shopper and whose advice was sought and trusted, was facilitated by the increased role of widely advertised brands in America and generally by the often-documented esteem Americans have for bigness among distributors as well as manufacturers. Brands are very important in Europe as well, but specialty stores which are trusted as the suppliers of high-quality goods nonetheless still play a large role in European trade. This divergence in buying habits may be related to differences in attitudes toward prices. There are indications that in durable goods, house furnishings, and clothing a higher price is more widely identified with better quality and with the valued feature of durability in Europe than in America. German buyers especially appear to look upon low prices of many products with some suspicion. In the United States buying at a lower price, or at a discount, is more often considered to be an indication of clever or successful shopping.

Supermarkets are usually smaller in Europe than in America. The major difference probably lies, however, not in the stores themselves, but in the way they are used by shoppers. Shopping for groceries by car just once or twice a week is common in America, where the housewife frequently purchases a great variety and quantity of goods in one shopping trip. This pattern is less common in Europe not only because of a lesser availability of the car but also because ownership of freezers or freezing compartments in refrigerators is still much less frequent in Europe than in the United States. In Europe most meat is still bought in small butcher shops and most bread in small bakeries. It is true that self-service is spreading in Europe, but it has not begun to take on American proportions, and the desire for personal service and home delivery is a far larger factor in European than American retail trade.

Food habits are known to be very persistent. In the United States, for instance, children and grandchildren of immigrants tend to prefer or at least to be fond of the food of the "old country." Tradition also plays a great role in the taste and eating habits of each European country. As a major example it may suffice to point to the preference for rich food by the Germans, which is attested to by numerous conferences of experts of nutrition and public health who have deplored the fact that the Germans eat too much and too rich food. In several European countries two substantial meals eaten at home every day are the rule. The introduction of ready-made or precooked or frozen food products in Europe after World War II was initially far from successful because many of them were first advertised by emphasizing their convenience. The stress on saving labor and time for the housewife created guilt feelings; to appear lazy was not acceptable. The acceptance of such food products increased slowly only when their quality, often with additional home preparation, was emphasized and when the speedy preparation of meals began to be considered an achievement.

In most European countries regulations prohibit the opening of food stores in the evening, or on Saturdays or Sundays, and these regulations are rarely objected to. This acceptance stands in sharp contrast to the many legal battles that have taken place in the United States to permit stores—even nonfood stores—to remain open Sundays. In the United States, in contrast to Europe, an ever-growing number of stores of all kinds remain open evenings. This difference in buying habits is related not so much to affluence as to differences in patterns of living. For example, the American housewife who holds a job outside the home depends on evenings and weekends for her shopping expeditions.

The discussion of the housewife's shopping habits may be supplemented by a note on housekeeping. Several surveys indicate that most European women still see their major function to be the fulfillment of their duties at home. These include the preparation of daily meals for the family as well as extensive and frequent cleaning of the house. Husbands expect to find their home always in good order, usually without their contributing much to the housekeeping chores. Neglect of the house is seen as a violation of the accepted standard of conduct. To be sure, labor-saving home appliances have spread, and the endeavor of their sellers to make life easier for the modern woman has met with success. The disappearance of household servants is deplored in all the affluent countries, but European women in general consider that although housekeeping may involve a certain amount of drudgery it still provides great rewards. Many aspects of homemaking are treasured by the European housewife, and this retention of traditional values surely plays a role in her disinclination to take a job outside her home (see Chapter 10).

It is hardly possible to make a statement as to whether brand and store loyalty are more or less pronounced in Western Europe than in the United States. Nor is there any available evidence as to differences in the extent and influence of advertising, except for the absence of large-scale television advertising in most European countries. One particular effect of advertising in the United States—namely, reliance on brand names—has already been mentioned: Those who buy in self-service supermarkets want identifiable brands to a greater extent than did those who formerly relied on personal service. The extent of the influence of advertising represents a controversial topic in Europe as in America. While there is reason for concluding that advertising has but little influence on deep-seated attitudes and reflects rather than creates values, it probably has contributed in the United States to a greater heterogeneity of wants and to their spread to an ever-growing number of products and product types. At the same time, in Europe as in America, advertising may well have served to increase the market share of the large producers. No universally valid answer can be given to the much discussed question as to whether advertising in itself serves to increase demand for types of products and not just for specific brands and makes. No doubt, there are many goods the demand for which has been greatly augmented by advertising; cosmetics, for both women and men, may be mentioned as an example. But it should not be forgotten that there also exist products the use of which has grown very greatly without the benefit of commercial advertising, for example, contraceptives and marijuana.

For some time in the United States and also in Europe, there has existed a two-way process of influence, from consumers to business as well as from business to consumers. Business firms watch and study consumers, not only their past purchases but also incipient trends in their preferences and attitudes, and often adjust their policies, and their advertising as well, according to how consumers feel and think. What is sold in large quantities is not always what the producers would prefer to produce and sell. Interaction prevails in this respect as in all forms of communication and learning. Both the traditional doctrine of consumer sovereignty and the thesis of Galbraith that large producers control and manage their customers[4] presume a unidirectional process of influence, which in fact represents the exception rather than the rule.

Information has been obtained in the United States on the extent of what may be called circumspectness in purchasing. In a study carried out in 1954 purchasers of such appliances as television sets, refrigerators, and washing machines were questioned in detail on shopping around, seeking information, discussing prospective purchases in the family and with friends, and shifts in brand preferences. Similar surveys were recently conducted with purchasers both of appliances and of automobiles.[5] Both sets of studies indicate that there are careful and deliberate buyers who spend many months to find out as much as possible and from as many sources as possible about what to buy, where to buy it, and how much to pay. They indicate equally, however, that there are very many other buyers who conclude a purchase within a few weeks after it enters their minds, and who contact but one single store or seller and proceed with a minimum of information-seeking or deliberation. The findings contradict the assumption that outlays of relatively large amounts of money, which are made infrequently, and which involve products used over long periods, such as cars and appliances, are always or even usually carefully considered.

Who are the American buyers who were found to make major outlays with—and who are those who make them without—extensive deliberation and information-seeking? It was not possible to single out any income or demographic groups which overwhelmingly fell in the one or the other classification, and the association of circumspectness to identifiable personality traits was likewise not successful. It was, however, found that users of a product who were replacing a similar or identical good with which they were satisfied generally ranked low in time and effort spent in in-

---

[4] Galbraith.[21] Interaction, rather than either consumer or producer sovereignty, has been discussed by Katona,[38] pp. 29ff. Galbraith's thesis is derived from his notion that the wants of an individual do not originate with him. This is, of course, correct in the sense that higher-order wants are learned rather than innate. But the consequence drawn by Galbraith is contradicted by the psychology of learning. What is learned depends on what the learner has experienced, that is, on information received from teachers, the printed page, by word of mouth, or even from advertising —but the learner still chooses and selects what he learns from any or all of these sources of information. (See Katona,[35] chap. 7.)

[5] George Katona and Eva Mueller[33]; also studies by J. W. Newman conducted in 1968 and 1969 (not yet published).

vestigating before buying. Satisfactory previous experience with a product or a store was considered the best basis for making a decision to buy. These findings alone provide less than a full explanation of the presence or absence of careful purchasing behavior. One reason for that latter seemed simply to be that many Americans were greatly interested in minimizing the time and effort they put into shopping.

It appears then that the traditional notion of the rationality of consumers, in the sense of weighing alternatives and choosing among them on the basis of as much information as possible, holds good only for some, possibly not even the majority, of the purchases of durable goods. With respect to items frequently purchased—incidentals, convenience goods, also many food products and minor clothing items—it was found that such rationality is commonly superseded by habitual or routine buying behavior. Regarding a variety of choices of brands, which are not important to the consumer, it may be in his best interest to act habitually, or even to rely on advertising, rather than to make time-consuming "rational" choices. But the consumer cannot be considered to behave irrationally either, in spite of the occasional occurrence of impulse buying. For example, studies indicated that the young American housewife, a large factor in retail purchasing, is generally much better educated than her parents and thus quite critical and careful in her selection of many, if not all, of her purchases.

Unfortunately for the purposes of our comparative studies, little information is available on deliberation or choice, or their absence, in European purchasing behavior. A study by Klaus Schreiber, conducted in West Berlin, suggests that in many respects the behavior of the buyers is similar on the two sides of the Atlantic.[6] This is probably true of the major American finding: Neither the thesis of the rational economic man who carefully studies, weighs, and evaluates his every purchase, nor the notion of an irrational, impulsive, and careless buyer is generally applicable.

[6] Schreiber[70] finds that everyday purchases are usually habitual, while careful decision making prevails, especially with respect to prices, when relatively expensive durable goods are purchased. What is apparently missing in most purchases is knowledge of and therefore consideration of differences in quality.

PART 3

Acquisition of Income

CHAPTER *9*

Work and Leisure

*A*CCORDING to an ancient Aristotelian proposition, there are two strictly separated spheres in human life and society: the realm of labor, necessity, compulsion, production and the realm of enjoyment, leisure, consumption. The former is characterized by coercion, discipline, order; the latter, by freedom, discretion, individuality. The implications Aristotle drew from this dichotomy were as simple as they are unacceptable today. For him some people were chosen by destiny for labor and coercion, whereas others were destined for the life of leisure. Marx, although perceiving the need for extending the realm of freedom or choice, at the expense of the realm of necessity, agreed with Aristotle on one point: Labor and leisure, producing and consuming, are two distinctly different areas; the one governed by the laws of society, the other subject to individual choice.[1]

[1] The preceding ideas draw on observations by R. Dahrendorf.

The Aristotelian tradition has had its impact on modern social science. Today economists still overrate the cleavage between income acquisition and income allocation; they tend to ignore that in affluent societies consumption aspirations influence working and occupational decisions. Conversely, the social role of the individual — his education, social background, and occupation — also exerts an influence on his consumption patterns.

The amount of income is no longer a fact predetermined by employers; income is no longer something over which the income receiver has no control. Modern man is not a passive object of economic forces. The choice the economy grants to the consumer in matters of spending and saving extends as well to the realm of earning. In the 1950s and 1960s, large-scale unemployment became a matter of the past; almost every able-bodied person with a minimum level of education could find permanent work if he or she so desired. He could indeed choose among several available jobs. Full employment as prevalent today for most Americans and practically all Western Europeans makes it possible to exchange unsatisfactory jobs for more pleasant and rewarding ones.

Modern economic behavior in the area of income acquisition may be divided into two categories: (1) the quantitative dimension, namely, the choice between work and leisure in terms of regular working hours, overtime and second jobs (to be discussed in this chapter), and women's participation in the labor force (Chapter 10); and (2) the qualitative aspect related to occupational mobility with emphasis on education, the most powerful instrument for upgrading the quality of work and achieving social advancement (Chapter 11). The quality of labor input more than its quantity, the level of skills more than the number of persons employed or hours worked, characterize the scope of the private household's contribution to economic dynamics. The modern man is in a position to adapt himself and to participate more intensively than ever in the changing world of production as well as of consumption and leisure.

JOB SATISFACTION

There is evidence to invalidate or at least to question the conventional conception of work as drudgery and coercion. Manual labor is progressively being replaced by "clean", supervisory, skilled, and white-collar jobs. Working conditions in industrial economies have steadily improved in the last fifty or more years; there is a trend toward reduced physical effort, toward an improvement in the work environment—less heat and noise, better lighting and ventilation—toward more security against personal injury, and toward more rewarding social relations with supervisors and fellow workers. Part of this has resulted from specific efforts of employers, unions, and employees, facilitated by the improved bargaining position of labor, and part from the intersectoral shifts in employment and technological changes, discussed in Chapter 2. The shrinking of the agricultural sector, the transition from blue-collar to white-collar jobs, and, even more important, the advanced machine technology, in spite of widespread fears and eloquent warnings about "alienation" from the job, have enhanced job satisfaction, provided challenge, and increased motivation to work.

A recent American study based on interviews with a representative cross section of members of the labor force revealed a significant positive relationship between change in technology and job satisfaction. Respondents were queried extensively about the "machinery" they were using on their job and about changes during the preceding five years as well as about their satisfaction with their jobs (Table 9-1). About one-half of all members of the labor force said that they were more satisfied than five years earlier. This proportion was higher among those who had experienced a change in machines than among those who had not. Those who had changed their jobs likewise expressed greater satisfaction than those who had not. Similarly, a study conducted among workers of five British firms in the late fifties reported a growing measure of satisfaction. Many more men said they were satisfied with their work and their working conditions at that time than before the war.[2]

In Germany, likewise, the trend was found to be strong enough to have been observable in a time series of answers to the same question. Within the few years from 1951 to 1960 the proportion of German adults associating with their work such highly motivating attributes as "satisfying" or "meaningful" increased, while the proportion describing their work as "a heavy burden," "a necessary evil" or just as "a way to make money" or "to sustain oneself," de-

---

[2] Ferdynard Zweig[89] writes: "Many men whom I interviewed referred to their bad past. 'I enjoy my work now, but if you had asked me the same question before the war I would have said definitely not', or 'In my life I had jobs to endure, believe me. It was different in those days', or 'Compared with now the pre-war days were slavery. It is comfortable now, you can please yourself;' such were typical comments."

TABLE 9-1   *Influence of Change in Machine Technology on Change in Job Satisfaction in the United States, in percent*

Change in satisfaction	All*	Same job for past 5 years and		Different job and	
		Machine change	No machine change†	Machine change	No machine change†
More	51	58	40	67	64
Same	34	34	45	16	20
Less	9	8	9	11	9
Not ascertained	6	‡	6	6	7
Total	100	100	100	100	100
Proportion in sample	100	8	54	14	24

*Members of the labor force, including self-employed.
†Includes those who do not work with machines.
‡Less than one-half of one percent.

The question was: "Taking everything into consideration, how satisfied are you with your job now as compared to five years ago—are you more satisfied, about the same, or less?"

SOURCE: Mueller et al.[57]

A member of the labor force is assumed to use machinery (including typewriters, computers, laboratory equipment, etc.) not only when he operates it but also when he perceives the equipment as important for his work. A "machine change" is defined here to include: (1) a machine taking over tasks previously involving human labor; (2) the introduction of faster, more accurate, more powerful, or more self-regulating machines; or (3) machines performing higher quality work or putting out goods and services not previously produced.

clined (Table 9-2). And from 1960 to 1969 the proportion of those considering their work "wholly satisfying" increased from 50 to 59 percent.

Evidence from Germany suggests that job satisfaction becomes significantly stronger as one gets older.[3] There is generally a gradual shift of interest throughout the life of the worker. In earlier stages of the life cycle, outside interests predominate; then, when a family is being raised, the home is of greatest importance. In later years, interest in the work increases, although it tends to fade out in the years preceding retirement.

The shift from industrial drudgery to modern forms of participation in the labor force has profoundly affected the erstwhile dismal connotation of labor and employment, as transmitted by Puritan and, in general, by Christian values.[4] True, there are still many who

---

[3] In a survey conducted in 1961 the proportion of people below the age of thirty who said they were fully satisfied with their work was 46 percent as against 64 percent of those above sixty. See Press Release of April 25, 1961, by Institut fuer Demoskopie, Allensbach.

[4] Cf. the infliction of labor on mankind as punishment for Adam's sin.

complain about their work, and working long hours is only rarely considered attractive or desirable for its own sake. Yet coupled with increasing opportunities for material advancement and for furthering long-term occupational goals, the weakening of the unfavorable image of work is of truly paramount importance to modern economies. Since work has become less disagreeable and at the same time more profitable, labor force participation is now more attractive than it has ever been.

What are the goals people have in mind when they evaluate their jobs or occupation? Obviously, several criteria are applied at the same time: income, security, satisfaction, being left with enough leisure, and others. Still, it is of interest to learn about differences in the saliency of these goals. Are immediate or deferred, material or nonmaterial, gratifications foremost in people's minds? Is a good job considered most of all a means of making as much money as possible, or a long-term, secure base of existence, or primarily a meaningful, satisfactory activity?

TABLE 9-2 *Characterization of Jobs by German Workers*

(Percentage of German adults sixteen years and older in the labor force)

The job is considered . . .*	1951	1957	1962
Satisfactory activity or "calling" (inner commitment)	47	50	60
Heavy burden, necessary evil, way to make money	51	46	38
Don't know; not ascertained	2	4	2
Total	100	100	100
The present work is considered . . .†	1960	1962	1969
Wholly satisfying	50	55	59
Partly satisfying	43	40	37
Not satisfying	7	5	4
Total	100	100	100

*The question was: "Do you consider your job primarily a heavy burden, a necessary evil, a way to make money, a satisfactory activity, or an inner commitment?"
SOURCE: EMNID-Institute, *EMNID-Informations*, no. 14, 1965.
†The question was: "Would you say your present work is wholly satisfying to you, or only partly satisfying, or not at all satisfying?"
SOURCE: Institut fuer Demoskopie, *Allensbacher Berichte*, March, 1969.

Table 9-3 suggests similar evaluations of jobs in the United States, Britain, and Holland, while Germany is conspicuous for its conservatism. Every third household head in the United States, Britain, and Holland opts for security as the most important criterion of an occupation. Another third in each of the three countries names meaningful work (in Holland: prestige, recognition), whereas high income is mentioned by only 10 to 15 percent of respondents. In Germany, however, an overwhelming majority of 70 percent opts for security. This finding indicates again the prevailing German concern with the preservation of the progress already achieved. Involvement in one's work is mentioned by only 10 percent of the Germans and thus appears to be a matter of secondary concern.

American data clearly suggest that job security becomes less salient with rising occupational status. Fifty-four percent of people with less than a high school degree are mostly security oriented, as opposed to only 15 percent of college graduates and 6 percent of holders of advanced degrees, among whom concern with meaningful and satisfactory work increases to no less than 78 percent. Similarly, in the United States, but in contrast to England, Germany, and Holland, concern with security diminishes drastically with rising income. In Germany, the distribution of answers does not change much in different income and age groups, suggesting the

TABLE 9-3   *Job Preferences of Head of Household, in percent*

Country	Economic security	High income	Short working hours	Advancement opportunities	Satisfying work	Don't know	Total
United States (1966)*..	34†	11	9	8	35	3	100
England (1968)*	33	13	3	15	35	1	100
Germany (1968)......	70	14	1	5	10	....	100
Holland (1968).......	31	12	5	9	37‡	6	100

*Employed heads only.

†Includes those who indicated "steady income" and "no danger of being fired or umemployed" as most important.

‡Prestigeful work rather than satisfying work.

The question in the United States was: "We're interested in how people rate different occupations. Would you please look at this card and tell me which thing on this list about a job you would most prefer?"

The question in other countries was: "Here is a list of items that people have said are important in following an occupation. Would you tell me which one do *you* think is most important?" The choices offered were not quite the same in all surveys, as indicated in footnote ‡ above.

SOURCE: United States, Katona et al.,[37] chap. 6, 1966. European surveys conducted by the authors.

prevalence of rather fixed cultural norms resistant to socioeconomic change. The material rewards of the job and its steadiness are valued distinctly higher than the immaterial ones. The substantial involvement of workers in the Anglo-Saxon countries and Holland with work satisfaction, and their somewhat higher concern with career advancement indicate sensitivity to the challenges of new technology which may well be less pronounced in security-minded Germany.

THE DESIRE FOR MORE WORK

The most radical of work-leisure choices is the decision to work or not to work. For male adults who have finished their education and are much below the normal retirement age, this decision very rarely is a matter of true option. For them, in our society, work is rigidly prescribed behavior. Furthermore, most typically the pace of the work and the working hours are largely beyond the individual's discretion. Those who take a job usually have to work full time. However, there do exist some choices regarding whether or not to work overtime and regarding second jobs (moonlighting), especially in societies where the regular workweek has declined to approximately forty hours.

In the past few years, the reduction of hours worked appears to have come to a standstill in all the countries studied. For the United States, government figures indicate, contrary to the popular impression, that the length of the workweek declined very little between 1947 and recent years and is now increasing. From 1948 to 1965, the number of people other than farmers working more than forty-eight hours per week increased sharply, rising from 4.0 million to 9.4 million, or from 12.9 percent to 19.7 percent of the full-time nonfarm work force.[5] Regular working hours are longer in Europe than in America (see Table 9-4). Apparently the shorter the time spent on the regular job, the more frequent is moonlighting. The freedom to take a second job suffers from the indivisibility of most jobs; it is usually impossible to break them up into short and irregular hours to fit into one's regular working schedule. A person is often left with a choice only between too much or nothing.

For the United States, there are data about the extent of "discretionary" labor. In 1965, in the most important group, males twenty-

[5] Henke,[30] pp. 721–727.

TABLE 9-4   *Average Hours per Week Spent on Jobs by Full-time Workers***

Country	First job	Second job†
United States	42.3	1.12
France	44.4	0.88
Germany	45.7	0.47
Belgium	47.2	0.30

*Working time includes all work for money whether done outside or inside the home. It excludes meals at workplace, regular breaks, and prescribed nonworking periods during worktime, and time spent at workplace before starting or after ending work.

†The figure on hours per week spent on the second job is an average for all those fully employed. Survey data from the United States for 1968 indicate that about 14 percent of males in the labor force held a second job.

Note: Times of survey: United States, November–December, 1965, and March–April, 1966; France, February–March, 1966; Germany, September–October, 1965; Belgium, February–March, 1966.

SOURCE: UNESCO comparative study of time budgets, conducted 1965/1966 in eleven Eastern and Western countries. For details of the study see Szalai et al.[81]

five to forty-four years of age, 40 percent of all workers worked overtime (on a given job).[6] In 1968 in the same group 9 percent worked at least 200 hours a year on a second job, and 54 percent of married workers had working wives.[7] A very large proportion of families in the lower-middle age group made some extra effort to earn money beyond the husband's regular income.

Do the actual, largely institutionally fixed working hours coincide with the preferences of different peoples? To what extent are today's economies capable of absorbing the available labor supply and of satisfying prevailing aspirations for participation? Some answers were obtained in surveys conducted by the authors in the United States and Europe (Table 9-5).

The overall impression is that of a large reservoir of unused willingness for more participation in the labor market. In all countries, there was only a small proportion of people preferring to work less.

[6] Lebergott,[44] p. 105.
[7] Katona et al.,[37] 1969.

Most of those who said they would not like to work more were satisfied with the number of hours they were working. Britain stands out with by far the largest percentage of heads of households (55 percent) who expressed a desire to work more hours per week if they could get paid for it. Both Germany and the United States also had fairly high percentages (40 and 34, respectively) who expressed the same desire. Holland and France, by contrast, had relatively small percentages (28 and 25, respectively) who said they would prefer more work, although it should be said that in those countries as in all the others, the proportion of those who preferred to work more exceeded those who preferred to work less.

There are indications that the top position of Britain on the above list indeed reflects highly developed motives to acquire as much income as possible. F. Zweig speaks of a "constant quest for overtime" and describes the British worker as follows: "Money mindedness plays an ever increasing part in a man's attitude to his work. . . . Some skilled men take up unskilled work if they can earn more at it."[8] One reason for this desire to accumulate earnings might well be that England is the only large European country where unemployment is still a major problem.[9]

Let us turn briefly to the number of hours actually worked by people at different employment levels and in different income groups. Data presented in the Appendix (Table C-2) suggest that, contrary to widely held opinion, workers at lower levels of employment in all four countries studied work longer hours than those at higher levels. To be sure, it might be argued that higher-level workers are not in a position to distinguish accurately between work and leisure because they spend some of their so-called "nonworking" time in activities related to their jobs (digesting information, social gatherings, etc.). Even allowing for that, the evidence is unequivocal: Employed unskilled workers in the United States and Germany spend more time on the job than skilled workers, and in

[8] Zweig,[89] p. 68.

[9] A survey conducted in 1965 by the Cologne Forschungsstelle fuer empirische Sozialoekonomik indicates that in Spain as in England 55 percent of all members of the labor force expressed a desire to work longer hours. Almost 40 percent of the Spanish labor force, according to an estimate, held several jobs in 1966, and more than two regular jobs were no rarity. In some jobs—among unskilled workers and also government employees—working time is short and earnings inadequate. Only in large private corporations has the forty-eight hour week been generally adopted; yet prevailing remuneration even for this part of the labor force suggests the need to supplement income through additional employment.

TABLE 9-5   *Desire to Work More or Less*

(Percentage distribution of heads of households)

Country	Would like to Work more	Work less	As much as now	Not ascertained
United States (1966)	34	10	56	*
United Kingdom (1968) ...	55	10	31	4
Germany (1968)	40	6	45	9
Netherlands (1968)	28	17	39	16
France (1966)	25	15	56	4

*Less than one-half of one percent.

The question was: "Some people would like to work more hours a week if they could be paid for it. Others would prefer to work fewer hours per week even if they earned less. How do you feel about this?"

SOURCES: Surveys conducted by the authors; for France, unpublished data collected by the Cologne Forschungsstelle fuer empirische Sozialoekonomik.

all countries low-level white-collar employees (e.g., clerks and sales people) work longer hours than managerial and professional personnel. According to additional evidence collected only for the United States, the negative relation between working time and socioeconomic status is confirmed when one looks at differences in hourly earnings: The higher the hourly earnings, the shorter the working time. Differences in hours worked among income groups are equally great among people employed by others and the self-employed, although the latter, as might be expected, work considerably longer hours.

How do these factual differences in working time between the higher and lower economic strata relate to *preferences* regarding the work-leisure choice? What kinds of people in the different countries studied would prefer to work longer hours?

It was to be expected that the desire for more paid work would be particularly pronounced among the younger age groups and the lower-income groups. Both relationships were confirmed in Germany, England, and Holland as well as in the United States (Appendix Table C-1). Low-paid workers not only actually work longer hours, they most frequently would like to expand their working time even more. Excluding people beyond fifty or fifty-five years there is a strong and apparently unsatisfied desire particularly among lower-income groups to put in more work. This desire is gradually decreasing as the economic situation of the workers is improving.

The desire to increase the number of working hours is associated not only with low income but even more so with manual labor. A higher proportion of blue-collar workers than of white-collar workers would like to work more. For blue-collar workers, working overtime is a very real part of their lives. It is common for them to find an outlet for their working aspirations on the job, and the availability of overtime undoubtedly accounts for their longer actual working time. White-collar administrative activities on the other hand are usually confined to regular office hours. More often than not, white-collar workers who want to extend their normal working time have to turn to supplementary jobs, i.e., to engage in moonlighting.

Thus far three characteristics have been discussed which distinguish those who actually and potentially work more than regular hours from their less ambitious colleagues: physical capacity for activity, as represented by age; occupational role as traditionally reflected by the color of the collar; economic position, as indicated by level of income.[10] Beyond these characteristics, there is evidence that the workers' financial expectations as well as their unsatisfied consumption aspirations also matter considerably in shaping the degree of working ambition. Table 9-6 shows that in three European countries the desire to work more was more common among low-income workers who expected advances in their financial situation than among those who had no such expectations. Even after controlling for income, there were more respondents expressing a desire for more work among those who did than among those who did not indicate that they had unsatisfied wishes.

The reason for the observed relation between optimism regarding one's personal financial future and desire for more work is far from obvious. It may be understood by recalling that optimism is related to aspirations and to the notion of being in control of one's own fate; a person who is confident of his capacity to shape his own destiny is willing to work harder. Only in Holland, where work aspirations are the lowest among the countries studied, does the optimistic outlook seem to make little difference; apparently the values supporting inertia are powerful. The relationship between

---

[10] Mott[54] says that the moonlighter has a particular personality profile. He is "surgent, dominant, tough-minded, and not easily given to resignation. He is so energetic that he can maintain two jobs, be active in voluntary associations, and still shun the other more sedentary leisure activities of the nonmoonlighter in favor of the more rigorous ones." (p. 93)

TABLE 9-6   *Relation of Wanting to Work More to Financial Expectations and Unsatisfied Wishes*

(Percent of workers under age 50 wanting to work more*)

	Germany		England		Holland	
Among respondents who ..	Lower income	Higher income	Lower income	Higher income	Lower income	Higher income
Expect to be 4 years hence:						
Better off.................	62	38	73	60	40	29
Same, worse off, don't know ..	47	43	60	54	37	28
Unsatisfied wishes:						
Expressed................	58	44	67	61	45	31
Not expressed.............	45	38	68	53	26	23

*In England under age forty-five.

Note: The split between lower and higher income was as follows: Germany—DM 12,000 per annum; England— £ 1,200 per annum; Holland—hfl. 10,000 per annum.
SOURCE: Surveys conducted by the authors in 1968. Comparable data not available for the United States.

consumption aspirations and the desire to put in more work is easier to understand. The connection between the two is pronounced in all the subgroups studied with the sole exception of low-income workers in Britain. In that country consumption aspirations are high among all groups but do not appear to influence the desire to work more among those with low incomes.

The relation between desire for more hours of work and both aspirations for a higher standard of living and optimistic expectations is pronounced among lower-income workers. Few avenues of fulfilling their aspirations are open to most people in the lower-income and lower-skill strata other than to increase their working hours. The number of people among whom such behavior is found, primarily ambitious manual laborers, is, however, steadily on the decline in affluent economies. People with higher incomes, fewer of whom were interested in more work although just as many had high levels of aspirations, find other, more productive outlets for their energies and ambitions. They tend to strive for occupational advancement by acquiring additional education and training. This dynamic form of participation serves the needs not only of the individual but of modern technology as well. The latter calls not just for more of the same skills, but for higher skills; not just for hard-working, but for better-trained, innovative, and mobile labor. Application of knowledge represents the essence of productive capital and the driving force behind economic growth.

There remains one further area of choice between work and leisure, namely, the choice as to whether or not to retire early. In the United States, the desire to retire before reaching the most common retirement age of sixty-five is rapidly increasing (Table 9-7). A similar change has been occurring in Western Europe although perhaps less rapidly.

The trend toward early retirement is related to the greatly improved old-age security that has resulted from the almost universal coverage by governmental social security, widespread private pension plans, and growing amounts of individual savings. Among the reasons given in the United States for desiring to retire early, by far the most frequent was reference to the respondents' expectation that they would be financially comfortable after retirement. Reasons of health and dissatisfaction with the job were much less frequently mentioned.

The French people are known to be retirement-minded even at a relatively low level of old-age security. Almost three out of four French heads of household over thirty-five years of age, in contrast to two out of four British, say that they want to retire at a certain age rather than work as long as they can. More than half of all Frenchmen interviewed would like to retire before the age of sixty-five as against only a third of the British.

The proportion of respondents who felt that financial provisions for their old age would be adequate also varied considerably among different countries, largely in accordance with the factual situation in each country. Satisfaction with their expected retirement income was expressed more frequently by the Americans and Germans than by the British and Dutch (Table 9-8).

A large proportion of Americans with high levels of aspiration were found to desire early retirement. They expect, at a relatively

TABLE 9-7 *Plans of American Heads of Household to Retire before 65 Years of Age, in percent*

Age of respondents	1963	1966	1968
45–54	23	33	35
55–64	21	22	26

The question was: "At what age do you think you will retire from the main work you are doing?"
SOURCE: Barfield and Morgan,[3] p. 9.

TABLE 9-8   *Opinions   about   Security   during Old Age, in percent*

	Proportion of confident people
United States (1966) ..	62
Germany (1968)	70
Britain (1968)	45
Holland (1968)	52

Question in the United States: "Some people feel sure that they will be fairly comfortable at that time while others think that retirement will cause financial problems for them. How is it with you?"

Question in England: "Do you feel that by the time you retire the financial provisions for old age will be sufficient to meet your needs, or not?"

Question in Germany and Holland: "Do you think you will be able to make ends meet when you retire, or do you feel that the financial provisions for your old age will not be sufficient?"

SOURCE: Surveys conducted by the authors.

early age, to have acquired adequate means for comfortable living after retirement. In addition, many Americans expect to earn some money, through part-time jobs or business activities, after they have retired from their main job.[11] The fact that at present many retired Americans are in dire need does not affect the expectations of those who are working. In the United States the desire for early retirement is an indication of optimistic attitudes rather than of an absence of high aspirations.

To sum up: Regarding the issues discussed in this chapter similarities between the United States and Western Europe appear to be much more pronounced than differences. This is true of increased satisfaction with the job, of the number of hours worked, of desires for more or less work, as well as of plans for early retirement. We turn now to the question of gainful employment by married women where the opposite is true: differences are much more pronounced than similarities.

[11] In 1966, 43 percent of American family heads, thirty-five to fifty-nine years old, expected to work for money after their retirement, cf. Barfield and Morgan.[3] There is no doubt that fewer Europeans would have such expectations.

CHAPTER *10*

Married Women
in the Labor Force

S OCIAL norms in all Western societies prescribe full-time paid work for adult men prior to retirement age and also, though somewhat less rigidly, for unmarried women. There are no such norms for married women, and their participation in the labor force shows striking differences in different countries.

Married women represent an increasingly crucial, yet only partly tapped, reservoir for labor force participation. This reservoir is particularly valuable from the point of view of manpower policy. It can be expanded in national emergencies or at times of high levels of business activity, and it can be contracted whenever necessary with a limited amount of social friction, since families who go from two earners to one still have an income. In the Anglo-Saxon countries, World War II enlisted married women to the labor force to a very great extent. Since the end of the war, the number of employed married women has increased in most Western countries.

135

This increase has been a consistent feature of the postwar period and reflects basic attitudinal changes.

The choice between outside employment and homemaking for the woman is all too often the alternative between living at the margin of one's peer group or living in material comfort, though subject to the discipline of the employment routine. It represents a radical choice between much more or much less participation in market processes. In no other area can one compare as clearly the relative strength of the pressures emanating from consumption aspirations and the traditions of family life.

Comparative statistics on female labor force participation leave much to be desired. The proportion of *all* women working is rather similar in the United States and in Western Europe with the exception of the Benelux countries and Italy, where it is lower. The comparison for five countries is shown in Table 10-1 for all females between the ages of twenty and sixty-four; the age group below twenty was purposely excluded so as not to prejudice the picture in disfavor of the United States with its prolonged period of formal education. The increase in the total female labor force participation in the 1950s and 1960s was most pronounced in the United States and in West Germany. It was nonexistent, if not reversed, in France. The increase occurred almost entirely among married rather than unmarried women.

In the United States in 1968, 15.8 million wives in the 43.3 million complete families were in the labor force; in 1952, there were 8 million in the 35.2 million families. Thus the proportion rose from less than a quarter to more than one-third. These data collected by the Bureau of the Census are based on a rather restrictive definition of labor force participation (gainful employment in the week prior to the interview). When families were asked, in the Survey of Consumer Finances conducted early in 1969, whether the wife had done any work for money during the previous year, approximately one-half of the wives under the age of sixty-five answered in the affirmative. Comparable data on the employment of married women are not available in Western Europe. But data presented in Figure 10-1 below indicate that the proportions are lower in Germany and France than in the United States. The rate of increase in the number of working wives during the 1950s and 1960s was also smaller in Western Europe.

The trend toward early marriage which has occurred in all countries studied, but has been most pronounced in the United States, by no means halted the extent of female labor force participation.

TABLE 10-1   *Labor Force Participation Rates, All Females Age 20–64*

(Percent of women working for pay)

Germany:		
1950 .... 40.1		
1961 .... 43.9		
1963 .... 45.1		
France:		
1954 .... 43.9		
1962 .... 42.6		
1964 .... 40.2		
Netherlands:		
1960 .... 20.8		
Italy:		
1951 .... 27.5		
1963 .... 30.6		
United States:*	White	Nonwhite
1951	31.5	41.1
1960	34.1	41.2
1966	36.5	44.1

*The American definition of labor force participation is considerably more restrictive than the European definitions. Whereas the latter refer to any gainful employment during the previous year, United States figures relate to a given week. Very probably the American figures would be at least 10 percentage points higher by European reckoning.
SOURCE: *Yearbook of Labor Statistics,* International Labor Office, Geneva, Switzerland, various years.

Young people are now inclined to marry before they have the means to acquire a certain accepted minimum package of durables and house furnishings. One result is that the young wives follow working patterns after marriage that they would normally have followed before. The considerable rise in labor force participation of wives in their teens or early twenties may thus reflect more a change in the institution of marriage than a change in patterns of economic behavior. In the case of older married women genuine decisions are involved as to whether or not to work outside the home.

Modern mass-consumption societies stimulate employment by married women by offering both job opportunities and material as well as nonmaterial incentives. They also facilitate it by providing laborsaving consumer goods. It might be noted here how the mod-

ernization of households in the last few decades has been related to
both occupational and consumption aspirations. Laborsaving devices, as well as prepared foods and the like, help the housewife
save time and may be desired for the simple purpose of reducing
household drudgery in the absence of servants or of children old
enough to help and still living at home. A further motive, however,
is frequently that they enable the housewife to work outside the
home. The phenomenal rise in employment of married women,
particularly in the United States, would not have been possible
without the mechanization and simplification of homemaking.
This is an instructive and not untypical example of how one progressive behavior pattern in the area of consumption reinforces another in the area of occupation or vice versa.

A further impetus to the rising employment of women has been
provided by the increase in the variety and attractiveness of jobs
available to them. A growing proportion of women work in such
jobs as medical assistants, clerks, and secretaries, rather than in
purely manual occupations, which, as we have seen earlier, are considered less satisfactory.

Fig. 10-1   Rates of labor force participation of married
women by age.

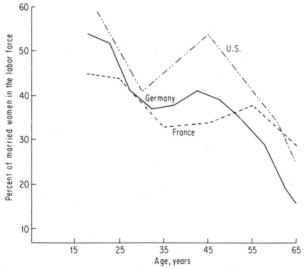

SOURCE: United States, 1964: Morgan et al.[52]; France, 1962:
Francaise Guelaud-Leridon[25]; Germany, 1965: Statistisches Bundesamt, *Hauptergebnisse der Arbeits-und Sozialstatistik* (Stuttgart and Mainz: W. Kohlhammer GmbH, 1965), p. 16.

Not only are the employment rates for wives higher in the United States than in Europe; there are also diametrically opposed behavioral patterns apparent on the two sides of the Atlantic with respect to the employment of married women in different age groups. In Germany, the number of working wives declines fairly steadily with age, from 54 percent of those in their twenties to 35 percent of those fifty to fifty-four years old. In the United States, the number similarly declines from 59 percent of those below twenty-five years of age to 41 percent of those twenty-five to thirty-four, the age group most needed at home to care for young children. The spectacular divergence then occurs when the American figure rises to 54 percent for women between thirty-five and fifty-four. In the age groups beyond thirty-five employment rates for married women increase only insubstantially in Germany and France, while in the United States there is a second peak in labor force participation after the age of thirty-five. American middle-aged women, to a far greater extent than their European counterparts, take advantage of the freedom of action they gain when their children go to school by resuming outside employment. In Germany, when women marry, they tend to abandon gainful employment permanently; in the United States, only temporarily. In France, the employment rate of married women according to age more closely resembles the German than the American pattern (see Figure 10-1).

These sizable international differences in the patterns of labor force participation of married women may be explained in terms of both material and nonmaterial motives. Material motivation may result either from needs or from aspirations. The former require little explanation: There are still many families with low incomes who have difficulties acquiring the necessities of life. The latter involve desires for a higher living standard and comparisons with reference groups. For German working wives, the scale appears to be heavily weighted toward wives' working only to satisfy needs: In reply to a survey question only one out of every four working mothers said that they planned to continue working any longer than was necessary,[1] and indeed German figures indicate a substantial decline in wives' employment once the household has reached a higher level of income. In the United States a high proportion of wives in middle-income families return to the labor force. Their motivation seems to be based on wants rather than needs. Even

[1] Pfeil,[62] pp. 181, 208.

wives whose husbands make $10,000 to $15,000 a year tend to turn to paid work fairly often; only among families with an income of more than $15,000 does the percentage of working wives drop significantly. This pattern suggests that in the United States material motives are effective on economic as well as age levels higher than those of constrained young families among whom most German working wives are found.[2] Thus the rise in the number of gainfully employed among middle-aged, well-off but not rich women points to the effectiveness of aspirations that extend beyond what is considered the absolute essential by the individual.

On the nonmaterial level our studies indicated that educational differences played a definite role in the high level of wives' participation in the labor force in the United States as compared to Germany and France. Three powerful incentives may operate to induce the educated wife to take up gainful employment: the higher income she can make compared to an unskilled worker; the fairly pleasant working conditions she is in a position to find; and dissatisfaction with the limitations of household work.

Appendix Table C–3 shows how age, education, and income relate to women's employment in the United States. Age and education are interrelated because at the present time those in younger age groups have had more extensive schooling than those in older groups. Nevertheless, education, and particularly college education, makes a difference in the rate of working wives within age groups as well. For instance, among wives under twenty-five years of age 78 percent of the college-educated, 70 percent of the high school graduates, and 43 percent of those with less than high school education were employed in 1968. Differences among educational groups, pointing in the same direction, existed also among women between the ages of forty-five and fifty-four, although the impact of education on the rate of employment among older women appears to be smaller than among younger women. It is noteworthy that, without regard to age, the higher her education the more a married woman tends to remain in the labor force even though her husband's higher-than-average income tends to exert an influence in the opposite direction. Thus in the United States the stimulating effect of education on employment of college-educated women is powerful enough to more than offset the opposite effect of the relatively high income of their husbands.

---

[2] For a more detailed analysis of American data, see Morgan, et al.[53]

For Germany, the positive effect of education on the wife's motivation to work is also confirmed by some available data. Only 34 percent of the women with some high school education and 21 percent with less education said that they would certainly continue to work even if it were not for economic pressure. Among women with a high school (gymnasium) diploma, which is equivalent to some college education, the proportion rose to 67 percent.[3]

A consideration of the role of income in the labor force participation of married women may provide further insights into the underlying dynamics of income acquisition. Let us repeat the two seemingly contradictory findings: First, labor force participation of women tends to decline as the husbands' incomes rise. Second, especially in the United States, labor force participation has risen greatly in the postwar period when incomes have also risen substantially. The apparent contradiction may be resolved by recalling the role of aspirations. In the United States material progress has not reduced aspirations, while in continental European countries there were some indications of growing saturation with increased well-being. It appears that in America the desire to acquire additional income is not generally reduced with rising income; it is reduced only if the income of a family improves greatly relative to other families, that is, if it attains the top decile or quintile of the income distribution. Married women in the United States who are financially comfortable but not really wealthy continue to work.

Since behavior is subject to factual pressures and is therefore only partly dependent on what people prefer to do, there is no one-to-one correspondence between attitudes and behavior. Nevertheless, a consideration of attitudes and preferences toward mothers' working outside the home serves the purpose of shedding light on the relative strength in different countries of traditions on the one hand as against more modern attitudes on the other. The matter of a married woman with children going out to work is delicate, controversial, and often determined by the attitudes of the husband. The question of whether or not they approved was therefore asked of the heads of households (husbands in complete families) in five European countries and the United States.

A comparison of attitudes toward the employment of mothers of schoolchildren is somewhat difficult because school systems differ in the various countries. In Anglo-Saxon countries, France, and

[3] Pfeil.[63]

TABLE 10-2   *Approval   of   Working   Mothers*
(Percent of heads of households)

| | Approval of working mothers with . . . | |
Country	Children at school*	Children at work†
United States (1968)	38	
United Kingdom	15 (1968)	55 (1966)
Holland (1968)	....	17
Germany (1968)	....	9
France (1966)	21	
Spain (1965)	....	12

*The question was: "If a family has children of school age living at home, do you think it is a good idea or a bad idea for the wife to go out to work?"

†The question was: "Suppose a family has children who live at home but are already at work, would you say it is a good thing for the wife to take a job or a bad thing?"

SOURCE: 1968 surveys conducted by the authors. 1965 and 1966 surveys conducted by Forschungsstelle fuer empirische Sozialoekonomik, Cologne.

Holland children customarily attend school for the entire day, in Germany and Spain for only half a day. Much greater difficulties arose because the data were not based on the same question in all countries. One question, asked in the United States and France, referred to mothers of children of school age; the other, asked in Germany and Holland, referred to mothers of children living at home but going out to work. Both questions were asked only in England, where it was found in 1966 that 55 percent of husbands approved of mothers working if the children were working as against only 15 percent (in 1968) if the children were at school (see Table 10-2). The latter question was doubtless understood to refer to younger children, including those six to ten years of age; the former, to teenagers. In the United States, where husbands were asked only about mothers of schoolchildren, it was still found that 38 percent approved of their working—two and a half times as many as in Britain. In Germany, Holland, and Spain, very small minorities approved of outside employment even by mothers with children at work. The French reacted somewhat more favorably, 21 percent approving even for mothers of schoolchildren; the proportion would certainly have been larger for mothers of children at work.

There is additional evidence suggesting that the German disapproval of working wives with children is rigid and uncompromising. In 1959, 59 percent of all adults interviewed said they would favor a law prohibiting employment of mothers with children below ten years of age. This statement was made slightly more frequently by women than by men. And 27 percent of respondents even disapproved of gainful employment of married women without children.[4] During the Second World War, the failure in Germany to mobilize women was in sharp contrast to Britain's success in doing so. After the war, an American group of experts was astounded to learn that the number of German women employed had remained practically unchanged throughout the war;[5] there had not even been a significant decline in the proportion of women in domestic service! Britain, in contrast, had increased the proportion of women in full or part-time occupations from 40 to 56 percent during the war.[6]

In all countries, younger respondents approved of mothers working far more frequently than older respondents. In the United States, the proportion was as high as 50 percent in the youngest group (below age thirty-five) and as low as 29 percent among those over sixty-five. The corresponding proportions in the other countries were: in Germany 14 and 6 percent, in England (in answer to the question about mothers of children in school) 21 and 7 percent, in Holland 22 and 10 percent. People's orientation toward the role of the wife in the household, like most other preferences and prejudices, may be assumed to develop fairly early in life and to remain relatively constant among individuals. The correlation between differences in attitudes and age probably reflects genuine attitudinal changes of the whole population, starting with the younger, more educated people. Thus the data cited give a hint of probable forthcoming changes in behavioral patterns.

The relationship between approval of mothers working and income is somewhat less conclusive, as might be expected on the basis of data on actual female labor participation. In all the countries studied except Holland, the highest income group approved

---

[4] Institut fuer Demoskopie, *Jahrbuch der oeffentlichen Meinung 1958–1964*, (Allensbach, 1965), p. 383.

[5] United States Strategic Bombing Survey Committee,[85] pp. 31–39.

[6] The authors of the American Bombing Survey report suggest that the Nazi government found itself hampered by its own preaching which had vigorously insisted for many years that women should stay at home. Accordingly, there were extensive official apologies for the faint attempts to forcibly recruit female labor. United States Strategic Bombing Survey Committee,[85] pp. 34ff.

less than other income groups, while groups in the middle everywhere leaned more toward mothers working than those in low-income brackets. Women in lower-income households generally have much less attractive choices in terms of job satisfaction and status than those in the higher brackets. For many a lower-income family, wives' employment apparently has the connotation of poverty and necessity, whereas at higher-income levels it is considered more often a legitimate outlet for the aspirations of a wife questioning her traditional role.

One final factor playing a great role in the proportion of husbands approving of mothers working is education; the more extensive the education the greater the approval. In the United States the percentage rises from 33 to 40 from the lowest to the highest educational group. This is true even though people with higher education are commonly people with higher income. Thus it seems that educational progress stimulates the desire to acquire additional income and to participate more actively in the economy. As will be shown in the next chapter, the extent of educational attainment in the United States is increasing at a fairly rapid rate. It will probably continue to stimulate women, including wives and mothers, to work outside their homes.

Here again we see the interacting influence of choices in different areas of economic behavior, in this case the areas of education and participation in the labor force. The great difference on the two sides of the Atlantic in the degree of husbands' approval of mothers working indicates that traditional values are far more powerful in Europe than in America. In Europe still today, full-time housework of the wife is considered the norm. To be sure, sizable minorities are departing from the norm and more will do so in future years.

CHAPTER *11*

Mobility and Education

PEOPLE may respond positively to the need or desire for greater income not only by adjusting upward their working time but also by spending their time in a more productive capacity or on a more productive job. The greater both the occupational and the geographic mobility of the workers, the greater the possibility of allocating existing labor resources to the most productive use. During the last two decades the three major forms of mobility — moving from one area to another, changing jobs or employers, and advancing in one's career — have become more common in all the growing economies on both sides of the Atlantic. A substantial part of the labor mobility has resulted everywhere from the large intersectional shifts in production described in Chapter 2, as well as from shifts of personnel within the same organization. Such mobility stems from the necessities of the situation rather than from any voluntary decisions on the part of the workers or from any of their own desires or aspirations. It will be shown in this chapter that the latter have played a greater role in determining labor mobility in the United States than in any of the other countries studied. Education represents the major key to upward occupational mobility. The modern man has considerable latitude regarding the acquisition of additional education, training, and skills. It thus became relevant to analyze the level of educational attainment and of educational aspirations in the countries with which we were concerned. Let us turn first, however, to certain aspects of mobility itself.

CHANGE IN JOBS AND GEOGRAPHIC MOBILITY

With rising prosperity fewer people are laid off or forced to leave a job. Separations occur as frequently at the initiative of the employee as at that of the employer. In 1961, about one-half of job terminations by American men, and an even larger percentage by women, were at the employee's initiative.[1] This proportion has, of course, since increased in the tight labor market characteristic of the second half of the sixties.

There are great differences in the rate at which different groups of people change jobs. For the United States extensive information is available (Appendix Table C-4) about residential and occupational mobility, both of which are highly related to age and to education. Younger people and people with extensive education change their jobs and their geographic location more often than older people or people with little education and do so frequently at their own initiative, whereas involuntary job changes are relatively frequent among older and unskilled workers. This may be related to the fact that many Americans who have received little or no education find it difficult to obtain steady jobs.

In Germany, young people are far more prone to change jobs than older ones, the cut-off point being approximately thirty-five years of age (Appendix Table C-5). Managerial, professional, and higher-level civil servants are distinctly lower than average in mobility, skilled workers and foremen higher. Job changes in Germany were found often to reflect a misallocation of occupational training. Large numbers of teenagers, after completing eight to

---

[1] *Manpower Report of the President* (Washington, D.C.), March, 1963.

TABLE 11-1   *The Utilization of Skills on the Job*
(Percentage distribution of members of German labor force, 1969)

| Labor force | Work in jobs . . . | | Total |
	for which they were trained	other than for which they were trained	
Education:			
Only elementary school	54	46	100
Secondary school and higher	72	28	100
Occupation:			
Unskilled workers	36	64	100
Skilled workers and foremen	69	31	100
Clerical and white collar	64	36	100
Managerial and executive	76	24	100
Net Income of Head per Year:			
Less than 7,200 DM	47	53	100
7,200–15,000 DM	59	41	100
15,000 DM and over	73	27	100
All members of the labor force	59	41	100

SOURCE: Institut fuer Demoskopie, *Allensbacher Berichte,* May, 1969, p. 7.

nine years of schooling, still today become apprentices in small crafts, as they did in earlier times. Apprentices are in high demand as cheap labor. Thus the number of apprentices who have completed their training tends to exceed by far the absorptive capacity for skilled labor in the respective trades. There is fragmentary but unambiguous evidence that the majority of workers skilled in the crafts (*Handwerk*) do not, therefore, find appropriate jobs.[2] Every third manual worker in Germany has undergone and completed an apprenticeship in a skill unrelated to his present job, and another third has received other less extensive but equally useless training. Thus more than 40 percent of all members of the labor force work in occupations different from those for which they were trained (Table 11-1). A misallocation of education and training, coupled with striking misconceptions about the nature of technological changes and their consequences for the worker,[3] account for the

[2] In 1962, about half of the 2,800 blue-collar workers of a particular steel mill were trained for different occupations, the majority of them for jobs entirely unrelated to those in which they were working, like clerks, miners, carpenters, bakers, masons, painters, butchers, tailors, shoemakers (see Lutz et al.,[47] pp. 231ff., and the sources quoted there).

[3] According to a survey of Infas in Bremen and Hessen, 80 percent of all interviewed German workers thought that not only they themselves but also their children would be able to work in the same occupation in 1980 as in the early 1960s.

greater part of involuntary job mobility among Germans skilled in the crafts.

There is evidence that workers in general are very hesitant to move from areas with few employment opportunities to more promising areas. Guy Routh in a report presented to the International Joint Seminar on Geographical and Occupational Mobility of Manpower of the OECD (1963) analyzed European and North American case studies of the relation of workers' attitudes to opportunities of changing jobs and places of employment, and he terms the findings "curious." He refers to an apparent preference for low wages and limited opportunities at one's place of residence, even when government authorities and employers have made great effort to make alternatives available elsewhere and have even solved the housing problem, which is a major obstacle to moving.[4] Adaptive mobility is not the rule, even in the presence of inadequate job opportunities. An individual is most often made aware of his need to readjust after he has been deprived of his means for adjustment, namely, when he is unemployed or, in the case of the businessman, bankrupt. "Financially and psychologically depressed, he is hardly in a position to make a sound decision regarding his most rational future place in the economy. . . . He is, in effect, forced to function irrationally."[5] Conversely, precisely the people who would be capable and willing to move, should the necessity arise, tend to find suitable employment in places where they are.

Where moves actually occur, they are often motivated by non-economic incentives. A recent American study, instead of confirming the stereotype of a society made mobile by the lure of monetary gains, points to affluence as strengthening the temptations of inertia. Fifteen percent of heads of households in 1962–1963 were found to have moved to different labor markets once or more in the preceding five years.[6] Yet little association was found between perceiving opportunities elsewhere and moving one's residence to take advantage of those opportunities. About 30 percent of all households were aware of better opportunities in different areas

---

[4] Routh.[67]

[5] Goesta Rehn, "Manpower Adaptability and Economic Growth," *The OECD Observer,* November 15, 1962.

[6] Lansing and Mueller,[43] p. 335. Moves in the study were defined as passing the boundaries of labor market areas; labor market is "an area within distinct geographical and occupational limits within which certain workers customarily seek to offer their services and certain employers to purchase them."

and yet did not move, as compared to 8 percent who actually did move because of the perceived opportunities. Of those who expressed an inclination to move, most did not have concrete plans; and reinterviews revealed that, even of those who had expressed the intention of moving within a year, most had not done so. People's willingness to leave an area has little to do with economic conditions there, except under extreme circumstances and perhaps also in the case of young workers just entering the labor force.

The proportion of American families changing their residence, whether combined with a change of the labor market area or not, was 21 percent a year in 1950–1951 and declined slightly to 19 percent a year in 1967–1968. "Migrants" (intercounty and interstate movers) constituted 6 to 7 percent of families per annum.[7] Residential mobility is concentrated among young households: As shown in Appendix Table C-4, in 1968 almost every second American family unit headed by an adult under thirty-five years of age moved, as opposed to only 6 percent of those with heads older than fifty-five. Education stimulates mobility of all kinds. On the other hand, income is negatively related to all forms of both residential and job mobility. Upper-income people, in part because of their being older, have more steady jobs than lower-income workers.[8]

Among Americans who had gone from one labor market to another in 1962–1963, 58 percent gave economic reasons for their move, 14 percent both economic and noneconomic reasons, and 23 percent noneconomic reasons (5 percent gave no reason). Among those giving economic reasons, 39 percent spoke of higher rates of pay and better prospects for advancement; and 16 percent of such things as lower cost of living or lower taxes, or better transportation or less traveling to reach the job. Twenty percent attributed their move to such necessities as looking for a first job, unemployment in their area, and desire for more or steadier work; and 25 percent to having been transferred by their employers.[9] These figures suggest that in the United States, voluntary moves ("being pulled") occur more frequently than involuntary moves ("being pushed").

One of the groups, namely, those transferred from one location to

---

[7] U.S. Bureau of the Census, *Current Population Reports*, ser. P-20, no. 188, August 14, 1969.

[8] Residential mobility in Europe is somewhat lower than in the United States. In Germany, in urban areas around 15 percent of families change their residence every year.

[9] Lansing and Mueller,[43] p. 62.

another by the same employer, represents one out of four of those moving for economic reasons and merits a closer look. It is one of the basic characteristics of a big organization that it allocates the total pool of available labor rather freely according to its needs. The initiative for career advancement and even change of residence comes from the employing organization; household decisions are replaced by management decisions. In a heavily concentrated industrial economy where mobility occurs under the guise of reshuffling of personnel, the workers' decisions play a much smaller role in determining change of job and residence than they do in an economy largely based on small business units and organizations. Correspondingly, there is a trend toward self-sufficiency within employing organizations. Seniority privileges in benefits and security impede separation, and the prevalent practice of "recruitment from within" and of hiring only at the bottom of the occupational structure, or at a few key maintenance and whitecollar levels, tends to prevent entrance into a large company at middle and higher levels of qualification.

With these changes in employment practices have come changes in incentives to attract labor. Organizations offering the promise of steady employment and career opportunities usually do not have to pay high initial wages. Richer career opportunities, higher job security, seniority privileges, and pension rights are incentives sufficiently valued to attract qualified employees in large numbers. The forward-looking applicant reacts not so much to immediate facts as to future chances. Since he is increasingly "locked in" in his employment—every separation may cost him accumulated seniority and pension rights and depreciate that part of his experience that is not transferable to a different employer—long-term considerations play an ever-increasing role in the choice of a job.

Given the various psychological and institutional obstacles to discretionary moves by workers over long distances, it is no accident that the large European labor migrations of the last decades, which contributed greatly to the economic growth of the receiving countries, were precipitated by the "push" of political upheavals or unemployment at home rather than by the "pull" to more favorable employment opportunities. The refugee stream from East to West Germany from 1945 to 1961 and the Indonesian and Algerian immigrations to the Netherlands and France, respectively, fall into the first category. The influx of South European workers to Central Europe, reaching its peak in the early 1960s, resulted as much from the unfavorable conditions in southern countries as from the attraction by the favorable conditions in Germany or Switzerland.

Even in a highly industrialized society there does, of course, still remain considerable latitude with regard to occupational mobility, and the amount of discretion possible in choosing and changing jobs was found to be closely related to the education of the worker. The relationship becomes evident at the moment of the initial choice of a job: The well-educated youth has a wide selection and is free to make the crucial first choice of entering into a career offering future advancement. The poorly educated, on the other hand, both in the United States and Europe, were found rarely to conduct a systematic search of available opportunities before making their initial employment decision. Their usual behavior was to accept the first job available, one not likely to offer much chance of advancement. Evidence indicates that, in terms of long-range occupational goals, the wisest reaction to early job opportunities is simply to refuse them all and stay in school. This, indeed, is what is being done to a greater extent each year, but to greatly differing degrees in different countries.

DIFFERENCES IN THE
LEVEL OF EDUCATION

There is no major area of behavior relevant for the economy that exhibits more striking differences among industrial societies than that of education. An educational revolution leaving its imprint on almost every aspect of society has been taking place in America for several decades. By contrast, in Western Europe educational progress has not begun to match the progress made in other areas of the social structure. Moreover, the gap in educational attainment between Europe and the United States has been growing ever-wider in the 1960s.

The level of education in different countries may be compared by considering either the number of years young people remain in school or the educational level of members of the labor force. On the first score, during the late 1950s American youth received an average of 2.6 years more formal schooling than their Northwest European counterparts in Belgium, Denmark, France, Germany, Holland, Norway, and Britain (Appendix Table C-6).[10] Of these

---

[10] European data on education have recently been compiled and analyzed by Denison.[14] We rely on his work for the evidence on educational differences between countries.

TABLE 11-2   *Mean Years of Formal Education of the Labor Force, 1950 and 1962*

Country	Males 1950	Males 1962	Females 1950	Females 1962
United States	9.68	10.68	10.01	11.08
Belgium	7.98	8.93	7.95	8.81
Denmark	7.46	7.82	7.55	7.83
France	8.09	8.65	7.89	8.51
Germany	7.93	8.24	7.95	8.19
Italy	4.23	5.10	3.89	4.88
Netherlands	8.43	9.11	8.35	9.02
Norway	7.90	8.40	7.70	8.28
United Kingdom ...	9.16	9.71	9.43	9.36

SOURCE: Denison,[14] p. 107. Reprinted by permission of the Brookings Institution.

countries Germany and Denmark, as well as Italy in Southern Europe, rank at the bottom of the scale in terms of the average number of years of formal schooling; the United Kingdom and Belgium, at the top.

Considering the educational attainment of the labor force as a whole, substantially the same picture emerges (Table 11-2). During the twelve years between 1950 and 1962, formal schooling increased one whole year for the average American male in the labor force (from 9.68 to 10.68 years), slightly more for the average female (1.07 years).[11] No European country matched the American rate of progress. Belgium, Italy, and Britain came close to it, Germany lagged far behind. The data contradict the widely held notion that it is easier for a country to show progress when it starts from a relatively low level than when it has to enhance a fairly high position.

Nowhere are the differences between the United States and Europe as striking as in the area of higher education. In the late 1960s close to 40 percent of youth eighteen and nineteen years old were enrolled in colleges in the United States. At the other extreme, in Germany only 4 to 5 percent go to a university. To be sure, German

[11] Entrants into the labor force in the fifties and the sixties not only enjoyed more years of formal education but also more hours of instruction per year than their fathers. When the data in Table 11-2 are adjusted for the higher intensity of recent education, educational attainment in the United States has increased in the twelve-year period by 1.66 years for males and by 1.75 years for females. Adjusted British figures for increase in educational attainment are likewise much higher than the unadjusted ones, although proportionately less so than the American data. Adjusted figures for other countries are not available.

universities represent higher education in a truer sense of the term than do some American colleges. In the last years of "gymnasium," often considered equivalent to an American high school, German youth receive some instruction given only in colleges in America. But in 1960 only 7 percent of German youth completed *A bitur,* the final examination before entrance into a university, usually taken at the age of eighteen or nineteen.

The intercontinental educational gap, as well as the rapid progress in educational attainment in the United States, are fairly recent phenomena. A rough estimate offered by Denison would put the 1925 United States index of educational attainment of the labor force no higher than the index in Italy in 1960, which was much below the 1960 indexes for the countries of Northwest Europe. Yet real national income per employed person in the United States in 1925 approximated the 1960 Northwest European level. Similarly, the educational lag of Germany behind some other European countries appears to be of recent origin. Germany has increased the education of its labor force within the last generation significantly less than any other major West European country.

In Figure 11-1 the educational attainment of older and younger people is compared in various countries on the basis of survey data obtained in the United States in 1968 and in Europe in 1963. The data show how many older people (age fifty-five or over) and how many younger people (age twenty-one to twenty-nine) remained in school at least twelve years (in the United States) or until the age of sixteen (in Europe). It was to be expected that the latter group would outnumber the former by far. The unexpected finding, indeed, was that the differential was so small in Germany: Only 35 percent of the younger group as against 23 percent of the older group remained in school to age sixteen. By contrast, in Britain, France, and Holland the proportion of the young generation staying in school beyond sixteen exceeded the proportion of the older generation by 20 to 30 percentage points. In Belgium and the United States, no less than forty out of every 100 young people stayed in school who, if they had been born one generation earlier, would have left with only elementary schooling.

There is not much difference between the two continents in the minimum number of years of schooling required by school attendance laws. However, voluntary continuation of education is practically universal in the United States and recently also in Belgium. In France, 42 percent of youths in 1950 and 70 percent in 1962, and

Fig. 11-1   Educational attainment—Proportion of adults in 1963 whose full-time education ended at age sixteen or older. (Proportion of young and old adults)

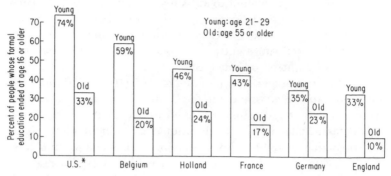

*In the United States, proportion of adults who completed twelve or more years of school, 1968.

Note: The figures for England appear low compared to the tables relating to years of schooling because elementary school in England starts at age five, as opposed to age six or seven in other European countries. American figures are understated because high school degrees are usually acquired at the age of seventeen or eighteen.
SOURCE: European data, *Reader's Digest,* [65] table 49, London, 1963. United States data, U.S. Bureau of the Census, Current Population Reports, *Population Characteristics,* ser. P-20, no. 182, April 28, 1969, p. 9.

in Germany only 39 percent in 1960 and 37 percent in 1963, were continuing full-time schooling beyond the eight or nine required years.[12]

EDUCATIONAL ASPIRATIONS

In the following report on educational aspirations in different countries we shall emphasize the sharp contrast between Germany and the United States partly because the most complete data are available for those countries, and partly because of their diametrically opposed trends in educational progress even though both experienced a rapid rise in income and living standards as well as extensive urbanization. Is this contrast due primarily to differences in opportunities and rewards for education or alternatively to people's preferences? Can the educational revolution in the American society be traced largely to certain attitudes, values, and beliefs, and the German educational lag to other attitudes and values stemming from different traditions? A comparative analysis of ed-

[12] Denison,[14] p. 81.

ucational aspirations as expressed in surveys may provide some of the answers.

There is hardly a strong case for attributing differences in educational attainment to differences in the environment. Education is no less necessary or useful in Europe than in America. In all the countries studied, social and occupational advancement is greatly fostered by high educational attainment and impeded by its absence. It is universally recognized that minimal education tends to lead to dead-end jobs. From the point of view of making progress in one's career, Europeans no less than Americans have reason to want to stay in school. Then, too, tuition charges in colleges and universities, high for American students and either low or nonexistent for those in Europe, might be expected to encourage more of the latter than of the former to continue their studies. True, there is more provision for on-the-job and part-time vocational training in Europe, and particularly in Germany, but much of it, as may be recalled, is not well suited to the requirements of the modern labor market.

Survey data gave evidence that not in the surface facts of the situation but rather in the underlying psychological attitudes, beliefs and values must be sought the reasons for differences in educational attainment. In the United States, Germany, and Britain questions were asked about how long it was either expected or desired that boys should remain in school (Table 11-3). In the United States in 1959, 66 percent of fathers with sons age twenty or below expected them to receive some college education. Only 24 percent would have been satisfied with a high school degree, and a mere 2 percent would settle for less. There is no question that aspirations have been expanded further in the last decade. Educational aspirations in Britain in 1968 were quite similar to those in the United States in 1959. Almost 60 percent of heads of households would expect their sons (if they had any) to work toward a university degree; 28 percent would like them to attain what roughly amounts to an American high school degree, and only 5 percent would settle for the minimum duration of education as required by law. Despite the fact that in Germany most managerial and supervisory as well as civil service careers are closely tied to a high level degree (*Abitur*) or equivalent formal education, only 41 percent of the respondents expressed the desire for their sons (or young people in general) to attain or exceed that degree. Nine percent of all respondents (but 16 percent of the lowest income group) spontaneously

TABLE 11-3   *Expected or Desired Education for Boys**

	In percent
United States, 1959:	
Less than 12 grades	2
12 grades	24
Some college, Bachelor's	
or advanced degree	66
Don't know, not ascertained	8
	(N = 1,128)
Germany, 1968:	
8–9 years (minimum required)	9
Mittlere Reife, vocational school†	49
Abitur‡	7
University degree	34
Don't know, not ascertained	1
	(N = 1,908)
Britain, 1968:	
9 years (minimum required)	5
11 years ("O"-levels)	15
12 years ("A"-levels)	13
University degree or equivalent	59
Don't know, not ascertained	8
	(N = 1,637)

*The following question was asked of fathers of boys under age twenty in the United States: "How much education do you expect your boy(s) to have before he (they) stops going to school?" In Britain and Germany all heads of households were asked: "Suppose you had a son aged ten. How long would you want him to stay on at school or college?"

†Corresponds to 10–11 years of formal schooling.

‡Corresponds to high school degree plus some college.

SOURCE: United States, Morgan et al.,[52] p. 588. Germany and Britain, surveys conducted by the authors in 1968.

voiced their disinterest in any education exceeding the minimum level. Almost half of the respondents would be quite content to have young people acquire a general education below the American high school degree (*Mittlere Reife*).

In all the surveys young fathers were found to have more education than older fathers and to express greater expectations for their sons. But in Germany the differences between the age groups were much smaller than in the United States or England. It was further found that the parents' income was very influential in raising educational sights in all countries.

Asked whether they were satisfied with the education they had or whether they would have liked more, the majority of adults expressed dissatisfaction in each European country with the exception of Germany (Table 11-4). Lowest in satisfaction was Italy—a finding which may be explained by the comparatively low level of educational attainment in that country. France, although not low in attainment, scores high in dissatisfaction (70 percent of all adults), followed by Britain and the Benelux countries. In Germany, by contrast, 60 percent of all adults said they were satisfied with their own education. That country stands out for the low priority its people give to education; they seem to be maintaining the traditional posture of an era gone-by when schooling was less closely related than now to career advancement. In all countries except Germany, respondents who left full-time school early (at age fifteen or younger) are significantly less frequently satisfied with their education than those who left school between ages sixteen and twenty. Yet in Germany, the poorly educated perceive their lack of formal schooling as a deficiency or handicap hardly any more frequently than the better educated.

The most powerful determinant of the educational lag in Germany and, to a lesser degree, in Western Europe seems to be the rigid remnants of class structure. Although in the early sixties blue-collar workers represented close to half of German heads of households only 5 percent of the students at universities and comparable institutions came from their ranks; blue-collar workers and farmers

TABLE 11-4 *Satisfaction with Education, in percent*

| | Proportion satisfied with own education | | |
| | | Among adults who left school | |
Country	All adults	Under age 16	Between ages 16–20
Belgium	46	43	49
France	30	25	41
Germany	60	59	61
Italy	27	23	45
Netherlands	44	38	53
United Kingdom ..	40	34	66

Note: The proportion of those neither satisfied nor dissatisfied was approximately 4 percent in each country; therefore it is not necessary to present the proportion expressing dissatisfaction.
SOURCE: Surveys conducted in 1963 by *Reader's Digest*,[63] table 50.

together, comprising 64 percent of all households accounted for only 7 percent of all university students.[13] On the other hand, 49 percent of all students were recruited from 7 percent of the population, consisting mainly of families headed by government employees and professionals. R. Dahrendorf pinpoints the difference as follows:

> There are in the Federal Republic [of Germany] approximately one million agricultural workers, from whose families in the winter 1958–59 exactly 80 university students were recruited. There are also one million civil servants in Western Germany; from their families, 52,199 students were recruited during the same period.[14]

What are the reasons for the almost unanimous indifference of the large blue-collar segment toward higher education?[15] It is not primarily because of cost considerations that working class parents are content with or even desire relatively little formal education for their children. Rather, there appears to be a lack of appreciation of education as a marketable commodity and as a value in itself, and even a fear of being alienated from their children should education lead to an advanced social status. Even where there are aspirations for occupational advancement, the sights are restricted to the next steps of the hierarchy, which, like foreman or clerk, do not require higher education. Only in exceptional cases did parents of particularly gifted blue-collar children aspire to a level of education beyond *Mittlere Reife* (eleven years of schooling). Parents often rationalized their lack of aspirations for their children by expressing doubts about their intelligence or ability. The essence of these findings may be summarized by the terms complacency, lack of imagination, and reluctance to take risks.

In America, children's education is also related to the father's occupation. A report prepared by leading social scientists considers college attendance of high school graduates who rank in the top one-fifth of a large sample in academic aptitude:

> If the parents of these relatively able youth are from the top socioeconomic quartile, 82 percent of them will go on to college in the first year after high school graduation. But, if their parents come from the bottom socioeconomic quartile, *only 37 percent* will go on to college in the first year after high school graduation. High school graduates from

---

[13] Claessens et al.,[12] p. 299.
[14] Dahrendorf,[13] p. 7.
[15] The evidence quoted in this paragraph is based on an investigation by Paul.[61]

the top socioeconomic quartile who are in the third ability group [i.e. the third quintile of the ability ranking] are more likely to enter college than even the top ability group from the bottom socioeconomic quartile.

Differences in attendance at graduate or professional schools are even more striking. Five years after high school graduation, those high school graduates in the top fifth by ability are *five times more likely to be in a graduate or professional school* if their parents were in the top socioeconomic quartile than if their parents were in the bottom socioeconomic quartile.[16]

Still, the differences in the educational attainment of children of blue-collar and white-collar workers in the United States are relatively smaller than in Europe (Appendix Table C-7). American blue-collar families do not exclude themselves from higher education. The number of school years even of children of unskilled workers is only 12 percent below the average; of semiskilled workers just slightly below the average, while those of skilled workers reach the average. To a great extent, the educational attainment of a child is due to factors that are independent of his family background, and his education helps him achieve a higher occupation even if he had a disadvantaged family background.[17]

The lesson is obvious and conforms to widespread perceptions of American as opposed to European social stratification. Class differences between manual workers and white-collar workers are still very real in Western Europe. Even where they have ceased to be reinforced by income, the habits, stereotypes, values, and aspirations of a working class or farming background are carried forward into the changed economic environment. In the United States, class differences have been weakened by the continuous spatial mobility prompted by immigration and expanding frontiers. Also, the movement to the suburbs, in which blue-collar workers have participated, has contributed greatly to a thorough realignment of living patterns incompatible with rigid class boundaries.

There remains on the American scene one specific stratum of society not participating in the educational revolution, and indeed being negatively affected by it. That subgroup, usually referred to as the "poverty sector," is not equivalent to the occupational category of "unskilled worker." It consists largely of people not in the labor force at all and handicapped especially by race, age, and

---

[16] U.S. Department of Health, Education, and Welfare,[84] p. 20.

[17] *Op. cit.*[84] p. 22.

physical or mental disability, or family breakup. In a society where even low-level occupations can be filled with high school graduates, job applicants with an education much below a continuously rising average attainment are bound to suffer. In Germany and most of Europe, educational underachievement short of illiteracy does not drive a man into a marginal existence; his competitors are not likely to offer substantially more. In the United States the rapid educational advancement of the large majority inevitably aggravates the situation of the people at the low end of the spectrum, who to a large extent are those who dropped out of school at an early age.

The educational revolution provides the impetus for its own continuation. For a young man to receive the same amount of education as his father had will usually mean settling for a lower occupational status and lesser advancement than was available to his father. The very fact that so many young people have received or are now receiving higher education in the United States compels those who do not want to fall behind to follow suit if only to preserve their present status. This argument, naturally, can only help to explain the proliferation of the educational revolution once it started and not its takeoff. However, it may shed light on the relatively widespread participation in higher education on the part even of those American families whose heads had little education.

EFFECTS OF DIFFERENT
EDUCATIONAL LEVELS

To what extent are the skills acquired by formal education in the United States put to productive use? An attempt to gauge the changing relationship of "necessary" and available qualifications of the American labor force over a ten-year period was undertaken by Eckaus. He compared the "estimates of worker traits requirements for 4,000 jobs" as published by the U.S. Department of Labor with the actual level of schooling of the American labor force. He concluded as follows:

> In 1940 and 1950, according to the Census of Population, the proportions of employed persons who actually had at least a full *high school education* were 31.2 and 39.0 percent respectively. Those *needing* that much education for their jobs according to this study were 28.5 and 32.4 percent of the labor force. On the other hand, the *higher education* represented in the labor force is quite fully employed: in 1940 and 1950

the percentages of employed persons having four or more years of college were 5.9 and 7.4 percent, respectively, while the percentages of those requiring such an education were 7.1 and 7.4 percent.[18]

There is some evidence that in the United States in the 1960s the income differential between labor market entrants with high school as compared to college education has been narrowing,[19] implying a lesser degree of utilization of higher education and a growing scarcity of lesser-educated workers as the number of college graduates has increased. A leveling of income differentials may well prove to be an important by-product of mass college education.

We may add that the underutilization of skills—if there is any—has not impaired job satisfaction. As a recent American survey suggests, job satisfaction rises significantly with education, as do favorable attitudes toward automation and toward the equipment and machinery used.[20]

The recent American trend toward college education of a very large proportion of young people raises a variety of further problems which can only be hinted at here. A college education is not necessarily good for all those who now receive it or who aspire to it. Remaining till the early or middle twenties in a theoretically oriented college environment and thus postponing participation in the labor force may not suit all students and may cause discontent and frustration for many. The United States may need to create alternative avenues of progress for young people for whom the present system of college education is not entirely appropriate.

Recently steps have been taken in several European countries, particularly in Belgium, France, and Britain, toward closing the educational gap between the two continents. Nevertheless, differences in the number of years spent in school by members of the labor force are likely to persist for several decades. Germany in particular, as Denison remarks, "is heading toward a position in which its labor force will have the least full-time education of any of the countries covered except Italy, and eventually little, if any, more than Italy."[21]

What effect, if any, have these differentials in education had on the economies of the different countries? The high productivity of the American economy compared to the West European economies

[18] Eckaus,[17] p. 181ff.
[19] Stafford.[74]
[20] Mueller et al.[57]
[21] Denison,[14] pp. 106ff.

has, over the years, been explained in various ways. Shortly after the war, lack of capital was the most widely accepted scapegoat for lagging European productivity. After European capital formation had grown greatly, a technological gap, supposedly caused by limited investments in research and development, and, more recently, the "managerial gap," have been blamed for the lag. Differences in the education of the labor force, or the insufficiency of investment in human capital in Europe, may represent a further reason for the differences in productivity.

Certainly, the relationship between education and economic growth is a complex one. The very fact that virtual educational stagnation and consistent economic growth have occurred at the same time in several European countries raises doubts that any simple model could be constructed relating educational attainment to economic performance. Behavioral studies on the impact of education on individuals should help to clarify the picture. Extending the legal minimum school age, for example, would have different consequences—psychologically, socially, and economically—than, say, providing additional funds for higher education or increasing teachers' salaries. There is much yet to be learned about the impact and implications of investing in education in different countries, at different levels, or for different groups of people. As has been said, "An investment that makes a literate and disciplined labor force out of illiterates may have a simply colossal productivity, but this says nothing about the returns on an investment which makes it possible for every salesgirl and every ditchdigger to have a college degree."[22]

We must conclude that mobility and education are areas of economic behavior demanding the most radical choices from modern man, choices which often result in large-scale and even quite sudden changes of job, status, and way of life. Since the consequences and effects of these changes extend far into the future and are quite uncertain, it is little wonder that the gap between the perceiving and the seizing of opportunities is greatest in these areas of behavior. We found that the largest percentage of Americans and the smallest percentage of Germans chose to make the decision to change their way of life by increasing the length of their schooling. In America, as we said, the educational spiral created its own momentum. Within the individual, the felt need for additional educa-

---

[22] Machlup,[48] p. 120.

tion was found to rise with the level of education already attained. Just so within society, the felt need of more people to attain a higher level of education was found to rise with the number of people who had already a higher level.

In Germany an equally powerful self-reinforcing process was conspicuously absent. The educational backwardness of Germany can be attributed primarily to the failure of occupational aspirations of the people to rise at a pace with the rich opportunities created by a modern and rapidly growing economy. This failure is indicated by the persistence of many traditional beliefs and values, by the small proportion of children from blue-collar and farm families taking advantage of an essentially tuition-free system of higher education. Furthermore, the absence of massive popular support for legislation that would raise the minimum school age and would create preschool education as well as far more comprehensive and effective vocational training is noteworthy. The conclusions about the causes of differences in education coincide with and reinforce our previous findings about the German people being more static in their financial expectations and consumption aspirations than other Western European nations and particularly than the United States. However, whereas the stagnant outlook of the Germans measured by perceptions and expectations concerning their economic situation may be subject to change over a period of five or ten years, the impact of low levels of education is bound to extend far into the future; those who leave schools at present will be in the labor force for several decades to come.

PART 4

Conclusions

CHAPTER 12

Profiles of Consumer Cultures

*I*N our concern with the interaction between man and his economic environment we have attempted to answer some of the crucial questions of a comparative analysis: In what way do decisions by private households either reinforce or impede socioeconomic change? And is the behavior of the modern man substantially the same whether he lives in Detroit or Frankfurt, or does his response to affluence and economic and technological changes vary from country to country?

To recapitulate some of the similarities in the countries studied: In all of them there are not only greatly improved standards of living but modest wealth as well; not only less unemployment but also more secure jobs and favorable prospects for advancement; not just some provisions against sickness and emergencies but a vastly improved system of social security; not only higher levels of education but also unprecedented opportunities for education. In short, there have been great changes in the same direction in what Marx has called the "basis" on which economic processes rest. There have also been changes in people's values, habits, and behavior patterns which may have both anticipated and followed the other changes.

Although in all affluent countries, and among most socioeconomic strata, there are many people partaking in the offerings of the modern mass-consumption and mass-knowledge society, we found the various countries and also various subgroups of each country to be making use of these opportunities to a greatly varying extent. We found no one-to-one correspondence between a given change in the environment and the response to it. Our findings confirmed the hypothesis that it is such noneconomic variables as attitudes and expectations that must be held largely responsible for differences in the behavior of people in nations which are generally similar in affluence and technological progress.

In this chapter we shall recapitulate and summarize some of the most important data about economic behavior which in Parts 2 and 3 we dealt with sequentially in cross-national comparisons. Here we shall treat them in terms of their prevalence and consequences in each of the four nations in which we collected our own survey data: the United States, Germany, Britain, and Holland. Our findings, seen in the context of the economic performance of each of the four countries, may provide a clearer picture of the broad implications for society of consumer dynamism or consumer traditionalism.

THE UNITED STATES: ADAPTATION TO THE KNOWLEDGE SOCIETY

The economic behavior of the American people has supported and facilitated the transition from an industrial to a postindustrial or knowledge society in a unique manner. The United States is the only nation in which the major portion of the population is engaged neither in agriculture nor industry. Not only are about 55 percent of the labor force engaged in pursuits customarily classified as services (finance, trade, government, etc.) but, for the first time in history white-collar workers outnumber manual workers. Professional and technical workers have increased since 1940 at a rate twice that of manual laborers, and the subgroup of scientists and engineers has risen even three times as fast as the working population as a whole. These facts indicate the amount of adaptive effort that has been made continuously by the American people.

The nature of the effort has been characterized by a rush to secondary and higher education and an explosion of educational aspirations. To repeat the major data in this area:

▪ The average duration of the formal education of a member of the American labor force in 1962, 10.7 years, was 1 entire year longer than in Britain, 2 years longer than in France, and 2½ years longer than in Germany.

▪ American students in their late teens are receiving much longer full-time formal schooling than the average Western European of the same age, namely, 2 years more than in England and in France, 2½ years more than in the Netherlands, and almost 4 years more than in Germany.

Americans, by sharply increasing their demand for education, responded to and even anticipated the challenge of the knowledge society to replace unskilled or semiskilled workers by highly skilled personnel in large numbers. The man who can be trained within a few weeks to do routine operations on a simple machine is a creature of industrial economies in their early stages. The postindustrial society is dependent on a labor force possessing general knowledge rather than experience through "learning by doing." The flexibility it requires can be provided only by basic or theoretical knowledge.

The surge in educational aspirations among Americans is certainly only to a small extent attributable to conscious career planning anticipating the basic and continuing shift toward demand for higher-level skills. It is a reasonable assumption that education was high on the list of American desires for some time before the actual run on education started but could be afforded only after mass incomes had risen and higher education had become heavily subsidized by the government (GI bills and increased state and federal support of public as well as private colleges). Although the signals of the labor market—the lure of a higher standard of living for the better educated—certainly mattered, the main incentive for the newly educated subgroups was both the individual's desire to get ahead on the broad front of socioeconomic status and the high premium placed by society upon success and achievement.

The extraordinary vigor with which Americans invest in human capital is in sharp contrast to their relatively low rate of saving out of disposable income, which oscillated between 5 and 7 percent between 1960 and 1968, as compared with (1967) 20 percent in Japan, 15 percent in the Netherlands, 14 percent in Germany, 8 percent in France, and 6 percent in Britain. If, however, we look upon the cost of education as the formation of human capital to be added to liquid savings, the international differences narrow down considerably. In the United States higher education is an expensive affair; the college attendance of children often requires extensive financial planning and advance saving. The expenses are frequently taken out of accumulated savings. In addition, both for individuals and the society education can be considered as a way of providing for the future, or of transmitting assets from one generation to the next.

The relatively low United States saving rate in the face of high mass incomes and high consumer discretion might even be viewed as a transitory phenomenon, associated with an *increase* but not with a high *level* in education. While the present generation typically has to pay for increased levels of their children's education without having had very much education themselves, the next generations will be in a better position: While paying for their children's education, they will reap the benefits of their parents' sacrifices.

In the past, the process of industrialization has required huge sums of capital. Should the economic growth of postindustrial societies be less dependent on tangible capital than on human skills, and particularly on the supply of technical and scientific manpower, the practice of substituting education for monetary savings would constitute highly appropriate behavior. Little is known as yet of the extent to which the abundant supply of human capital enables the United States to specialize in production that is human-capital intensive. Signs of such a development are unmistakable and are recently of serious concern to Europeans who worry about the large surplus in the American "knowledge balance": To a large extent the United States sells abroad licenses, patents, know-how, and specialized technical equipment which are the products of American research and development.

The scope of Americans' participation in economic processes extends beyond that of Western Europeans in other areas as well. Again, to recapitulate:

▪ More American than European middle-aged married women hold jobs. In the United States about 55 percent of all married women age forty-five to fifty-four are employed (1964) compared to 40 percent in Germany (1965) and 35 percent in France (1962). Labor force participation of women is still rapidly on the rise.

▪ In spite of the relatively abundant possessions and high standard of living of the average American family, there are no signs of saturation or of slackening effort to supplement the basic income of the head of the household. In the last twenty years actual working time has hardly diminished. Rather, the number of nonfarm hourly and salaried employees working more than forty-eight hours a week has risen from 13 to 20 percent of the full-time labor force. Further shortening of the workweek has virtually disappeared from the agenda of collective bargaining and, where it occurs, tends to be partly balanced by moonlighting.

■ Spending for automobiles—a costly discretionary purchase— attracts a much higher share of the consumer budget than it does in Europe. In America 15 percent of disposable consumer incomes are spent on transportation and communication as opposed to 8 percent in France, 9 percent in Germany, 12 percent in Britain.[1]

What is the origin of the exceptionally smooth and rapid adaptation to the opportunities of change on the part of Americans?

The psychological reflection of change, i.e., its perception and the extent of optimism and confidence with regard to future improvements, represent powerful explanatory factors which we singled out earlier: Close to half (43 percent) of all American heads of household anticipate being better off four years from now, but only a third of the Britons, a quarter of the French, Germans, and Dutch. Whereas every third American both feels better off than four years ago and anticipates being better off four years hence, only every fourth Briton, every fifth Frenchman, every sixth Dutchman, and every eighth German feels similarly embedded in a continuum of progress. The feeling of cumulative progress proved to be positively related to discretionary purchases, consumption aspirations, and expressed willingness to put in more work. It suggests differences in the psychological basis of economic behavior and will concern us again in connection with the characterization of the British and German consumer cultures. The continuous extension of work and educational efforts as well as the rising level of innovative consumer demand by Americans stand out sharply in cross-cultural comparisons. The American, confident of his own power to advance his well-being, steps up his wants at an equal pace with, or even faster than, his accomplishments. Impatience goes

---

[1] These data, for the year 1965, represent the item communication and transportation in international statistics of budget composition. In the United States, this category was almost as high in 1950 (14 percent) as fifteen years later. This suggests that transatlantic differences are not due to the differential in real income alone.

along with optimism and thus is conducive to dynamic adaptation and the reinforcement of wants and efforts. This pattern was not found to be common to other affluent societies.

A well-known observer of the American scene concludes:

> . . . in the American Dream there is no final stopping point. . . . At each income level . . . Americans want just about twenty-five per cent more (but of course this "just a bit more" continues to operate once it is obtained). . . . The family, the school and the workplace—the major agencies shaping the personality structure and goal formation of Americans—join to provide the intensive disciplining required if an individual is to retain intact a goal that remains elusively beyond reach.[2]

The tendency toward adaptive economic behavior patterns may be rooted partially in social attitudes and beliefs in benign social relations and the value of cooperative behavior. As Almond and Verba found in the cross-cultural study mentioned in Chapter 3, the belief that people are generally cooperative, trustworthy, and helpful is much more frequent in the United States and Britain than in Germany or Italy. The high level of political participation, affiliation, and cooperation has been observed by political theorists ever since de Tocqueville:

> No sooner do you set foot upon American ground than you are stunned by a kind of tumult; a confused clamor is heard on every side, and a thousand simultaneous voices demand the satisfaction of their social wants. Everything is in motion around you; here the people of one-quarter of a town are met to decide upon the building of a church; there the election of a representative is going on; a little farther, the delegates of a district are hastening to the town in order to consult upon some local improvements.[3]

De Tocqueville and many observers after him turned to the class structure of the democratic American society to explain the speed with which the participative potential of the society was translated into aspirations and wants.

> In democratic times enjoyments are more intense than in the ages of aristocracy, and the number of those who partake in them is vastly larger; but, on the other hand, it must be admitted that man's hopes and desires are oftener blasted, the soul is more stricken and perturbed, and care itself more keen.[4]

[2] Merton,[51] pp. 136, 137.
[3] De Tocqueville,[83] vol. 1, pp. 249–250.
[4] De Tocqueville,[83] vol. 2, p. 139.

In the next chapter we shall return to the darker side of American dynamism described with great insight in the preceding quotation. Suffice it to say here that the American society in 1970 still stands out from European nations, which served as de Tocqueville's yardstick, in that differences in social status, real as they may be, appear to place lesser limitations on aspirations in the former than in the latter. Furthermore, even those differences in social status as do exist are not as frequently transferred from one generation to the next.

American society has been largely formed over the centuries by European immigrants who sought escape from the political oppression and economic limitations of their old-world existence. The reformist and dynamic ferment of European society has thus been overrepresented among the migrants. The exodus of enterprising individuals of all shades helps to explain both the American tradition of adaptation and the European lag.

GERMANY: PROSPERITY
WITHOUT ADAPTATION

The German and the American responses to affluence stand in the sharpest contrast to each other. In Germany there is a gap between the reality of a rapidly developing mass-consumption society and its perception by the people. Attitudes and behavior patterns taken over from agrarian and early industrial modes of living are still predominant, particularly among the manual workers.

Let us first summarize our findings on how Germans perceive their national well-being, their economy, and their own personal level of living. The Germans by far most frequently among Western nations deny that they are living in an extraordinarily favorable era of rising real incomes. Many of them fear an economic crisis, which fear apparently grows stronger with rising prosperity! In July, 1966, even before a slight recession had left its imprint on public opinion, 62 percent of respondents deemed it certain or probable that there would be an economic crisis during the next twenty to thirty years; only 16 percent considered such a crisis improbable or impossible. In 1962, the respective figures had been 48 and 36.[5]

The focus of the Germans' worries about the economic future is

[5] Cf. Institut fuer Demoskopie, *Pressedienst,* November, 1966. In the United States in 1968, 43 percent of family heads said that a recession was *not* likely to happen again and 26 percent that it was likely (an additional 31 percent had no opinion).

the value of the currency. Many more people mentioned inflation as a cause for concern than unemployment or the environment— crime, pollution, noise, etc. "There is no other area in which (German) people react as sensitively as toward rising prices."[6] Much of this concern is habitual and not in touch with ongoing trends. The continuous concern with the value of the money provokes complaints even at times when the price index remains stable. From the beginning of 1958 to the middle of 1959 costs of living did not rise. Stability, however, was recognized by only 38 percent of German adults, while 53 percent claimed there had been price increases.

The overriding concern of Germans with preserving the status quo was further apparent when attitudes toward their jobs were analyzed. As reported in Chapter 9, 70 percent of the Germans, as compared to only 30 to 40 percent of Americans, British, and Dutch, mentioned security as the most important criterion for choosing an occupation. The threat of inflation is taken so seriously that many people seem willing to sacrifice the prospect of rising real incomes for monetary stability. Shortly after the slight recession of 1966–1967, Mr. Schiller, the Minister for Economic Affairs, proposed to have wages raised 5 percent to stimulate consumer demand and compensate wage and salary earners for the lag of income increases behind soaring profits. More than 50 percent of the population, blue-collar and white-collar workers alike, were opposed to the proposal! At the same time, the government was chided for not controlling prices—and this in an economy the success of which is often attributed to the absence of controls. "Irritation about even small rates of inflation appears to obstruct the comprehension of economic dynamism."[7]

Insecurity about the economic future breeds an apprehensive posture toward consumption and spending. Higher living standards are a by-product of progress on which Germans tend to look with reserve, almost with suspicion. The maintenance and preservation of past gains is foremost in people's minds rather than any longing for better living. In 1957, 48 percent of German adults stated flatly that they would be satisfied if their economic situation would remain as it was for the next five to ten years. This proportion rose to 60 percent in 1961 and to 70 percent in 1963. When asked whether they considered the present average standard of living in Germany to be too high, too low, or just right, the proportion

[6] Noelle-Neumann,[58] p. 40.
[7] *Ibid.*, p. 44.

of those who disapproved of prevailing levels of consumption as being too high increased from 52 percent in 1958 to 62 percent in 1963.[8] The suggestion given by the interviewer in 1963 that "We Germans attach too much value to a good life and to consumer durables and are not living within our means" was approved by 61 percent and rejected by only 29 percent of the people.[9]

Thus it is not surprising to find consumption aspirations of Germans lagging behind accomplishments. A symptom of the lag is an uninterrupted, steep increase in the proportion of households which are close to feeling "saturated," together with a continuously high rate of saving. Asked whether respondents intended to make large outlays during the coming year, the negative answers increased from 16 percent in 1956 to 20 percent in 1959, 31 percent in 1962, and 46 percent in 1967.

There are further indications of a strong preference for saving and a cautious and conservative handling of financial affairs in Germany:

▪ The rate of saving out of disposable income, which oscillated in the early fifties below 10 percent, reached 14 percent at the end of the fifties, and has stayed at that level (declining slightly in 1967), as compared to a 1967 rate of 7 percent in the United States, 5 percent in Britain, and 10 percent in France.

▪ Only 14 percent of their most recent durable purchases, as reported by German consumers in 1968, were financed by installment debt, compared to 58 percent of cars and 45 percent of household appliances purchased in the United States.

▪ In 1963, 74 percent of German households had a savings account, as opposed to 56 percent in the United States (which increased to 64 percent in 1967), 29 percent in France, and 13 percent in Belgium.

▪ Whereas in 1968 real GNP per capita in Germany surpassed that of the other large Western European countries, automobile density—expressing the strength of aspirations for the key consumer item in an affluent society—still lagged behind Britain and France.[10]

There can be no doubt that low consumption aspirations impede

---

[8] EMNID Institute, *EMNID-Informations*, no. 5, 1963.

[9] Cf. Institut fuer Demoskopie, *Pressedienst*, February, 1963.

[10] On December 31, 1968, the density of passenger cars per 1,000 inhabitants was 189 in West Germany, 194 in the United Kingdom, and 210 in France, (Bundesministerium fuer Wirtschaft, *Leistung in Zahlen, 1968*, Bonn, 1969, p. 32).

labor force participation. Germans probably are more critical of married women taking a job than most other Western nations, and the actual labor force participation of married women, although hardly below the West European average, falls far short of meeting the immense demand for labor exerted by the booming economy. Large numbers of South Europeans fill the gap and derive sizable incomes from rendering productive services the demand for which cannot be satisfied domestically. The proportion of foreign labor had reached 6 percent of the domestic labor force in 1966, representing one of the largest voluntary migrations of recent history.

Prosperity and high rates of growth have prevailed in Germany in spite of consumer conservatism. It would be speculative and premature to argue that the highly cautious reaction of German consumers to progress and change will one day pose a threat to economic prosperity. We have just seen how German industry compensated for the lack of participation of its constituents and reduced its dependence on domestic labor by filling its needs from abroad. Its independence from a rapid growth in domestic consumption has followed a similar pattern. The slow increase in domestic demand for consumer goods occurred at a time when German businessmen were opening up large export markets and when business investment was high. Consumer restraint and high rates of saving are welcome from a business point of view as long as there are absorptive and elastic export markets. The heavy long-term foreign trade surplus of Germany may be viewed in this light.

In the long run, however, the consequences of consumers' reluctant adaptation to change cannot fail to have an impact on economic processes, or indeed on consumers themselves, as is evident if we look once more briefly at the picture of education:

■ In 1962 the average male in the German labor force had received 8.2 years of formal education, compared to 10.7 years in the United States. The average increase in duration of formal education over 1950 was only about 4 percent, as against 6 percent in England, 8 percent in France and 10 percent in the United States; the lag behind the other countries was greater at the end than at the beginning of the period.

The conspicuous neglect of education and the heavy emphasis on saving, both evident in an international comparison, are paving the way for a situation that may serve to constrain tomorrow's investment and production decisions. The formation of human capital, as required in a knowledge society, is being neglected. There is little prospect that this lack, too, may be compensated for by looking to foreign markets. Differences in organizational culture and language problems set limits to the importation of highly trained personnel.

Although lack of adaptation to affluence is by no means confined to manual workers, it has been most pronounced in this group. If middle-class living were the major goal for the blue-collar segment, income should determine consumption styles. The scarcity of middle-class symbols in the higher-income blue-collar group and the emphasis on home entertainment and minor home appliances provide sufficient evidence of class constraints on aspirations. These are largely due to the educational background of the manual worker and his children. In addition, the inadequate and highly elitist system of secondary and higher education makes it very hard to cross class frontiers.

Why was a large proportion of the German people unimpressed by the "economic miracle" occurring around them? An explanation may be sought in the particular economic constellation of the postwar years. Germany's postwar economy was founded more on reconstruction than on innovation. Following the destruction of plants, equipment, and trade relations during the war, the priority was on revitalizing old organizational structures and well-known production processes. Protestant virtues like diligence, persistence, thrift, and sense of duty were particularly well suited to the period of reconstruction. The very success of the postwar economy reinforced not only the old social and power structure but static value systems as well. All groups of the population profited from the boom, although, to be sure, to a varying extent. The large number of successful entrepreneurs and *nouveau rich* capitalists of the first postwar decade demonstrate that there were royal rewards for bold investments, geographic and occupational mobility, and risk taking. Yet there were also modest but still perceptible rewards for a nonadaptive discharge of one's duty. The German example provides ample evidence that affluence and a secure environment are not sufficient conditions for adaptation. Where prosperity occurs in spite of conservatism, conventional values may be confirmed and strengthened rather than weakened.

To what past experiences may one trace the differences in outlook, trust, and participation, which find their correlate in economic behavior in different societies? Does recent history explain German character types? This is a possibility—but probably not a full explanation. Certainly, the upheavals following both world wars were particularly violent in Germany. The inflation of the early twenties and the depression of the early thirties marked traumatic experiences, the first primarily for the upper class, the second particularly for the lower class, with the middle classes heavily hit both times. The aftermath of World War II brought devastation, occupation, inflation, and—for a sizable proportion of refugees—expulsion from their home provinces. These experiences, however, were followed by a particularly rapid and steady upward trend in employment, income, and affluence in the fifties and sixties which should have left their mark. It is probable that the reserve of Germans toward modern ways of perception and interaction is of a more remote, rather than recent, origin. German national unification was achieved only in the second half of the nineteenth century. The long persistence of feudal authority exercised by oppressive and parochial princes may well have been instrumental in creating insecurity, defensiveness, and inward orientation.

This pattern manifests itself repeatedly in the political sphere. Konrad Adenauer used to win his election campaigns with the slogan "No experiments," a slogan carefully selected after studies by experts of German attitudes during the fifties and early sixties. The recent 1969 election campaign revealed only a slightly changed emphasis in priorities: The slogan of the conservatives "Safely into the 70s" was matched by the socialists' "Safe jobs, stable economy." This defensive posture contrasts with the British conservatives' proclamation, "We never had it so good," appealing to a population which, as we shall see, places much emphasis on consumption and progress.

BRITAIN: PARTICIPATION WITHOUT PROSPERITY

The British consumer exhibits a realistic perception of change. Notwithstanding the widely deplored stagnation of the economy, difficulties in the modernization of industry, critical balance of payments problems resulting in restrictive government policies, and even some unemployment, consumer optimism is more pronounced than in the more prosperous continental nations. Britons participate intensively in the areas of consumer goods and labor markets, and they adapt fairly well to changing career patterns and skill requirements. In short, they approach American behavior patterns somewhat more closely than any other Western European country. To recapitulate our basic findings:

■ In early 1968, only a few months after the shock of the devaluation, the frequency of optimistic assessments of their past and expected financial situation was closer to the confident mood prevailing in the United States than to continental skepticism.

■ Labor force participation of married women is, by Western European standards, relatively high in Britain, and more widely approved. There is also much willingness to work overtime.

■ The years of formal education of the labor force are 9.7, the highest in Western Europe and again resemble the American more closely than the continental European pattern. Participation of the lower classes in higher education, although they are still underrepresented in proportion to their size, is much more frequent than anywhere else in Western Europe. Among British college students, around 25 percent are from blue-collar backgrounds as opposed to only 5 percent in Germany.

■ Britons consume much higher proportions of their income than the other prosperous Western European countries. The rate of saving out of disposable income oscillated between 1960 and 1967 around 5 to 8 percent, roughly in line with American rates but much lower than in Germany and the Benelux countries, and slightly lower than in France.

■ A sizable proportion of British consumers are inclined to purchase goods on the installment plan; in this too Britain, together with Scandinavia, stands in contrast to the rest of continental Europe.

Despite all these favorable factors, the British economy is not capable of accommodating the participative impetus of the population. While the people desire higher income and consumption standards, the economy fails both to mobilize available labor resources and to respond to consumption aspirations. Its mediocre performance is due partly to balance of payments problems and management practices. Partly, however, it is due to the immobility of the labor force. The workers, supported by their leaders, resist leaving unproductive, overstaffed jobs for other, more productive and more profitable ones. Much of the basically favorable response to progress of the British common man is negated by his lack of mobility, geographic and occupational, which probably results from both the traumatic experience of mass unemployment in the thirties and the prevailing organization of the housing market. According to the

British anthropologist Geoffrey Gorer, for the generation now in a position of power in the labor movement, unemployment is considered so destructive that the employed members of the working classes and their leaders tend to engage in all sorts of legal and semilegal devices to "spread the work," to protect their "mates" as much as themselves.[11] Memories of the depression are most vivid in the obsolescent labor-intensive industries such as railroads, shipbuilding, docking, mining, textiles and the like, industries which must contract. Yet closing an unprofitable industry represents unemployment to the workers, even if there be opportunities elsewhere. Many of the strikes which have plagued Britain are concerned with the working man's resistance to attempts by management to abolish featherbedding and other forms of overstaffing.

Another major reason for working class resistance to residential and job mobility can be found in the scarcity of low-cost housing. A large and growing proportion of the British working classes are housed in subsidized apartments known as "council houses." If a family moves to a new district it is placed at the bottom of the waiting list for a "council house." Gorer concludes that British housing policy and housing laws make a move from one area to another hazardous and expensive, particularly if it is a move from an area of contracting industry to an area of expansion. Geographic mobility is impeded not only by the risk of losing low-priced housing but also by regional differences—differences in dialect and vocabulary, in preferred foods, in patterns of leisure. For many members of the British working class, according to Gorer, moving to a new region within the country entails much the same dislocation as moving to a foreign country does for the more mobile middle class.

In addition, British business and management apparently fail to mobilize available labor resources. Evidence for this, beside regional unemployment, is "disguised unemployment" in the form of people continuing to work in unrewarding small trades and crafts for lack of attractive opportunities elsewhere, an unsatisfied quest for overtime, and a considerable "brain-drain" to foreign countries siphoning off some returns of the relatively extended and efficient

[11] Geoffrey Gorer "What's the Matter with Britain?" *The New York Times Magazine,* December 31, 1967: "It seems clinically accurate to describe the 1931 depression as traumatic for the British working class, using the word in exactly the same way as it is used in classical psychoanalysis: an experience so overwhelming in its horror that all later behavior, both conscious and unconscious, is devoted to averting its repetition."

system of higher education. A vicious circle is at work here. Featherbedding and immobility of labor contribute to keeping the price level of British goods too high to compete effectively in foreign markets or even to combat the penetration of home markets by imported goods. The resulting adverse balance of payments forces the government to restrict domestic purchasing power and to curb installment purchases for the purpose of preventing consumer demand from competing unduly with the export trade or from bringing about large imports. These measures had to be erratic in timing and created an aura of arbitrariness and insecurity even for business investment. Thus industry, despite tax incentives and a relatively low tax rate on corporate profits, has not invested enough in plant and equipment. Furthermore, industrial management has failed to be sufficiently productivity conscious. Its understanding of how to apply research and scientific discovery to increase productivity has been notably inadequate.[12]

Thus, the growing wants of British consumers are out of line with the priorities of economic policy. When consumption aspirations are not matched by employment opportunities, they tend to depress the rate of saving and even, in the British case of balance-of-payment deficits and inflationary pressures, turn out to be a threat to stability and growth. Business and managerial inertia in conjunction with bad labor relations tend to transform the virtues of a fairly dynamic, aspiring, and participative consumer sector into a handicap.

A short summary of the differences in the reaction to economic change of the German and British people may be instructive. The British are most worried about large-scale unemployment, though they tend to consider the present situation as satisfactory. They accept the unglamorous but moderately prosperous performance of the economy. Germans, in spite of more rapidly rising mass incomes, are less cheerful. They are irritated by even modest rates of inflation which they consider as threatening. They see their own prospects in a dimmer light than the British and consequently adapt less to it in terms of upgrading their education, skills, and job choices. Yet their labor relations are not deadlocked as the British are. The German overemployment setting makes a change of job almost a routine affair. The compulsory mobility of the war and postwar years of large proportions of refugees and expellees made

[12] Caves et al.[9]

geographic mobility very common; it markedly reduced parochialism. Most important, German labor and their representatives are more ready and willing than their British counterparts to cooperate with business and government in the interest of gains in productivity. Whereas the older British worker put the blame for the hardships of the thirties on the ruling classes, most German employees and their leaders find no easy scapegoats for the economic catastrophies of the past. On the whole, German labor relations are characterized by avoidance of conflict, if not paternalism and subordination. The British labor scene, in contrast, was shaped by laissez-faire indifference of the bourgeois capitalist toward the welfare of his employees.[13] A strong and militant labor movement was the response to the lack of social commitment of the upper classes. Although British welfare policies have changed drastically over the last few decades, alienation and distrust between management and labor remain great enough to seriously prejudice a mode of interaction which would make it possible to increase the pie substantially rather than just stirring up conflict on how the existing pie should be divided.

HOLLAND: ". . . BETTER HAPPY THAN RICH"

The recovery of the Dutch economy after World War II was no less spectacular than the recovery of the German economy. In the twenty years between 1948 and 1968 the Dutch real GNP per capita increased by 90 percent, a growth rate which must be assessed in the light of a great increase in population. The Dutch managed to give their rapidly growing population a share in the national prosperity.

The damages of the war and the breakdown of her colonial empire disrupted Holland's international trade, which has always been and still is of vital importance to her. The loss of the Dutch East Indies required that Holland's industry establish new trade relationships. In this respect the Netherlands was eminently successful. In 1967 exports represented 46 percent of GNP in Holland as against 23 percent in Germany, 21 percent in England, and 6 per-

---

[13] (Still in the 1930s) ". . . the concepts that starvation must be avoided, but as closely as possible, and that recipients of relief should be made to feel humiliation and dissatisfaction at not working, governed the distribution of the inadequate dole," Gorer, *op. cit.*, p. 16.

cent in the United States. Rotterdam is now the largest harbor in Europe, and three Dutch concerns (Shell, Unilever, Philips) are among the world's largest industrial enterprises.

During the last two decades labor discipline has been high, unemployment has virtually disappeared, welfare legislation has brought greater social security, and the length of the average working day has been reduced.[14] From 1945 until 1959 the government had the main responsibility for setting wages. All collective wage agreements had to be approved by the government, the policy of which was to introduce successive waves of general wage increases whenever the economic situation of the country justified them. In the course of the 1960s greater responsibility was granted to business and trade unions, and the principle of a "differentiated wage policy" in accordance with developments in the various sectors of business gradually replaced the general wage policy of the central government.

In terms of their sense of personal financial well-being and optimistic outlook the Dutch rank considerably below the Americans, although higher than the Germans (see Chapter 4). In our surveys, in 1968, a larger proportion of the Dutch than of the Germans expressed the feeling that they were better off than they had been either one year or four years earlier. Among these respondents, however, less than one-third expected further improvement, again more than in Germany, but many fewer than in the United States. This tendency not to expect to be better off in the future appears to have been still more frequent four years earlier, according to a survey conducted by the Netherland Institute of Public Opinion. An important event in the recent economic history of the country was the much discussed "wage operation of 1964" when every worker in the country was given a 10 percent wage increase. Soon after this measure went into effect, NIPO asked people all over the country if they thought that their situation would improve further. Only 11 percent expected further improvement; 37 percent expected no change, 44 percent expected a deterioration, and 8 percent did not know. When asked in an earlier survey about the reasons for the 10 percent general pay increase, the most frequent answer was that higher wages were the consequence of rising prices. Only 3 percent said that wages were raised because the workers wanted and deserved a larger share in the growing prosperity.[15]

[14] Goudsblom.[24]

[15] NIPO press bulletin no. 984, February 17, 1964; no. 977, January 10, 1964.

Several times during the 1960s NIPO asked questions in nationwide surveys about "prosperity" *(welvaart)* in the country as well as in the respondents' personal situation. The proportion of respondents indicating that they felt the country was prosperous reached its highest level, about 84 percent, in 1961–1962; in 1966 and 1968 it was only around 60 percent; in 1969, 71 or 72 percent. On the other hand the proportion of people feeling that they personally were well off has been steadily rising and reached a level of 73 percent in 1969.[16]

Additional findings indicate that the Dutch people's assessment of their economic well-being depends considerably on their satisfaction with marriage and family life, health and work, which are spoken of as the "package of happiness." In a NIPO survey, therefore, people were also asked whether they "felt happy." Not fewer than 76 percent said that they did. Among the reasons for happiness, satisfaction with marriage and family life as well as with health was cited very frequently, satisfaction with material possessions considerably less frequently, and satisfaction with income rather infrequently.

An observer of cultural differences between Europe and America recently wrote: "Better happy than rich is a typical European motto."[17] Nowhere is this more applicable than in Holland. The President of the Board of Directors of the Dutch National Bank is quoted as having said that the Dutch people, if they were aware of the widening gap between the American economy and the Dutch economy, were not concerned. What is important to them is that the Dutch situation has been constantly improving.[18]

An unpublished survey carried out among the managerial staff of a large business corporation in the Netherlands confirms these notions of the contentment of the Dutch people. Three-quarters or more of the managers of one large company reported satisfaction with their salary, their ability to do a good job, and their home life. In contrast, only 5 percent said that "ambition and desire to get ahead" was a major factor in their lives.

Nevertheless, during the last ten years there has been much argument in the press and among politicians as to whether Holland was

[16] Some of these findings have been published in Elseviers Weekblad, Christmas edition, 1969.

[17] Haenni.[26]

[18] Kuin.[42]

really prosperous. Whenever the balance of trade or the balance of payments happened to be precarious, the Dutch were told, sometimes in nationwide appeals to desist, that they were consuming too much and living beyond their means. Such statements appealed to those who preserved and cultivated the traditional Dutch sense of orderliness, thrift, and diligence. The Dutch are reluctant to accept buying on credit and slow in buying new products that are seen as luxuries. On the whole, the Dutch are inconspicuous consumers. They are the laggards in fashion in Western Europe and notorious buyers of low-quality goods, even among foreign products (canned food, textiles, and second-hand and even damaged cars).

Critical attitudes toward innovations extend to the area of female employment. The share of married women in the labor force is lower in the Netherlands than in any other country of the Common Market or Britain. Women are still expected to be concerned with traditional patterns of housekeeping and domestic life which, of course, are becoming increasingly difficult to maintain. Employed married women devote very much time to homemaking, which means that they work very long hours. It has also been said that the slow decline in the birth rate testifies to a lack of adaptation to modern life.

The Dutch word for prosperity *(welvaart)* has a materialistic connotation. Popular essays describing affluence as a cause for unease have been well received by the large number of sophisticated people who place great value on cultural activities. An official report by the Committee on Social Affairs of the Ecumenic Council of Churches in the Netherlands makes the statement that prosperity represents a danger to the human mind. In view of the great influence exercised by the churches in the Netherlands, it is very well possible that such criticism of prosperity has had an impact on consumer attitudes. Surveys have indicated the percentage of Calvinist families owning TV sets to be lower than the percentage of Catholic families.

More relevant are the low educational aspirations of the workers, particularly in the less-developed provinces of the country. Under the headline "Parents Satisfied with Lag in Education" the leading Dutch newspaper published the results of a survey carried out by the University of Groningen in the province of Overijssel.[19] Ac-

---

[19] *Nieuwe Rotterdamse Courant,* Rotterdam, December 19, 1969.

cording to that survey, parents as well as school teachers showed little interest in or appreciation of an improvement in school performance.

To be sure, the wind of change is blowing in Holland as elsewhere. In 1969, in response to widespread disruption at the universities, a nationwide discussion started on education, school reform, and vocational training. In business and industry there is much talk of the management gap between Europe and America. Participation has come to be an issue throughout the country — in labor-management relations, universities, and also in the Catholic Church. The desire for participation has thus far, however, been manifest primarily among organized groups and still very little among individuals in their behavior either as workers or as consumers.

CHAPTER *13*

Consequences of
Dynamic Adaptation

W E may summarize again: Dynamic forms of adaptation consist of acceptance of change, social learning, striving for further change, and a continual stepping-up of levels of aspiration as each higher goal is achieved. They stimulate the economy by inducing consumers to replace their possessions at a fairly rapid rate and to be receptive to innovations in products and services. They raise the level of educational aspirations, thus resulting in a rapid growth of human capital. Such dynamism is clearly not an unmitigated blessing. Grave economic as well as social problems may both accompany and follow upon such dynamic adaptation. Among the economic problems are inflation, occasional recessions, and an adverse trend in the balance of trade, and among the social problems alienation of population groups not partaking of the affluence, as well as the possibility of increased stress and tension among the total populace. These may represent prices to be paid for dynamic growth.

The discussion of the problems related to economic and social dynamism will concern itself primarily with the United States, where this phenomenon first developed and is more pronounced than in any other country. Consideration will also be given to Germany, where a production-oriented economy flourishes, in contrast to the American consumer-oriented economy.

EXPORTS AND IMPORTS

Whether or not an economy is consumer-oriented exerts an influence on foreign trade. Thus imports of manufactured consumer goods into the United States have been growing and may be expected to grow further. American consumers want not only a great variety of goods but also diversity and distinctiveness in the goods they purchase. Large imports of small foreign cars as well as of sport cars represent the example that first comes to mind. Photographic equipment, novelties, and gifts made in foreign countries have also received increased acceptance by the American consumer because they represent something different and therefore attractive. Dynamic behavior implies not only absence of saturation but also continuous upgrading and proliferation of wants. The desires extend to a great variety of goods and services, and therefore enterprising foreign sellers—above all Germans and Japanese—find great opportunities in the American market.

Regarding the trend of exports of consumer products manufactured in the United States, the behavior of the automobile industry is of particular interest. In the 1950s and 1960s Detroit gave no thought to producing at home a car suitable for foreign markets. Even though in these decades the American car industry suffered repeatedly from relatively low utilization of its capacity and demand for cars increased rapidly all over the world, the possibility of large car exports from the United States was not even considered. General Motors, Ford, and Chrysler purchased foreign companies producing cars and built large factories for their foreign subsidiaries. They exported capital and know-how rather than goods. American car manufacturers even turned to importing the products of their foreign subsidiaries into the United States. The relatively high American wages and the high foreign tariffs are hardly sufficient to explain this behavior. American know-how and economies of scale have made it possible for several other American industries to export finished products, especially machinery, in spite of these handicaps. Yet the preference noted in the automobile industry to produce almost exclusively for the domestic market and to restrict its exports primarily to capital and management has been observed in nonconsumer fields as well. Producers of machinery and computers also built factories abroad and acquired foreign companies at a greatly increased rate in the 1960s.

Germany, after the devastation of World War II, constructed an efficient industrial plant. From 1950 to 1964 the German index of production rose from 100 to 249 for industrial goods and from 100 to 178 for consumer goods. The orientation toward foreign rather than domestic markets was attested to by the fact, for example, that for a number of years the Volkswagen Company let German customers wait several months for the delivery of cars they had ordered, while its foreign sales outlets were kept well supplied. As in the German Empire at the beginning of this century or in the Weimar Republic during the interwar years, the German entrepreneur today does not shy away from the difficult task of opening up new foreign markets. The introduction of German products abroad, say in a South American country, is expected to bring forth a steady growth of orders.

Major differences in the export-import situation of several highly developed countries are also shown by traditional economic analysis. Houthakker and Magee made a careful statistical study of the foreign trade of twenty-six countries during the period 1951 to 1966.[1] The findings resulting from their analysis of American trends are relevant in our context. First, in line with our statement above that a large proportion of Americans with rising incomes are attracted to buying foreign products, they find that "the U.S. has an exceptionally high income elasticity of demand for imported finished manufactures" (p. 122). Second, in line with the little interest shown by American industry in exporting those consumer goods which improving foreign economies are interested in purchasing, American "exports do not participate as much in the growth of the world community as do other countries' exports" (p. 118) and "the income elasticity of other countries' demand for U.S. exports is abnormally low" (121f). Houthakker and Magee conclude from the two findings that "the U.S. is gradually becoming a net importer

---

[1] Houthakker and Magee,[31] pp. 111–125.

of finished manufactures" (p. 122). They found the foreign trade of Great Britain to resemble that of the United States in many respects and the relation between foreign trade and income elasticity to be at the opposite extreme in Japan.[2]

Needless to say, several important transactions beyond exports and imports enter into the balance of payments. The large American gold losses in the 1960s were due primarily to an outflow of funds.[3] Because of her large export surplus, Germany resorted to a revaluation of the mark both in 1961 and in 1969. Following the 1961 measure, the higher prices of German exports and the lower prices of foreign imports had an impact on foreign trade for a short period only. At the same time, other greatly desired steps could also be taken, such as an increase in wages and salaries without large price increases, resulting in a somewhat higher share of wages and salaries in national income. However, the revaluation of 1961 proved to be only a temporary panacea. Price increases in Germany were smaller in the following years than in most of the countries with which it traded, and the German export surplus again grew substantially. The orientation of industry toward exports rather than toward domestic markets continued. The foreign currency reserves increased greatly, and the more they increased the less valuable they became. A second upward revision of the mark was opposed by many Germans who took pride in large exports and feared any disturbance of the status quo. Nevertheless, growing concern by experts with the disadvantages of large exports in a full-employment economy as well as substantial international pressures led to a revaluation of the mark again in 1969.

What the consequences of this latest move will be will depend largely on whether the present export orientation of German in-

[2] Houthakker and Magee found the German data unusable for their purposes. It should be noted that their analysis did not include the developments in the late 1960s when the American export surplus declined greatly, while that of Germany and Japan reached new peaks.

[3] Both the United States and Germany year after year have had sizable negative items in their payments balance. An outflow of funds from the United States results from expenditures by defense installations abroad, from foreign aid, from Americans traveling abroad, and from remittances by immigrants. Germany makes payments to foreign countries in the form of restitution payments, travel, remittances by foreign workers, and foreign aid. Finally, a third set of transactions, in addition to foreign trade and the continuous negative items just listed, is of crucial importance for the balance of payments of both countries. These are capital investments abroad and foreign capital investments in the home country, as well as transfers of liquid funds from one currency to another.

dustry will persist, or whether the German consumers' aspirations toward higher income and higher-consumption standards will grow and thus provide new outlets for industry. At the end of this chapter we shall return to the question of probable future trends of German consumer attitudes. First, let us turn to problems of dynamism that have arisen in the United States.

WORRIES AND MISGIVINGS OF AMERICANS

Concern with the balance of trade or the balance of payments, and even with losses of gold, is felt primarily by government and business leaders, rather than by the American people in general. Our interest is in determining what worries and misgivings are most pronounced among the people and to understand how they might be related to dynamic attitudes.

Hadley Cantril has studied the "patterns of human concern" through surveys conducted in several countries in which questions were asked about wishes and hopes as well as fears and worries about the future. Concern with one's own health and the health of members of one's family was found to be the major worry of Americans, exceeding economic worries and fears which were mentioned by only a small proportion of respondents.[4]

In 1968 the Survey Research Center included a few questions in its economic surveys in the United States on people's concerns and worries. In replying to an introductory question, "What would you say are the most important things that may influence business conditions during the next twelve months," respondents referred by far most frequently — as many as 60 percent of respondents — to the war in Vietnam. Notions of a favorable influence of the war on domestic business conditions were less common than concern with its possible adverse impact, although there was little evidence of any clear ideas of how that impact might manifest itself. References were made to higher taxes and inflation, as well as to domestic tasks to which, because of the war, insufficient funds were being devoted. The urban crisis, riots, and violence as well as race problems were also mentioned by a sizable proportion of respondents as problems that might possibly interrupt the satisfactory trend in the economy.

When asked about their own economic well-being, the great

[4] Cantril.[8]

majority of Americans expressed satisfaction. This was true with respect to their pay or income, their standard of living, their occupational progress, and their retirement prospects. These opinions supplement the data presented in Chapter 4 on the optimistic outlook of the American people.

It appears, then, that the major concerns of Americans are not with their own well-being or their personal financial prospects. It is rather with the environment in which they live. Their worries relate primarily to matters over which they as individuals have little, if any, control.

What is known about the worries of Western Europeans indicates that, in addition to their health, they are greatly concerned about their own economic future and about inflation. Even though social security legislation is old and extensive, the German people are greatly concerned with economic security, as was especially clear during the slight recession of 1967. Worries about a loss in the value of money, especially as it might affect the well-being of the aged, were also widespread in Europe, while fears about the quality of the environment were rarely expressed.

Inflation, which accelerated greatly in the United States in 1968–1969, is of course a matter of concern to the American people. But in the opinion of the majority it is brought about by forces beyond their influence, which forces they understand dimly at best. They are of the opinion that there is little, if anything, that they can do to influence it in any way. There seems to be little awareness that their own most usual reaction to rising prices, namely, refraining from or postponing some discretionary expenditures, does in fact serve to slow down inflation. As was noted in Chapter 4, inflation is viewed as a bad thing; because of inflation it becomes harder to make ends meet or, in case of an income increase greater than the price increases, to enjoy well-deserved rewards. Therefore most Americans agree that they are hurt by inflation. But when asked, in October, 1969, whether they were personally hurt by inflation "very much, a little, or not at all," only 15 percent said that they were hurt very much, 13 percent that they were hurt much, 55 percent that they were hurt little, and 13 percent that they were hurt not at all.[5]

---

[5] In addition, 4 percent said "Don't know." There were some differences in the answers among income groups, with somewhat more low-income people saying that they were hurt very much and more upper-income people that they were hurt a little or not at all. The opinion that one was hurt a little or not at all was associated with feeling better off and expecting to be better off (see Katona et al.,[37] 1970).

Only a very small proportion of the population expressed any willingness to make personal sacrifices in order to slow down inflation. The proportion approving increased income taxes for that purpose was 9 percent; the proportion agreeing that income increases during the next year should be limited to the extent of price increases was, as reported in Chapter 4, 24 percent among those who expected income increases of at least 5 percent.

Further survey findings indicate that most people are not willing to accept a substantial increase in unemployment as the price to be paid for arresting inflation. They believe that there are greater evils than inflation, such as the urban crisis, which might be aggravated by increased unemployment of inner city inhabitants and blacks.[6]

Recessions, even though they had been short and mild, have frequently interrupted the upward trend in the American economy during the post-World War decades. They are often seen by economists as reactions to earlier excessive spending by all sectors of the economy, including the consumers. One of the authors pointed to the possibility of "dangerous dynamism" in a book published in 1960.[7] However, he argued, and the same argument is valid ten years later as well, that the dangers arising from cumulative wants and easy credit are mitigated by the fact that levels of aspiration usually rise slowly rather than in substantial spurts. Psychological studies have indicated that most people want a little more than they have, rather than very much more very quickly. Moreover, only a rather small proportion of American consumers engaged in excessive borrowing either in the 1950s or the 1960s. For this the good record of repayment of consumer debt and the limited number of consumer bankruptcies, income garnishments, and repossession of goods bought on credit provide ample evidence. Even though many Americans buy on the installment plan according to the income they expect to have, rather than on the basis of their current

---

[6] The increase in interest rates in 1968–1969, of which most Americans were aware, was generally viewed as dampening economic prospects. Only 12 percent of the population thought that interest rates should be raised in order to slow down inflation. The notion that interest rates are business costs and therefore high interest rates induce business to raise prices was much more widespread. The great majority of people thought that high interest rates made it difficult if not impossible to buy houses for owner occupancy. At the same time, felt needs for purchasing houses were growing because many people born during the first few years after the end of World War II had formed families by 1969.

[7] Katona,[34] pp. 189ff.

income, the burden of consumer debt was felt to be onerous by a small minority only. This should continue to be the case at least as long as people's optimistic expectations about income gains are not disappointed.

On the other hand, absence of good news, or bad news about inflation, higher taxes, higher interest rates, and the like did occasionally stifle consumers' willingness to buy. Recessions occurred in 1957–1958, 1960–1961, 1966–1967 and again in 1970, at least in the areas dependent on consumers' discretionary demand, such as automobiles, appliances, and housing. The recessions did not last long, partly because of features in consumer behavior that tend to stabilize economic trends. Consumers get habituated to good news during prolonged periods of prosperity so that the stimulating influence of good news diminishes in time, and the development of a boom psychology is arrested. Similarly, in periods of reduced economic activity, the confident and optimistic evaluation of long-range trends tends to persist, and the high level of consumer wants and desires contributes to the return of an upward trend in the economy. Is there justification to assume that these past experiences will be repeated in the future as well? The possibility must be mentioned that if very many people continuously raise their aspirations, disappointment might become more common.

One example of a source of frustration may be found in the fact that the pyramid of corporate structure limits career opportunities. A corporation has only one president, but several vice presidents who aspire to the top; it has fewer vice presidents than department heads; similarly, down the list. Many people must fail to reach their goals, and the disparity between available opportunities and the desire for advancement and higher income may create stress and tension. The greater the dynamism and the felt need for more and more expensive goods and services, the greater the chance of disappointment.

People's wants and desires compete with one another and cause conflicts about which to satisfy first. In spite of large advances over the last two decades, the American people do not feel rich. For many, making ends meet has become more difficult because what they feel they must have has grown more rapidly than their resources. The plethora of incentives and strivings is in itself a source of difficulties and of tension.

There exists a further reason for strain inherent in a dynamic society. The desire for stable and predictable conditions still persists. This is true not only among the minority who oppose and resist change. It is not the rule for people in general to be consistent or consciously to resolve conflicts in their own attitudes and desires. They want stability and assurance about the future at the same time as their wants and aspirations escalate so that standing still is no longer acceptable to them. They do not realize that in an era of continuous rapid social change stability and predictability are hardly possible.

Even the many people who give unqualified optimistic answers about their job or the standard of living they expect in five or ten years indicate, if questioned in detail, that they are aware that the future is uncertain and that they not only dislike uncertainty but find it threatening. Dynamism has its rewards, for the individual as for the economy, but it may also augment uncertainty about the probability of fulfillment of great expectations. What has been learned about the impact of aspirations in the recent past hardly provides assurance that future progress will be smooth and undisturbed.

An additional threat to American society must be mentioned: There are indications that the rich are getting richer. Concentration of great wealth among relatively few people constitutes a danger to democracy. Huge gains obtained by a few without much effort may also weaken the economic incentives of the many whose expectations of receiving well-deserved rewards for hard work constitute the major hope of dynamic America.

It was noted in Chapter 2 that during the depression years of the thirties and the following war years some progress had been made toward a more equal distribution of income, but that no further progress had taken place since the end of the war—even when income was calculated without including capital gains, either realized or unrealized. In the late 1950s and the early and middle 1960s the prices of real estate, common stock, and mutual funds advanced rapidly, due not only to inflation but also to the substantial growth of American resources and productivity. Some capital gains were made by a fairly large proportion of American families because close to one-third of all families had some investment in either stocks or real estate.[8] But the investments of the great majority of

[8] Ownership of owner-occupied, one-family houses is excluded from consideration even though it represents a common asset the value of which has grown greatly. Home ownership by about two-thirds of all families does reduce the concentration of wealth somewhat but does not make the owners rich. It should also be noted that because of the great increase in real estate prices it has become increasingly difficult for young people to satisfy their desire to purchase houses for owner occupancy.

these families and especially of those who became stockholders in the 1960s are quite small. Even assuming that the small investor achieved the same rate of capital appreciation as the large investor, the magnitude of wealth accumulated by the two groups differed greatly. Appreciation by, say, 300 percent in ten years on an investment of a few thousand dollars does not make a person rich. A 300 percent profit on an investment of $100,000 or more is something quite different.

Awareness that some people had made substantial capital gains on stocks and real estate spread in the 1960s and an increasing proportion of the American population, being attracted by the lure of easy profits, then expressed an interest in speculation, particularly on the stock market.[9]

The tendency of the rich to become richer is not restricted to capital appreciation. Numerous new industries have provided opulence to those who participated in them at an early stage of development. It may suffice to name IBM and Xerox, the two most conspicuous examples of corporations which have grown in a fairly short time from small beginnings to mammoth size. Compensation for technological or management functions in growth industries, and also compensation for many top managers in business in general, advanced far beyond any increases in wages and salaries in the 1960s.[10]

POVERTY AND THE DECAY
OF THE ENVIRONMENT

In concluding our discussion of the consequences of the American ways of adapting to changed circumstances, we must take a look at

[9] According to Survey Research Center studies conducted in 1969, 20 to 25 percent of the approximately 15 million stockholding families indicated that they were primarily or largely interested in speculation. The sharp decline in stock prices in the spring of 1970 disappointed the hopes of millions of stockholders and greatly reduced the value of the rich people's assets.

[10] Some additional evidence is available of a recent trend toward an increased concentration of income from the annual *Surveys of Consumer Finances*. When income before taxes, without capital gains, is ordered by size, it appears that in 1968 family units with more than $16,200 income fell in the top decile and family units with more than $13,000 in the top quintile. In 1960 these limits were much lower, $11,000 and $8,600, respectively. The gain is approximately 50 percent. In comparison, families in the middle and lower-middle income deciles gained much less, namely, only 25 to 30 percent.

two major and immediate problems of contemporary American society—poverty and the decay of the environment. Dire poverty still persists among a minority of people who are handicapped by their age, the absence of a male earner, a lack of skills, or discrimination because of race. Poverty is intertwined with broken families, illness, lack of education, and the evil conditions which produce it tend also to perpetuate it. The growing affluence of the majority makes the poverty of the minority all the more intolerable.

True, affluence permits the channeling of ever-growing tax funds from the well-to-do to the poor (especially in the absence of war), and the proposed guaranteed minimal income for everyone might provide a cushion that would eliminate dire want and misery. But poverty consists not only of economic deprivation but also of the exclusion of the poor from the mainstream of society. Alienation may be the consequence of a great disparity in the standard of living of the poor and the majority of people. Continuous and rapid improvement in the well-being of the majority augments the difference between the poor and the well-to-do and is something the poor themselves are aware of. Because of it, feelings of deprivation and dissatisfaction may grow, and satisfaction with gradual improvement may diminish. The impatience characteristic of all Americans extends to the poor who want an end to poverty now, not in the years or decades to come. And the rich themselves are affected by having poor neighbors. The division of the country threatens the whole society and the economy as well.

Slums in the immediate neighborhood of the residences of well-to-do people constitute one clearly visible aspect of the decay in the environment. Modern technology has contributed to this decay by polluting the air and the water and by inducing trade and industry to move to outlying areas and away from the districts between downtown and suburbs which continually deteriorate. There is a wide gap between city and suburb, but the quality of life threatens to deteriorate even in the suburbs. Several years ago J. K. Galbraith in *The Affluent Society* contrasted the poverty of the public sector with the opulence of the private sector. He pointed out that the resources invested in schools, hospitals, public transportation, and recreational facilities have lagged behind the needs and behind the abundance of the possessions of individuals—their cars, appliances, and gadgets. Although the amounts of money invested in education, in medical care, as well as in welfare payments have grown greatly in postwar America—and no doubt would have increased still more in the absence of huge war expenditures—there is ample reason for dissatisfaction with the growth rate of the public sector. At a time when individuals continue to achieve further improvements in their well-being, the need for larger government expenditures for public purposes cannot be denied.

The imposition of restrictions on private spending would, however, hardly serve the purpose of enlarging public spending. It would seem unwise to reduce incentives for hard work and for progress in education, and those incentives arise from the confident expectation that one's own and one's children's standard of living will continue to advance. Nor can it be taken for granted that there is any conflict between private aspirations and the improvement of the environment. The concerns and desires of individuals need not be confined to what is usually considered the private sphere. Improved private well-being—well-furnished homes, cars and appliances, eating out and expensive leisure-time pursuits, to mention only a few former luxuries now available to very many people—are not the only areas to which personal wants may be directed. Psychological studies indicate that the realm of the ego often extends to include one's group. The wants and aspirations of individuals may then concern not only the family but also the environment, the community, or the country. Such a transition of interests from the private to the public sector is most easily seen with respect to wishes for better parking facilities and good highways provided by the community or the state. Better schools and better hospitals may also become goals for more and more individuals. The affluent may have broader perspectives than the poor, whose concerns are commonly restricted to immediate personal needs. Among well-to-do people concern with their environment is growing. Medical care, prevention of air and water pollution, as well as of crime and violence, have already become private concerns of some people, and this process may increase greatly in the near future.

This optimistic view is, however, not the only one that may emerge from the analysis of the sociopsychological characteristics prevalent among the American people. It may be argued that a reorganization of national priorities will not take place because Americans favor individual action. The optimism, independence, and self-reliance which make so many Americans feel that their progress has resulted largely from their own efforts may also result in their feeling no need for governmental protection for themselves and little interest in welfare legislation for others.

In a survey conducted by the Survey Research Center late in 1969, when a representative sample of Americans was asked whether the government should spend more, the same amount, or less on welfare payments, their opinions were found to be greatly divided—about one-third calling for each of the three courses of action. These opinions contrast with the general support given to increased government expenditures for education, and also for highway construction and slum clearance, with which programs people identify themselves to a larger extent. American attitudes toward welfare payments also appear to differ from European attitudes. In Europe the concept of a welfare state is widely accepted, and there is no widespread public sentiment against welfare legislation on ideological grounds. There exist budgetary restraints, but it is generally accepted that the poor, the unemployed, and the aged have a claim against the state. These opinions may be related to Western Europeans being not only somewhat less affluent than Americans but also less self-reliant and less secure. In America, the tradition of individualism favors voluntary help in the form of philanthropy rather than government action. There is limited acceptance of increased taxes for the support of others who cannot, or, as some respondents said, will not support themselves.

The question is whether affluence, in addition to generating funds for combating poverty and environmental decay, will increase or decrease people's willingness to do so. Americans have successfully tackled many of their economic problems. They have not yet faced with equal vigor their environmental and social problems.

We noted above that there need be no conflict between the pursuit of private and public goals. Just so must it be said, in response to the condemnation of the American consumer economy as materialistic, that affluence need not interfere with interest in nonmaterial pursuits. There is no support for the romantic notion that spiritual and cultural values are fostered by poverty and misery, and are impeded by affluence. The antidemocratic thesis that high culture must always originate with the upper classes and loses its strength when it trickles down to many people is not tenable. When the immediate problems of living are solved for very many people, who also have much free time at their disposal, tastes and values may change and cultural interests come to the fore. This process again is not inevitable; people may spend their free time seeking nothing more than fun. But there has been progress in postwar America toward greater interest in art and culture. Excessive materialism is not a necessary consequence of increased well-being or of striving for further well-being.

The interruption of the upward trend of the American economy in 1970 aggravated the prevailing social problems. A recession set in, as was noted in Chapter 6, because of growing consumer apprehension. Inflation and layoffs, as well as the expansion of the war in Indochina and domestic unrest changed the short-term economic outlook even of the many people whose incomes continued to grow. Expectations about an improvement in material well-being over the long run were affected to a much smaller extent. Yet the American people have become increasingly aware of the necessity to overcome the gap between the young and the old, the poor and the rich, and the whites and the blacks. Possibly, psychological predispositions to strive toward a solution of the social problems have been strengthened by the recession of 1970. At the time this book goes to press, there is no evidence either to support or to contradict this hopeful view.

THE OUTLOOK

Among the various highly developed countries studied, what is the prospect for the persistence of the differences revealed between the more dynamic and the more traditional societies? It is possible that studies in future years would reveal much smaller differences between the United States and Germany. Continuing prosperity may induce more Germans to put more trust in themselves, to believe in their own ability to control their fate, and to have a confident and optimistic outlook. Overcoming the differences in educational achievement and educational aspirations may take longer than arousing greater consumption aspirations, but even in that respect some fluidity in the national character may produce change.

All this, however, is no more than speculation. For the moment it must be said that available data point toward the conclusion that the differences will persist for quite a while. A comparison of the attitudes and expectations of younger and older people in the various countries is relevant. The first finding is that in all countries studied younger people, say, those under thirty-five, exhibit more dynamic attitudes than older people, those fifty or fifty-five and older. The younger people are more optimistic about their future income and well-being; they have a larger number of special wishes; more of them would prefer to increase the amount of time they spend working; more of them approve of working mothers. The question is whether the extent of the divergence in the attitudes of the younger and the older people differs in the various countries, and especially whether there is a greater divergence in Germany than in the United States. The findings are unequivocal: The differences are greatest in the United States.[11] If the comparative analysis of American and German expectations and aspirations had been restricted to the younger people of the two countries, rather than being based on data from the entire population, similar or even somewhat greater differences in attitudes and aspirations would have emerged between the United States and Germany. Younger Germans appear to be less dynamic than younger Englishmen and much less dynamic than younger Americans. Therefore, for the time being, there is justification for predicting a continuation of different trends in the consumer economies and in occupational and social mobility in the United States and Germany.

Our findings confirm what Servan-Schreiber so well expressed when he wrote: "We [Europeans] continue to suffer progress rather than to pursue it."[12] Americans pursue it, welcome it, and adapt to it. Their manner of adaptation brings about not only more and more progress but also many problems and tensions at the same time. The sociopsychological approach to the study of the economies of affluent societies, where the attitudes, expectations, and aspirations of the consumers play so great a role, has proved rewarding: It has provided an understanding of different trends in the various countries, unexplained by technological or financial differences. There is every reason to believe that such an approach will be a useful supplement to the more traditional forms of economic analysis in the future as well.

[11] See the data presented in the Appendixes.
[12] Servan-Schreiber[71], p. 185.

Appendix A (to Chapter 4)

Four surveys were carried out in 1968 with carefully drawn representative samples in the United States, Germany, Holland, and England. Findings from these surveys are reported in Chapters 4, 5, and 10. The questionnaires, prepared by the authors of this book, were identical in most respects (except for translation into German and Dutch). Some changes, however, were made as dictated by different conditions prevailing in different countries; they are discussed in the text as well as in the appendixes. Sampling and interviewing were carried out by the Survey Research Center in the United States, by the DIVO Institute in Germany, by the NIPO Institute in Holland, and by Research Services Limited in Great Britain.

In the United States 1,322 families were interviewed in August, in Germany 1,908 families in April, in Holland 1,410 families in February, and in Great Britain 1,749 families in April, 1968. The head of each selected family was interviewed whenever possible. The analysis of the data was directed by the authors. Comparable findings were also used from a survey conducted in the United States in 1967 with 3,171 families.

Although a great effort was made to employ identical sampling and interviewing methods in all countries, it was not possible to eliminate all differences. The training of and the practices usually employed by interviewers of the European survey organizations differ somewhat from those in the United States. The Survey Research Center specializes in the use of the fixed question-free answer interviewing method, in which many open questions are used and the answers received to them are recorded verbatim whenever possible. In Europe, questions in which fixed alternatives are presented are much more common; the interviewer's job then consists of making check marks. Some results of such differences have been noted in connection with the analysis of reasons given for income gains (see Table 4-1 and the subsequent discussion). Furthermore, the frequency of "Don't know" and "No change" responses depend to some extent on the techniques of interviewing; therefore the very large differences in these respects, shown in Table A-2 for Germany and Holland, may be partly spurious. The comparability of the major findings as presented in the five charts in Chapter 4 is, however, hardly affected by these differences.

The detailed data on attitudes and expectations in the four countries are presented in Tables A-1 to A-4. They are supplemented by Table A-5 in order to illustrate the relation of being and expecting to be better off to income and age. The younger a person is and the higher his income, the more frequent is improvement as well as expectation of improvement in his personal situation both in the United States and in Western Europe.

TABLE A-1   *Evaluation of Changes in the Personal Financial Situation*
(Percentage distribution of families in four countries)

Country	Better off	Same	Worse off	Don't know	Total	Index*
Compared to four years ago						
United States	53	23	21	3	100	132
Germany	36	39	24	1	100	112
Holland	49	25	19	7	100	130
England	45	20	31	4	100	114
Compared to one year ago						
United States	36	40	22	2	100	114
Germany	16	64	19	1	100	97
Holland	26	49	21	4	100	105
England	30	34	35	1	100	95

*An index has been constructed as follows: "Better off" minus "Worse off" plus 100. This is equivalent to giving a weight of 2 to "Better off" responses, a weight of 1 to "Same" and "Don't know" responses, and a weight of 0 to "Worse off" responses. In the Index presented in various charts of Chapter 4, 100 was not added to the difference in frequency of "Better off" and "Worse off" responses.

The questions were: "We are interested in how people are getting along financially these days. Would you say that you and your family are better off or worse off financially than you were a year ago? Now thinking back four years, would you say that you people are better off or worse off financially than you were then?"

SOURCE: All tables in this chapter from surveys initiated by the authors in 1968.

TABLE A-2 *Expected Changes in the Personal Financial Situation*
(Percentage distribution of families in four countries)

Country	Better off	Same	Worse off	Don't know	Total	Index*
Four years from now						
United States	43	28	8	21	100	135
Germany	24	40	18	18	100	106
Holland	22	21	14	43	100	108
England	35	26	18	21	100	117
One year from now						
United States	36	42	10	12	100	126
Germany	12	66	14	8	100	98
Holland	19	44	14	23	100	105
England	23	43	23	11	100	100

*See footnote to Table A-1.
The questions were: "Now looking ahead—do you think that a year from now you people will be better off financially, or worse off or just about the same as now? And four years from now, do you expect that you and your family will be better off, worse off, or just about the same as now?"

When the expectations of young respondents (family head under thirty-five) are compared with those of older respondents (family head over fifty in Germany and Holland and over fifty-five in the United States and England), naturally, larger differences emerge than when middle-aged families are compared with all families as is done in Table A-5. To illustrate: In the United States 79 percent of younger people, but only 13 percent of older people, expected to be better off in four years. The respective data for Germany are 46 and 11, for England 66 and 12, and for Holland 43 and 10. The discrepancy in the expectations of younger and older respondents is clearly largest in the United States.

TABLE A-3 *Opinions about the Future Course of Business*
(Percentage distribution of families in four countries)

| Country | In the next five years there will be . . . | | | | | |
	Good times	Uncertain, good and bad	Bad times	Don't know	Total	Index*
United States	35	29	27	9	100	108
Germany	19	60	19	2	100	100
Holland	15	45	23	17	100	92
England	8	50	35	7	100	73

*See footnote to Table A-1.
The question was: "Which would you say is more likely, that in the country as a whole we'll have continuous good times during the next five years or so, or that we will have periods of widespread unemployment or depression, or what?"

The higher the education the more frequent are income increases, optimistic income expectations and, primarily, Cumulative Gains (as defined in Chapter 4). In the United States 18 percent of those with less than twelve grades of education, 39 percent of those with high school education, and 46 percent with higher education fall in the Cumulative Gains group. In Europe as well those with little education are infrequently represented among those with Cumulative Gains, but higher education is much less common than in the United States.

In order to indicate the presence or absence of spurious correlations, multivariate analysis is presented in several instances in this book. It takes the form of multiple classification analysis (MCA).[1] In this chapter such an analysis is needed only in one case, the association between past and expected progress, discussed on page 49. Is this association due to the fact that past and expected progress are both particularly frequent among upper-income people and younger age groups? Table A-6 shows that income and age explain much, but by no means all, of the relation between past and expected progress. There are very large differences in the unadjusted frequencies of optimists among those who did and those who did not experience progress. Among the frequencies adjusted for income and age there are still substantial differences, albeit smaller ones.

American data relating to earlier years but similar to those presented in this chapter have been published in several past publications. Monographs issued each year by the Survey Research Center of The University of Michigan under the titles *1968 Survey of Consumer Finances, 1967 Survey of Consumer Finances,* etc., contain survey findings on being and expecting to be better or worse off as well as on price expectations in the United States. *The Mass Consumption Society* by George Katona, contains an extensive discussion of attitudes toward and reactions to inflation (Chapter 14), of changes in the peak lifetime income and their relation to optimistic expectations (Chapter 12), and also of earlier answers to the question about reasons for income increases (pp. 112 and 134).

The methods of probability sampling used in the United States have been described in the monographs *Survey of Consumer Finances.* Similar methods were used in Germany, England, and Holland. The basic unit of sampling was the dwelling unit and in

[1] Andrews, Morgan, and Sonquist.[2]

TABLE A-4 *Past and Expected Changes in Financial Situation*

(Percentage distribution of families in four countries)

Country	Cumulative Gain	Intermittent Gain	Reversal	Stagnation	Deterioration	Continuous Deterioration	Don't know	Total	Index*
Four years ago and four years from now									
United States	31	15	9	10	8	3	24	100	135
Germany	12	19	10	19	14	6	20	100	111
Holland	16	11	7	8	7	5	46	100	115
England	24	13	12	9	10	10	22	100	117
One year ago and one year from now									
United States	20	21	8	23	11	4	13	100	126
Germany	4	15	3	48	15	7	8	100	97
Holland	10	15	4	27	12	6	26	100	107
England	13	18	7	18	18	15	11	100	98

Cumulative Gain $++$

Intermittent Gain $+=$ and $=+$

Reversal $+-$ and $-+$

Stagnation $==$

Deterioration $=-$ and $--$

Continuous Deterioration $--$

$+$ Indicates "better," $=$ "same," and $-$ "worse" responses.

The first sign relates to past and the second sign to expected changes.

*Construction of the Index: Frequency of Cumulative Gains and Intermittent Gains minus Deterioration and Continuous Deterioration, plus 100.

Note: Data obtained in Belgium in 1966 on changes compared to a year earlier and expected changes during the next year were quite similar to the data in Holland.

TABLE A-5 *Past and Expected Changes in the Personal Financial Situation Among Upper-Income Families, and Middle-Aged Families in Four Countries*

Country	All families		Upper-income families*		Middle-aged families†	
	% Better off	Index	% Better off	Index	% Better off	Index
Better off than four years ago						
United States	53	132	71	160	62	142
Germany	36	112	44	124	40	117
Holland	49	131	61	149	58	142
England	45	114	64	143	54	128
Expect to be better off in four years						
United States	43	135	55	147	48	141
Germany	24	106	29	112	27	112
Holland	22	108	32	117	26	113
England	35	117	53	138	45	131
Better off than four years ago *and* expect to be better off in four years						
United States	31	135	44	156	34	147
Germany	12	111	17	119	15	116
Holland	16	115	25	129	19	124
England	24	117	40	143	30	134

Country	*Annual income	% of all families	†Age	% of all families
United States	over $10,000	28	35–54	39
Germany	over 15,000 DM	29	35–49	34
Holland	over 12,000 hfl.	30	35–49	31
England	over £1,200	32	35–54	37

each dwelling unit the head of each family unit was interviewed.[2] Survey data are subject to processing errors, nonresponse errors (of 15 to 20 percent in the surveys discussed here), and reporting errors, the effects of which cannot be measured but which good survey methodology attempts to minimize. The data are also subject to sampling errors, the size of which depends on the size of the sample and also on the size of the proportion being estimated. Sup-

[2] A family unit consists of all related persons living in a dwelling unit and may consist of a single person only. For the sake of simplicity the term "family" is used in this book in place of the term "family unit."

plementing the detailed information on sampling errors published in the *Survey of Consumer Finances* it may suffice to report here that in Survey Research Center surveys the sampling error of data from a sample of approximately 1,500 cases is 3.1 percentage points if the proportion is approximately 50 percent, and 1.8 percentage points if it is approximately 10 or 90 percent. Sampling error means here two standard errors; it indicates the range, on either side of the survey finding, chosen to obtain a 95 percent level of confidence. When data from two surveys, each having approximately 1,500 cases, are compared, the difference must be 4.4 percentage points or larger to yield a 95 percent level of confidence. If a lesser degree of confidence is deemed satisfactory, a range of one standard error may be used; it yields a 68 percent level of confidence.

Information on subgroups of the population has a larger sampling error than information on the entire population because it is based on a smaller number of cases. The most important subgroups taken into consideration in this book are age and income groups. The number of cases in these groups is presented in Table A-7. When data of two groups, each having approximately 400 cases, are compared, the difference must be approximately 7 percentage points in order to be significant at the 95 percent level of confidence.

TABLE A-6 *Multivariate Analysis of Expectations to Be Better Off in Four Years, United States, in percent*

Expectations	Unadjusted frequencies	Adjusted frequencies*
Among those who say they are better off than four years ago	58	50
Among those who say they are in the same situation as four years ago	19	32
Among those who say they are worse off than four years ago	32	39
Average (all families)	43	43

*Multivariate analysis yielding adjustment for income and age.

Beta coefficient indicating the strength of the adjusted association of past trend with expected trend is .15; of income with expected trend, .11; and of age with expected trend, .44.

(For similar data based on surveys conducted in 1967, see Katona,[38] no. 2, p. 26.)

TABLE A-7   *Number of Families in Age and Income Subgroups**

Country	Age of head	Number of families	Annual income	Number of families
United States	Under 25	101	Under $3,000	260
	25–34	253	3,000–4,999	211
	35–44	246	5,000–7,499	293
	45–54	266	7,500–9,999	199
	55–64	214	10,000 or more	308
	65 or older	240		
Total sample = 1,322				
Germany	15–34	394	Under 7,200 DM	223
	35–49	647	7,200–9,599	346
	50–64	639	9,600–11,999	421
	65 or older	228	12,000–14,999	371
			15,000 or more	547
Total sample = 1,908				
Holland	15–34	325	Under 6,000 hfl	159
	35–49	443	6,000–7,999	212
	50–64	334	8,000–9,999	276
	65 or older	164	10,000–11,999	186
			12,000 or more	418
Total sample = 1,410				
England	16–34	370	Up to £ 749	475
	35–44	319	750–1,199	416
	45–54	323	1,200–1,849	373
	55–64	345	1,850 or more	189
	65 or older	390		
Total sample = 1,749				

*Information on surveys conducted by the authors in 1968. Subgroups do not always add to total sample because some respondents' age or income was not ascertained.

Appendix B (to Chapter 5)

Studies of the relation of perceived and expected financial progress to various aspects of discretionary behavior were initiated in the United States a few years ago. The findings of studies made before 1968 were reported in three publications[1] in which perceptions of past income changes and expectations for the future were related to the following transactions: recent purchases of durable goods on the installment plan; intentions to buy new cars; intentions to buy two or more durable goods; short automobile turnover rates (less than three years between the last purchase and the expected next purchase of a car by the same family). The frequency of these forms of behavior was much higher among families with perceived Cumulative Gains—better off than one year earlier and expectation of being better off one year later, as well as higher income than four years earlier and expectation of higher income four years later—than among families with other trends. The outstanding position of those with Cumulative Gains was less pronounced but still significant when income and age were held constant.

Similar studies were continued by the authors in the United States in 1968 when, for the first time, such studies were also carried out in Germany, Holland, and England. Some major differences between the American and European studies were mentioned in Chapter 5 and may be summarized here: In order to concentrate on innovative discretionary behavior, purchases of and purchase plans for new cars and color TV sets were studied in the United

---

[1] Katona et al.,[37] 1967; chap. 8; Katona and Mueller,[39] chap. 9; Katona.[38]

States; the European studies extended to all cars and all TV sets. Purchases of and purchase plans for several durable goods during the same year, incurrence of installment debt, and automobile turnover rates were studied in the United States, but not in Europe.

There were also some differences in the time span for which past purchases as well as buying intentions were analyzed. The European surveys were conducted somewhat earlier in the year 1968 than the new American survey. Since the questions about past purchases related to the years 1967 and 1968, in Europe purchases over fourteen to sixteen months and in the United States over nineteen months were taken into account. Questions about buying intentions in the United States related to the following twelve months. In Europe respondents were asked first whether the family expected to buy a car or a television set during the next four years; then, in case of an affirmative answer, they were asked in which year they expected to make the purchase. Respondents who said they would buy in 1968 or 1969, that is, during the next twenty or twenty-two months, were considered as planning to make major discretionary purchases.[2]

In order to provide an indication of the proportion of families who felt they were well provided for, questions were asked in all four countries about unsatisfied wishes. These questions relate to desires and wants, which may be much less definite than expressed buying intentions. In all four countries, respondents were asked: "Now, I have a question about your wishes: Are there any particular things you (and your family) would like to buy or spend money on, or do you have most of the things you want?" The proportion of families responding affirmatively to the first part of this question is presented in the tables under the subheading "unsatisfied wishes expressed without suggestion." Additional probes were then made to find out what kinds of things respondents wanted. Of particular interest both to the people and to the economy are wishes for better housing. Respondents who had not previously indicated a desire for better housing were therefore asked: "You did not mention wanting a better house or apartment; in this respect are you fairly well satisfied or not?" The second line under "unsatisfied wishes" presents the proportion of families expressing a housing wish (either to the probe or earlier). The final line indi-

[2] An additional difference consisted in the inclusion among purchase plans of somewhat indefinite intentions ("We might buy") in Germany and Holland, but not in the United States and England.

cates the proportion of families expressing no unsatisfied wishes and therefore satisfaction with the things they had, even after the probing questions.

The findings obtained in the four countries are shown in Tables B-1 to B-4. Because of the differences in the questions used as well as in interviewing methods, the rate of purchases or purchase plans in the United States is not comparable to that in Western Europe. As we said in Chapter 5, however, the purpose of the tabulations was not to compare rates of purchases but rather the proportions of families in the different trend groups who either had made or intended to make major purchases.

In each of the three European countries the frequency of intentions to buy a car is almost twice as high among those who perceived Cumulative Gains than among other families. People classified under the headings Stagnation and Deterioration participated infrequently in discretionary transactions; those with Intermittent

TABLE B-1 *Past and Expected Change in the Personal Financial Situation Related to Discretionary Behavior*

(Proportion of American families in percent; unadjusted frequencies as of August, 1968)

Behavior	Cumulative Gains	Intermittent Gains	Stagnation	Deterioration	All families
	Four years ago and four years hence				
Purchases in 1967–1968:					
New car	21	17	9	9	16
Color television set	11	16	6	8	10
Two or more appliances	16	11	4	9	12
Intentions to buy:					
New car	13	13	5	10	11
Color television set	13	8	4	3	8
One appliance	25	23	14	13	21
Two or more appliances	13	8	2	1	8
Unsatisfied wishes:					
Expressed without suggestion	59	60	35	46	56
Regarding housing (including probe)	28	28	10	16	24
None	38	38	64	54	42
Proportion of sample in each group	31	15	10	11	100
	One year ago and one year hence				
Intentions to buy:					
New car	16	11	8	9	11
Color television set	15	10	7	4	8
Incurred installment debt*	52	41	29	48	37
Short automobile turnover rate*†	45	35	29	19	33

*Based on surveys conducted in 1967.

†The date when the last car was purchased and the date when the next car was expected to be purchased were determined for all car-owning families. The percentage indicated represents those car-owning families with a turnover rate of less than three years.

TABLE B-2   *Past and Expected Change in the Personal Financial Situation Related to Discretionary Behavior*

(Proportion of German families in percent; unadjusted frequencies as of April, 1968)

Behavior	Cumulative Gains	Intermittent Gains	Stagnation	Deterioration	All families
		Four years ago and four years hence			
Purchases:					
Car	16	11	4	6	9
TV set	14	11	12	12	12
Intentions to Buy:					
Car	20	16	9	8	13
TV set	12	12	8	7	9
Unsatisfied Wishes:					
Expressed without					
suggestion	55	40	34	38	40
Regarding housing					
(including probe)	40	33	28	35	33
None	26	41	44	37	37
Proportion of sample					
in each group	12	19	19	20	100
		One year ago and one year hence			
Purchases:					
Car	22	10	7	9	9
TV set	16	14	11	12	12
Intentions to Buy:					
Car	23	21	10	12	13
TV set	11	11	10	7	9
Unsatisfied Wishes:					
Expressed without					
suggestion	58	47	36	42	40
Regarding housing					
(including probe)	43	35	31	33	33
None	27	32	41	34	37
Proportion of sample					
in each group	4	15	47	22	100

Gains occupy a middle position. These findings are consistent in all three European countries, the differences in the relationships being insignificant among them.

Unsatisfied wishes show somewhat larger differences among the various groups in Germany and Holland than in the United States. This finding is also true of desires for better housing. It is interesting to note that despite the greater housing shortage in Europe, the absolute level of the frequency of housing wishes is only slightly higher in Europe than in the United States.

The kinds of wishes expressed in the European countries differed somewhat from those in the United States. Durable goods were mentioned much more frequently among American than European respondents. The desire for more travel or vacation was the second most frequent wish expressed in the European countries, whereas in the United States it ranked relatively low.

Although our main concern was with perceived trends that extend both to the past and the future, it may be mentioned that on both sides of the Atlantic past financial improvement was much less related to discretionary behavior than expected improvement. The difference in this respect was particularly pronounced in intentions to buy a car, which were found to be much more frequent among families with optimistic expectations than among other families. This finding again points to a psychological rather than an environmental explanation of the differences in the American and European data.

The differences in the frequency of intentions and wishes be-

TABLE B-3   *Past and Expected Change in the Personal Financial Situation Related to Discretionary Behavior*

(Proportion of Dutch families in percent; unadjusted frequencies as of February, 1968)

Behavior	Cumulative Gains	Intermittent Gains	Stagnation	Deterioration	All families
Four years ago and four years hence					
Purchases:					
Car	23	18	8	15	16
TV set	15	15	12	12	14
Intentions to Buy:					
Car	32	21	10	10	18
TV set	9	7	7	8	8
Unsatisfied Wishes:					
Expressed without suggestion	75	62	40	45	58
Regarding housing (including probe)	41	29	18	20	29
None	13	24	29	16	22
Proportion of sample in each group	16	11	8	11	100
One year ago and one year hence					
Purchases:					
Car	20	21	15	15	16
TV set	17	14	12	14	14
Intentions to Buy:					
Car	32	28	15	12	18
TV set	10	7	7	10	8
Unsatisfied Wishes:					
Expressed without suggestion	75	57	50	59	58
Regarding housing (including probe)	45	27	22	27	29
None	12	20	38	30	22
Proportion of sample in each group	10	24	33	10	100

TABLE B-4   *Past and Expected Change in the Personal Financial Situation Related to Discretionary Behavior*

(Proportion of British families in percent; unadjusted frequencies as of April, 1968)

Behavior	Cumulative Gains	Intermittent Gains	Stagnation	Deterioration	All families
	Four years ago and four years hence				
Purchases:					
Car	35	18	9	14	21
TV set*	–	–	–	–	–
Intentions to Buy:					
Car	32	16	7	10	18
TV set	14	12	3	4	8
Unsatisfied Wishes:					
Expressed without					
suggestion	59	47	35	54	53
Regarding housing					
(including probe)	33	26	14	21	25
None	33	46	60	42	41
Proportion of sample					
in each group	24	13	9	20	100
	One year ago and one year hence				
Purchases:					
Car	39	24	11	18	21
TV set*	–	–	–	–	–
Intentions to Buy:					
Car	36	21	11	13	18
TV set	18	11	6	4	8
Unsatisfied Wishes:					
Expressed without					
suggestion	64	49	40	57	53
Regarding housing					
(including probe)	37	27	17	25	25
None	27	43	55	38	41
Proportion of sample					
in each group	13	18	18	33	100

*Not asked.

tween younger and older people are quite similar in the various countries. For example, in the United States 73 percent of respondents under thirty-five expressed unsatisfied wishes as against 36 percent of those fifty-five years old or older. In Germany the respective proportions were 58 and 29 percent.

As in the case of the relation between past and expected trends in one's financial situation (Chapter 4), just so in the relation between trends in attitudes and discretionary behavior patterns, the obviously important factors of income and age had to be partialed out. Both progress in the financial situation and a relatively high frequency of discretionary transactions are most common among families at the upper-income levels and in the younger age groups. Again the Multiple Classification Analysis (MCA), mentioned in Appendix A, was used to transform the "unadjusted frequencies" presented in Tables B-1 to B-4 into data adjusted for income and age, i.e., "adjusted frequencies."

Major results of the multivariate analysis carried out with American and German data are shown in Tables B-5 and B-6. The beta coefficients in Table B-5 serve to indicate the relative importance of the various factors. Clearly, income and age have a great influence on the frequency of discretionary transactions. However, the effect of financial trends remains substantial. With respect to intentions to buy a car in Germany, the trend factor is as important as age, while income level—indicating ability to buy—exerts the strongest influence. With respect to expressed wishes, the influence of financial trend is second only to the age effect, older people having fewer unfulfilled desires than younger people.

Table B-6 indicates the extent of the relationship between discretionary behavior and felt financial progress in the United States and Germany both before and after adjusting for income and age. The differences in the adjusted frequencies between the trend groups are smaller than those between the unadjusted frequencies. For example, the unadjusted frequency of past purchases of a car in Germany is 16 percent for those with Cumulative Gains over eight

TABLE B-5 *Relation of Discretionary Behavior to Financial Trends, Income and Age*

(Beta coefficients* from multivariate studies)

	United States			
Predictor	Intend to buy new car	Intend to buy color TV	Intend to buy two or more durable goods	Auto turnover rate†
Income level	.28	.16	.21	.18
Age	.10	.06	.11	.20
Financial trend:				
4 years ago, 4 years hence ..	.04	.05	n.a.‡	n.a.
1 year ago, 1 year hence ...	.04	.09	.12	.10

	Germany		
Predictor	Purchased car	Intend to buy car	Unsatisfied wishes
Income level	.09	.20	.07
Age	.10	.10	.21
Financial trend:			
4 years ago, 4 years hence ..	.09	.08	.14
1 year ago, 1 year hence ...	.10	.10	.12

*The beta coefficients are analogous to standardized regression coefficients.
†1967 data; see Katona et al.,[37] 1967, chap. 8.
‡n.a. = not available.

TABLE B-6   *Adjusted* and Unadjusted Frequencies of Discretionary Behavior Among Families with Different Financial Trends*

(Proportion of families in percent)

Financial trend United States	Intend to buy new car 1968–1969		Intend to buy color TV 1968–1969		Intend to buy two or more durable goods 1967–1968†		Auto turnover rate†	
	Unadj	Adj	Unadj	Adj	Unadj	Adj	Unadj	Adj
4 years ago, 4 years hence:								
Continuous Gain	13	10	13	10	n.a.‡	n.a.	n.a.	n.a.
Stagnation	5	10	4	7	n.a.	n.a.	n.a.	n.a.
Deterioration§	10	13	3	6	n.a.	n.a.	n.a.	n.a.
1 year ago, 1 year hence:								
Continuous Gain	16	13	15	12	26	21	45	39
Stagnation	8	10	7	9	8	11	29	34
Deterioration§	9	11	4	5	15	14	19	25
All families	11		8		14		33	

Germany	Purchased car 1967–1968		Intend to buy car 1968–1969		Unsatisfied wishes	
	Unadj	Adj	Unadj	Adj	Unadj	Adj
4 years ago, 4 years hence:						
Continuous Gain	16	13	20	16	55	48
Stagnation	4	5	9	11	34	38
Deterioration§	6	8	8	10	38	41
1 year ago, 1 year hence:						
Continuous Gain	22	19	23	18	58	51
Stagnation	7	8	10	11	36	38
Deterioration§	9	10	12	13	42	44
All families	9		13		40	

*Adjusted for income and age.
†1967 data.
‡n.a. = not available.
§Includes both the Deterioration and the Continuous Deterioration subgroups.

years; the frequency is reduced to 13 percent when the data are adjusted for age and income. Nevertheless, that frequency is still substantially higher than the overall frequency of 9 percent among all families. It appears that part of the large difference in transactions between those with Cumulative Gains and those with other trends is accounted for by income and age. These factors do not, however, suffice to cancel out the differences in discretionary behavior among the various trend groups. This is true for all forms of behavior studied with the exception of the relation of four-year financial trends to intentions to buy new cars in the United States. We conclude therefore that personal financial trends, past perceptions, and especially expectations do make a difference in the frequency of discretionary purchases, which in turn represent an important indicator of the extent of consumer participation in the modern market.

Appendix C (to Part 3)

This appendix presents data supplementary to the discussion in Part 3 of people's choices regarding acquisition of income.

In Tables C-1 and C-2 it may be seen that both the number of hours worked and the expressed desire to spend still more hours at working to earn more money almost invariably, in every country, bore a strong inverse relation to both the age and the income of the respondents. (The single exception was in England where a smaller percentage in the lowest income group than in the next higher ones said they would like to work more.) The correlation between youth and the desire to increase income by longer working hours is corroborated by the fact that among all American household heads holding second jobs 49 percent were under age thirty-five in 1968.

Results from a survey conducted in the United States in early 1969, reported in Table C-3, summarize the relation of wives' labor force participation to income, age, and education. The proportion of wives working for money was found to vary inversely to both the income of the husband and the age of the wife and directly to the education of the wife.

Questions concerning job changes and geographic movements, asked in the Surveys of Consumer Finances, provide several indicators of mobility in the United States. The data in Table C-4 suggest that the young worker is almost twice as likely as the average worker to change jobs or move to a different county, the latter being the indicator used to denote mobility between labor markets. Within age groups, mobility and earned income are inversely related. This is particularly pronounced among those respondents under age thirty-five with less than $5,000 earned income who changed

TABLE C-1   *Preferences for More or Less Work*
(Percentage distribution of respondents)

Respondents	To work more	To work less	No change	Don't know	Total
*United States**					
Age:					
Under 35	49	7	44		100
35–44	33	10	57		100
45–54	27	12	61		100
55–64	23	14	63		100
65 and older	16	16	68		100
Annual Income ($):†					
All respondents under 50	39	8	53		100
Under 3,000	54	10	36		100
3,000–4,999	49	7	44		100
5,000–7,499	41	8	51		100
7,500–9,999	41	8	51		100
10,000 or more	27	9	64		100
All respondents	34	10	56		100
Germany					
Age:					
15–34	52	5	41	2	100
35–49	43	5	48	4	100
50–64	34	9	47	10	100
65 and older	28	7	36	29	100
Annual Income (DM):†					
All respondents under 50	46	5	45	4	100
Under 7,200	56	2	33	9	100
7,200–9,599	51	3	41	5	100
9,600–11,999	52	5	41	2	100
12,000–14,999	44	2	51	3	100
15,000 or more	39	8	49	4	100
All respondents	40	6	45	9	100
England‡					
Age:					
16–34	66	5	25	4	100
35–44	61	7	29	3	100
45–54	49	9	37	5	100
55–64	40	19	36	5	100
65 and older	40	14	24	22	100
Annual Income (£):¶					
All respondents under 55	59	7	30	4	100
Under 750	54	6	37	3	100
750–1,199	69	5	23	3	100
1,200–1,849	59	9	30	2	100
1,850 or more	46	9	39	6	100
All respondents	55	10	31	4	100

TABLE C-1 *Preferences for More or Less Work (Continued)*
(Percentage distribution of respondents)

Respondents	To work more	To work less	No change	Don't know	Total
Holland					
Age:					
15–34 ....‚.........	35	14	40	11	100
35–49	31	15	42	12	100
50–64	23	23	38	16	100
65 and older	19	16	31	34	100
Annual Income (hfl.):†					
All respondents under 50	32	15	41	12	100
6,000–8,000	42	13	34	11	100
8,000–10,000	35	17	37	11	100
10,000–12,000	30	14	42	14	100
12,000 or more	28	14	46	12	100
All respondents	28	17	39	16	100

* Asked only of those in the labor force. The "No change" group consists of respondents not expressing a definite preference in response to the two questions quoted below.
† Respondents under fifty years of age.
‡ Asked only of those fully employed.
¶ Respondents under fifty-five years of age.
SOURCE: Surveys conducted by the authors in: August, 1966, United States; March, 1968, West Germany; May, 1968, England; January, 1968, Holland.
    The questions were: In the United States: "Some people would like to work more hours a week if they could be paid for it; others would not. How is it with you? Some people would like to work fewer hours even if they earned less. How do you feel about this?" In Germany, England, and Holland: "Some people would like to work more than they do, if they could be paid for it. Others would like to work less, even if it meant less pay. Which of these two would you prefer to do?"

their jobs during 1968 more than three times as frequently as all members of the labor force. The higher the education, the greater the mobility.

Data available about job changes in Germany indicate that younger workers and blue-collar workers are more mobile than older and white-collar workers (Table C-5).

Table C-6 presents an estimate of the number of school years the average student in 1957–1958 would complete before leaving school. These calculations indicate the probable educational attainment of relatively recent entrants into the labor force.

Data on the years of schooling of American children according to the different occupations of their fathers are presented in Table C-7. Since these data were collected in 1959, it is questionable whether they are valid for children in school at the time of this writing.

TABLE C-2   *Working Time of Employed Men (Main Job Only)*

Country	Hours per week			
	Unskilled workers	Skilled workers	Low white-collar	High white-collar
United States	47	41	47	41
Germany	52	42	39	35
France	44	43	45	40
Belgium	47	46	41	36

SOURCE and time of surveys: See Table 9-3.

Hours of Working Time of Heads of Households: United States, 1964

	Hours per week
All heads of households	46
Employees with high hourly earnings ($3.00 or more)	42
Employees with low hourly earnings (less than $3.00)	47
Self-employed with high hourly earnings ($3.00 or more)	48
Self-employed with low hourly earnings (less than $3.00)	59

SOURCE: James N. Morgan et al.,[53] p. 19. The unemployed are excluded.

TABLE C-3 *Labor Force Participation of Wives: United States, 1968*

	Proportion of wives working in percent	Proportion in subgroup in percent
Earned income of head:*		
Under $5,000	67	18
$5,000–7,499	61	26
$7,500–9,999	52	25
$10,000–14,999	44	23
$15,000 or more	35	8
Age of wife:		
Under 25	64	13
25–34	54	25
35–44	50	20
45–54	54	19
55–64	40	13
65 and older	12	10
Education of wife:		
0–11 grades	41	36
12 grades	51	42
Some college or more	56	21
Age and education of wife:		
Under age 25:		
0–11 grades	43	3
12 grades	70	6
Some college or more	78	3
Age 25–34:		
0–11 grades	53	6
12 grades	51	11
Some college or more	59	7
Age 35–44:		
0–11 grades	53	7
12 grades	49	9
Some college or more	50	4
Age 45–54:		
0–11 grades	50	9
12 grades	55	9
Some college or more	60	3
All wives	48	100

*Heads in the labor force

The question was: "Did your wife do any work for money in 1968?"

SOURCE: Unpublished data from *1969 Survey of Consumer Finances.*

TABLE C-4 *Mobility According to Age, Income, Occupation and Education: United States, 1968*

(Percentage distribution of heads of families in labor force)

Respondents	Head changed job during the year	Changed house or apartment during the year	Moved to different county during the year*	Proportion of sample in subgroup
Age:				
Under 35	22	48	18	34
35–44	12	20	9	22
45–54	7	12	5	22
55–64	5	6	3	17
65 and older	6	7	3	4
Age and Earned Income of Head:				
Under age 35				
Under $5,000	46	63	23	8
$5,000–7,499	18	50	19	11
$7,500 or more	14	38	17	14
Age 35 and older				
Under $5,000	14	20	7	14
$5,000–7,499	12	9	3	12
$7,500 or more	5	12	6	30
Occupation of head:				
Professional, technical, kindred workers	12	32	18	16
Managers, officials (non-self-employed)	14	24	13	10
Self-employed	10	12	5	6
Clerical and sales workers	13	24	7	12
Craftsmen, foremen, and kindred workers	13	20	7	19
Operatives and kindred workers	14	31	9	18
Laborers and service workers	17	25	10	13
Education of Head:				
0–8 grades	9	17	5	20
9–11 grades	12	21	7	17
12 grades	13	26	10	32
Some college or more	16	32	15	31
All respondents	13	25	10	100

*Also included in second column of residential mobility.

The questions were: (1) "Have you changed the business you work in since this time last year?" (2) "When did you move into this house (apartment)?" (3) "How long have you lived in (county name)?"

SOURCE: Unpublished data from *1969 Survey of Consumer Finances.*

TABLE C-5 *Job Changes in Germany, 1965**

	Changed job in 1965, %
Age:	
16–20	15
21–24	25
25–34	20
35–44	5
45 and older	6
Occupation:	
Managers, professionals, higher-level civil servants	6
Clerical, lower-level civil servants	10
Skilled workers, foremen	18
Unskilled	12
All employees	12

*Self-employed excluded.
SOURCE: *DIVO Pressedienst*, October, 1966, p. 12.

TABLE C-6 *Average Years of Formal Education, 1957–1958*

	Number of years*
United States	12.90
Northwest Europe	10.26
Belgium	11.39
Denmark	8.84
France	10.74
Germany	9.13
Netherlands	10.43
Norway	9.99
United Kingdom	10.96
Italy	8.86

*Number of years spent in school during school career; calculations made for students in school in 1957–1958.
SOURCE: Denison,[14] p. 93.

TABLE C-7   *Average Completed Years of Education of Children by Occupation of Father: United States, 1959*

Occupations	Years of schooling	N
Professionals	14.42	59
Managers	13.99	39
Self-employed businessmen	12.86	62
Clerical and sales workers	12.93	100
Skilled workers	11.87	124
Semiskilled workers	11.34	164
Unskilled workers	10.45	219
Farmers	11.07	103
All occupations	11.82	939

SOURCE: James N. Morgan et al.[52]   The data are based on a sample of *households* whose heads have children who finished their schooling (not on a sample of children).

Bibliography

1. Almond, Gabriel A. and Sidney Verba. *The Civic Culture: Political Attitudes and Democracy in Five Nations.* Princeton, New Jersey: Princeton University Press, 1963.
2. Andrews, Frank, James Morgan, and John Sonquist. *Multiple Classification Analysis.* Ann Arbor, Michigan: Institute for Social Research, University of Michigan, 1967.
3. Barfield, Richard and James N. Morgan. *Early Retirement: The Decision and Experience.* Ann Arbor, Michigan: Institute for Social Research, University of Michigan, 1969.
4. Behrend, Hilde et al. *Incomes Policy and the Individual.* Edinburgh and London: Oliver & Boyd, 1967.
5. Berting, Jan. *In het brede maatschappelijke midden.* Meppel: Boom & Zoon, 1968.
6. Buiter, J. H. *Modern Salariaat in wording.* Rotterdam: Universitaire Pers, 1967.
7. Cagan, Phillip. *The Effect of Pension Plans on Aggregate Saving.* New York: National Bureau of Economic Research, 1965. Distributed by Columbia University Press.
8. Cantril, Hadley. *The Pattern of Human Concerns.* New Brunswick, New Jersey: Rutgers University Press, 1965.
9. Caves, Richard E. et al. *Britain's Economic Prospects.* Washington, D.C.: The Brookings Institution, 1968.
10. Chandler, J. H. "Perspectives on Poverty - An International Comparison," *Monthly Labor Review,* vol. 92, February, 1969.
11. Chombart de Lauwe, Paul Henry. *Pour une Sociologie des Aspirations.* Paris: Editions Denoël, 1969.
12. Claessens, Dieter et al. *Sozialkunde der Bundesrepublik Deutschland.* Düsseldorf, Cologne: Diederichs, 1965.
13. Dahrendorf, Ralf. *Arbeiterkinder an deutschen Universitäten.* Tübingen: J. C. B. Mohr (P. Siebeck), 1965.
14. Denison, Edward F. *Why Growth Rates Differ: Postwar Experience in Nine Western Countries.* Washington, D.C.: The Brookings Institution, 1967.

227

15. Devereux, Edward C., Urie Bronfenbrenner, and Robert R. Rodgers. "Child Rearing in England and the United States: A Cross-National Comparison," *Journal of Marriage and the Family*, May, 1969.
16. Dewhurst, J. Frederic and J. Coppock, and P. Yates and Associates. *Europe's Needs and Resources.* New York: Twentieth Century Fund, 1961.
17. Eckaus, R. S. "Economic Criteria for Education and Training," *Review of Economics and Statistics,* vol. 46, 1964.
18. Forschungsstelle fuer empirische Sozialoekonomik. *Daten zur Wirtshaftlichen Situation des Mittelstandes.* University of Cologne, 1962.
19. Fromm, Erich. *The Revolution of Hope.* New York: Harper & Row, 1968.
20. Galbraith, J. K. *The Affluent Society.* Boston: Houghton Mifflin, 1958.
21. _____. *The New Industrial State.* Boston: Houghton Mifflin, 1967.
22. Gesellschaft fuer Konsum-, Markt-, and Absatzforschung. *Der Verbraucher-Motor oder Bremse des Wirtschaftlichen Wachstums?* Nürnberg, Germany: June, 1967.
23. Goldthorpe, John H. and David Lockwood. "Not So Bourgeois After All," *New Society,* October/December, 1962.
24. Goudsblom, Johan. *Dutch Society.* New York: Random House, 1967.
25. Guelaud-Leridon, Francoise. *Le Travail des Femmes en France.* Paris: Presses Universitaires de France, 1964.
26. Haenni, Paul. "The Management Gap in a World Context," *Progress, The Unilever Quarterly,* no. 2, 1969.
27. Hamilton, Richard F., "The Behavior and Values of Skilled Workers," in Arthur B. Shostak and William Gomberg (eds.), *Blue Collar World.* Englewood Cliffs, New Jersey: Prentice-Hall, 1964.
28. "Affluence and the Worker: The West German Case." *American Journal of Sociology,* vol. 71, 1965.
29. Heald, Gordon. "How Consumer Confidence Affects Expenditure," unpublished paper, 1969.
30. Henke, Peter. "Leisure and the Long Workweek," *Monthly Labor Review,* vol. 89, 1966.
31. Houthakker, H. S. and Stephen P. Magee. "Income and Price Elasticities in World Trade," *Review of Economics and Statistics,* vol. 51, May, 1969.
32. Katona, George, *Psychological Analysis of Economic Behavior.* New York: McGraw-Hill Book Company, 1951.
33. _____ and Eva Mueller. "A Study of Purchase Decisions," in Lincoln H. Clark (ed.), *Consumer Behavior,* vol. 1, New York: New York University Press, 1954.
34. _____. *The Powerful Consumer.* New York: McGraw-Hill, 1960.
35. _____. *The Mass Consumption Society.* New York: McGraw-Hill, 1964.
36. _____. *Private Pensions and Individual Saving.* Ann Arbor, Michigan: Institute for Social Research, University of Michigan, 1965.
37. _____. et al. *Survey of Consumer Finances.* Ann Arbor, Michigan: Institute for Social Research, University of Michigan, 1966, 1967, 1968, 1969, and 1970.
38. Katona, George. "Consumer Behavior: Theory and Findings on Expectations and Aspirations," *American Economic Review* vol. 58, May, 1968.
39. _____ and Eva Mueller. *Consumer Response to Income Increases.* Washington, D.C.: The Brookings Institution, 1968.
40. _____. "Attitudes Toward Monetary and Fiscal Policy," *Public Policy,* Winter, 1970.

41. Kindleberger, Charles P. *Europe's Postwar Growth, The Role of Labor Supply.* Cambridge, Mass.: Harvard University Press, 1967.
42. Kuin, Peter. "Onderneming en Maatschappij," *De Accountant,* September, 1969.
43. Lansing, John B. and Eva Mueller. *The Geographic Mobility of Labor.* Ann Arbor, Michigan: Institute for Social Research, University of Michigan, 1967.
44. Lebergott, Stanley. "Labor Force and Employment," in E. B. Sheldon and W. E. Moore (eds.), *Indicators of Social Change.* New York: Russell Sage Foundation, 1968.
45. Lerner, Daniel with Lucille W. Pevsner. *The Passing of Traditional Society.* New York: Free Press, 1958.
46. Lipset, Seymour, Martin and Reinhard Bendix. *Social Mobility in Industrial Society.* Berkeley: University of California Press, 1959.
47. Lutz, Burkhard et al. *Berufsaussichten und Berufsausbildung in der Bundesrepublik.* Hamburg: Verlag Henri Nannen, GmbH, 1964.
48. Machlup, Fritz. *The Production and Distribution of Knowledge in the United States.* Princeton, New Jersey: Princeton University Press, 1962.
49. Maddison, Angus. *Economic Growth in the West: Comparative Experience in Europe and North America.* New York: Twentieth Century Fund, 1964.
50. Mead, Margaret. "The Pattern of Leisure in Contemporary American Culture," in Eric Larabee and Rolf Meyersohn (eds.), *Mass Leisure.* New York: Free Press, 1958.
51. Merton, Robert G. *Social Theory and Social Structure.* 9th printing, New York: Free Press, 1966.
52. Morgan, James N. et al. *Income and Welfare in the United States.* New York: McGraw-Hill, 1962.
53. ———. Ismail A. Sirageldin, and Nancy A. Baerwaldt. *Productive Americans.* Ann Arbor, Michigan: Institute for Social Research, University of Michigan, 1966.
54. Mott, Paul E. "Hours of Work and Moonlighting," in Clyde E. Dankert et al. (eds.), *Hours of Work.* New York: Harper & Row, 1965.
55. Mueller, Eva and Gerald Gurin. *The Demand for Outdoor Recreation.* Ann Arbor, Michigan: Institute for Social Research, University of Michigan, 1961.
56. ——— and Jane Lean. "The Savings Account as a Source for Financing Large Expenditures," *Journal of Finance,* vol. 22, no. 3, September, 1967.
57. ———with Jay Schmiedeskamp, Judith Hybels, John Sonquist, and Charles Staelin. *Technological Advance in An Expanding Economy: Its Impact on a Cross-Section of the Labor Force.* Ann Arbor, Michigan: Institute for Social Research, University of Michigan, 1969.
58. Noelle-Neumann, Elisabeth. "Geldwert und oeffentliche Meinung," in C. A. Andreae et al. (eds.), *Geldtheorie und Geldpolitik, Essays in Honor of Guenter Schmoelders.* Berlin: Duncker and Humblot, 1968.
59. Ord, Lewis C. *Industrial Frustration: Commonsense for Trade Unionists.* London: Mayflower Publishing Company, 1953.
60. OECD. *Capital Markets Study.* Paris, 1967.
61. Paul, H. "Talent Reserves of Blue Collar Children," Bielefeld: EMNID Institute, 1966.
62. Pfeil, Elisabeth. *Die Berufstätigkeit von Müttern.* Tübingen: J. C. B. Mohr (P. Siebeck), 1961.
63. Popitz, Heinrich, H. P. Bahrdt, E. A. Jüres, and H. Kesting. *Das Gesellschaftsbild des Arbeiters.* Tübingen: J. C. B. Mohr (P. Siebeck), 1961.

64. Postan, M. M. *An Economic History of Western Europe 1945 till 1964.* London: Methuen & Co. Ltd., 1967.
65. Reader's Digest. *The European Common Market and Britain.* London, 1963.
66. Rosenberg, Morris. "Misanthropy and Political Ideology," *American Sociological Review,* vol. 21, 1956.
67. Routh, Guy. "Geographical Mobility of Manpower," *Joint International Seminar on Geographical and Occupational Mobility of Manpower,* Castelfusano, Italy: rep. no. 2, November, 1963.
68. Schmoelders, Guenter. *Psychologie des Geldes.* Hamburg: Rowohlts Deutsche Enzyklopädie, 1966.
69. ———. *Der Umgang mit Geld im Privaten Haushalt.* Berlin: Duncker and Humblot, 1969.
70. Schreiber, Klaus. *Kaufverhalten der Verbraucher.* Wiesbaden: Betriebswirtschaftlicher Verlag Dr. Th. Gabler, 1965.
71. Servan-Schreiber, J. J. *The American Challenge.* New York: Atheneum, 1968.
72. Shapiro, Harold T. and Gerald E. Angevine. "Consumer Attitudes, Buying Intentions and Expenditures - An Analysis of the Canadian Data," *Canadian Journal of Economics/LaRevue Canadienne d'Economique,* vol. 2, no. 2, May, 1969.
73. Sozialenquete-Kommission. *Soziale Sicherung in der Bundesrepublik Deutschland.* Stuttgart: W. Kohlhammer GmbH, 1967.
74. Stafford, Frank P. "A Note on Recent Trends in Income Inequality." Unpublished manuscript, 1969.
75. Strumpel, Burkhard. *Wirtschaftliche Entwicklung als menschliches Verhalten-Ein Forschungsbericht, Beltrage zur Verhaltensforschung* (Economic Development and Human Behavior) Berlin: Duncker and Humblot, 1964.
76. ———. "Preparedness for Change in a Peasant Society," *Economic Development and Cultural Change,* vol. 13, no. 2, January, 1965.
77. ———. *Steuermoral und Steuerwiderstand der deutschen Selbständigen-ein Beitrag zur Lehre von den Steuerwirkungen* (Tax Evasion of German Self-employed and its Economic Effects). Cologne, Opladen: Westdeutscher Verlag, 1966.
78. ———. "Consumption Aspirations: Incentives for Economic Change," *Social and Economic Studies,* vol. 14, no. 2, June, 1968.
79. ———. *Steuersystem und Wirtschaftliche Entwicklung-Funktion und Technik der Personalbesteuerung im sozioökonomischen Wandel* (Tax Systems and Economic Development: An International Comparison of Reactions Toward Taxation). Tübingen: J. C. B. Mohr (P. Siebeck), 1968.
80. ———. Klaus Novy, and M. Susan Schwartz. "Consumer Attitudes and Outlays in Germany and North America," *Jahrbuch fuer Sozialwissenschaft,* vol. 21, 1970.
81. Szalai, Alexander et al. *The Multinational Comparative Time Budget Research Project.* Evian: Sixth World Congress of Sociology, 1966.
82. Ter Hoeven, P. J. A. *Arbeiders tussen welvaart en onvrede.* Alphen aan den Rijn: N. Samson, 1969.
83. Tocqueville, Alexis de. *Democracy in America.* The Henry Reeve text, Phillips Bradley (ed.), New York: Knopf, 1948.
84. United States Department of Health, Education, and Welfare. *Toward a Social Report.* Washington, D.C.: January, 1969.
85. United States Strategic Bombing Survey Committee. *Effects of Strategic Bombing on the German War Economy.* Washington, D.C.: Overall Economic Effects Division, 1945.

86. Zahn Ernest. *Leven met de Welvaart.* Amsterdam: Arbeiderspers, 1962.

87. _____. *Soziologie der Prosperität.* Munich: Deutscher Taschenbuch Verlag, 1964.

88. _____. "Wirtschaftliche Entwicklung und Gesellschaftliche Erwartungen," *Kölner Zeitschrift für Soziologie und Sozialpsychologie,* no. 2, June, 1967.

89. Zweig, Ferdynand. *The Worker in an Affluent Society.* London: Heinemann, 1961.

Index

Index